# 'PUFFIN' ASQUITH

Also by R J Minney:

BIOGRAPHY

The Tower of London
Rasputin
Hampton Court
No 10 Downing Street
The Edwardian Age
The Two Pillars of Charing Cross
Fanny and the Regent of Siam
Carve Her Name with Pride
The Private Papers of Hore-Belisha
Clive of India
Chaplin, the Immortal Tramp
Viscount Southwood
Viscount Addison, Leader of the Lords
I Shall Fear No Evil: the Story of Dr Alina Brewda
The Bogus Image of Bernard Shaw (*Leslie Frewin*)

NOVELS

The Road to Delhi
A Woman of France
The Governor's Lady
Distant Drums
How Vainly Men . . .
Nothing to Lose
Maki
Anne of The Sealed Knot (with Margot Duke)

TRAVEL

Hollywood by Starlight
Next Stop – Peking
India Marches Past
'Midst Himalayan Mists

PLAYS

Gentle Caesar (with Osbert Sitwell)
Clive of India (with W P Lipscomb)
A Farthing Damages (with John McCormick)
The Voice of the People
They had His Number (with Juliet Rhys-Williams)

*Photo:* Cornel Lucas

R J MINNEY

# 'PUFFIN' ASQUITH

A BIOGRAPHY OF
THE HON ANTHONY ASQUITH
AESTHETE, ARISTOCRAT
PRIME MINISTER'S SON AND
FILM MAKER

LESLIE FREWIN of LONDON

---



First published 1973 by
Leslie Frewin Publishers Limited,
Five Goodwin's Court,
Saint Martin's Lane,
London, WC2N 4LL, England.

This book is set in Bembo 12/14,
printed and bound in Great Britain by
R J Acford Limited, Industrial Estate,
Chichester, Sussex

ISBN 0 85632 044 7

*For those who knew him, worked with him and were his friends;*

*And for those who don't know what they have missed . . .*

# Contents

# List of Illustrations

Frontispiece Photograph by Cornel Lucas

—

Facing page

## LIST OF ILLUSTRATIONS

Facing page

# Acknowledgements

A great many people who worked with Anthony Asquith in his films as stars, technicians and writers, and others who were his admirers and close friends, have helped me to write this book: their names appear throughout these pages.

I am also deeply indebted to Miss Brenda Davies of The British Film Institute, Miss Gladys Pearce and numerous others, who advised and guided me.

For the Filmography at the end of the book my gratitude is due to Peter Noble and The British Film Institute for their kind co-operation and consent.

I must also acknowledge with grateful thanks the help accorded by the ACTT in providing several of their copyright illustrations.

R J Minney

# I

# Inherited Trends

THE STRANDS THAT formed the personality of Anthony Asquith were varied and at times conflicting, but he selected, blended, and welded them together with such exquisite skill that his quite natural and effortless image won him the admiration and affection of vast numbers of friends spread out over many continents and always evoked the exclamation, 'Dear, darling Puffin!'

But there was much more to him than just the kind, gentle, considerate person one met. Let us examine some of these strands. His father, Herbert Henry Asquith, the son of an unsuccessful Yorkshire millowner, won the distinction of a first in Greats at Oxford, struggled for some years as a barrister, and climbed steadily up the political ladder until he attained the supreme office of Prime Minister in 1908; seventeen years later he was raised to the Upper House as the Earl of Oxford. He was over fifty when Anthony, his youngest child, was born on 9th November 1902. The modestly hooked nose of the infant made his doting mother call him Puffin, a mode of address which he preferred to all others even in maturity.

His mother, Margot Tennant, had an impressive, indeed a dazzling background. Both her grandfather and her father were very rich men as a result of the industrial revolution in Scotland: her father, Sir Charles Tennant, left £3 million. Margot generally referred to her father as a self-made man. To an extent she was right, for he rose to riches by his own efforts and surprised his father by his rapid acquisition of great wealth. He became a Member of Parliament when he was fifty-six, hardly ever made a speech, and accepted a baronetcy only after leaving the House. Margot was his twelfth child by his first marriage; he married again when he was seventy-five and had four more daughters, two of whom, Peggy Wakehurst (the Dowager Lady Wakehurst) and Katharine Elliot (Baroness Elliot of Harwood), were Puffin's contemporaries – his aunts as well as his devoted friends, with whom he stayed at Glenconner, North Berwick, for holidays all his life. Lady Elliot, by no means old, awaits the celebration in November 1973 of the 150th anniversary of her father's birth.

In the great house built by Sir Charles in the Scottish baronial style in the heart of the Peebleshire moors the Tennant children were brought up. Margot inherited his looks, his tremendous vitality, and his lavish generosity, all of which were abundantly discernible in Puffin – he was small, he had curly hair, his vitality was so intense that he was often very restless, and his generosity at times strained his financial resources. It is from the Tennants that Puffin inherited his passion for music and the arts

Sir Charles's hospitality was on an immense scale. Often there were as many as fifty guests, all of whom brought their valets, ladies'-maids and grooms, and mountains of luggage filled with the dresses the women had to wear for various indoor and outdoor diversions. In that wealthy Victorian setting, Puffin's mother, his aunts and uncles spent their childhood and adolescence. Though not yet aristocratic the family was in time to become so. Many of Sir Charles's daughters married peers or men who eventually became peers; his eldest son, Edward, went to the House of Lords in 1911 as Lord Glenconner.

The financial and business world supplied some of the guests, but, because their host was in Parliament, others came from one or other of the two Houses, the worlds of art and literature, for Sir Charles had admirable taste for fine furniture and costly pictures. His own collection included Gainsboroughs, Reynolds, Raeburns, Romneys, and Hoppners. Among the younger generation there were the *jeunesse dorée*, a familiar term in that Victorian period. Lord Ribblesdale married Tennant's eldest daughter, Charlotte; Lord Lyttleton's son, Alfred, married Laura; and George Nathaniel Curzon of Kedleston was in love with four of the daughters, all of whom gaily, and innocently, flirted with him. But it was with Puffin's mother, Margot, that his friendship endured for many years. She did not marry until she was thirty, by which age many women had concluded that it was unlikely that they would ever marry. In her attitude to life she was markedly different from her sisters. She ignored the accepted conventions and often defied them. On the hunting-field her indifference to danger involved her in hair-raising escapades. She herself made a tally of the injuries she suffered: both collar-bones broken, as well as nose, ribs and one knee-cap; jaw dislocated; skull fractured and five concussions of the brain. After one final adventure when she heard 'a great cry of pain a long way off, followed by the roar of a donkey-engine in my brain', she gave it up.

But she had other skills. Drawing delighted her, and music even more: her piano-playing was much admired by her friends. Her keenest interest was in the world of letters. She read abundantly, but chose her books with discrimination. Her wit was quick and sharp and she often shocked people by her outspokenness. Only her disregard of the conventions, her preference for intellectual companionship, and her wit (without its barbs) were inherited by Puffin.

She was twenty when she was presented at Ascot to the Prince of Wales, later King Edward VII. He took her to the paddock to see the horses saddled for the next race. It was the first time she had ever been to a race meeting. 'My extreme ignorance delighted him,' she says. He took her to lunch with him in the Guards tent and they wandered afterwards among the costers, gipsies, and acrobats. The next day he sent her a gold shark-skin cigarette-case with a diamond-and-sapphire clasp, which unhappily she lost while riding in Rotten Row. They saw a great deal of each other in the years that followed.

For a time she was in love with Peter Flower, the brother of Lord Battersea. But things did not go at all well. He hunted, gambled, flirted, but otherwise led an idle life, was constantly in debt, won money from friends by jumping on to a mantelpiece across a blazing fire, and was madly jealous because Margot had danced with the Prince of Wales. She eventually said goodbye and stopped seeing him. Not long afterwards at a dinner given by Lord Battersea in the House of Commons, she met Asquith, Home Secretary in Gladstone's Liberal Government, a stocky, blue-eyed man, not yet so heavily-built as he became in later years. He was married and had five children, whose ages ranged from one year to twelve. A very few months after this meeting Asquith's wife caught typhoid and died.

There had been a succession of rumours in the Press about her marrying. Lord Rosebery was named and it was denied. Arthur Balfour was next mentioned: his reply to the enquiry was, 'No, that is not so. I rather think of having a career of my own.' Alfred Milner (later Lord Milner) proposed to her in 1892, but she refused his offer. Now it was Asquith, and it was true.

All who knew her found Margot fascinating and stimulating, but were sadly embarrassed and even angered by her blunt and often personal criticisms. Most were prepared to dismiss these as fleeting aberrations from her normal warmth and magnanimity. Marriage of course demanded a more intimate and continuing relationship. Friends on both sides prophesied that the marriage would end in failure; for, quite apart from the difference of eleven years in their ages and having to take on a young family of step-children, Margot would find she had little in common with her husband: he was not interested in hunting or any outdoor games, except golf which he did not play well. His friends felt that she was frivolous, too outspoken, and too wild in some of her activities to be a suitable wife for one who expected to attain the highest political office.

Both ignored these warnings. The marriage was solemnised in St George's, Hanover Square, on 10th May 1894. The register was signed by four Prime Ministers – Gladstone, Lord Rosebery, A J Balfour, and Asquith.

# 2

# At No 10 Downing Street

THERE WERE FIVE children of the marriage of whom three died. Of the remaining two, Elizabeth, a pretty little dark-haired child, was older than Puffin by six years: Puffin was tiny, delicate, very fair, with Sir Charles Tennant's hooked nose, and curly blond hair with a hint of red in the gold. At the time of his birth his father was out of office; A J Balfour was the Conservative Prime Minister. Three years later the Liberals were back in office with an immense majority. There wasn't even standing room on the Government side of the House to fit in their 377 elected members; together with their normal supporters – 29 Labour and the Irish phalanx – their total swelled to 513 out of 670. Campbell-Bannerman, in his seventieth year, was the new Prime Minister; Asquith was appointed Chancellor of the Exchequer. He did not, however, move with his family to No 11 Downing Street but preferred to remain in their large and comfortable house in Cavendish Square which had been bought for Margot by her father. But two and a half years later, when the failing health of Campbell-Bannerman led to

Asquith succeeding him as Prime Minister, the family did move into No 10 Downing Street: Asquith took the unprecedented step of going to Biarritz to kiss the King's hands.

On his return, nine Asquiths moved into the official residence of the Prime Minister in Downing Street. The children of his first wife were grown up now: Raymond, a barrister, was twenty-nine and was married from No 10 three months later; Herbert was twenty-six and devoted his time to writing poetry and novels; Arthur, two years younger, was in business and away much of his time; Violet, who had just come out, told me that she enjoyed the season enormously and from her room above the front door used to look at the men with whom she had danced the night before hanging up their bowler hats and umbrellas in the Foreign Office across the road: seven years later she too was married from No 10; the youngest member of the family, Cyril, was just seventeen, Margot's daughter, Elizabeth, was eleven and Puffin only five.

Margot did not like No 10 at all. She thought it squalid, inconvenient, and almost impossible to find one's way in it. With the help of the Board of Works she managed to make it comfortable. The large garden at the back was a joy and she was glad to escape from the noise of the traffic in Cavendish Square.

Puffin had fun in the garden with his young friends. They played football there and badminton and their little faces would pop up above the wall to persuade policemen in Horse Guards Parade to return their ball or their shuttlecock. In time, the policemen found it trying and some of them went so far as to complain. Margot herself recorded in her diary: 'All my dresses were either torn or dirtied by disentangling Anthony's aeroplanes from the sooty shrubs.' The aeroplanes were launched with calculated care and there were chortles of delight when they flew over the garden wall – delight that was not shared by the policemen.

The tremendous vitality Anthony had inherited from his mother had been obvious ever since he was able to crawl across the floor and it kept him restlessly on the go right through his life. Quite early, too, his father noticed a quality he possessed which made him say to Margot soon after they moved into No 10: 'Puffin has the best manners of any of my children. I dream every night of my life as you know, and last night I dreamt that as I walked into the room, I heard Baby say, "I don't like old men", and seeing me he added, "I hope you don't think this applies to you, father".'

Because of his delicate health Puffin was taught at No 10 by a governess named Anna Heinsius. He learned to talk French and German fluently by the time he was seven; he showed an artist's intense interest in design and colour, and his dancing lessons revealed his early passion for music. He loved to sit at the piano and evolve simple little compositions. Not until he was nine did he go to a school in Sloane Street. He was taken there in the morning and brought back to Downing Street for lunch. He got into fights, generally to defend a young boy from a hefty bully, and came home with a bleeding scar on his knee and his fair curly hair matted with blood. A year later, feeling that he was strong enough now to go to a boarding-school, his mother took him to Summerfields, which was not far from Sutton Courtenay, where she had bought an old pub and a cottage and converted them into a home, calling it The Wharf, and laid out a garden and lawn which stretched down to the Thames.

Next to No 10 Downing Street lived Lloyd George, who had succeeded Asquith as Chancellor of the Exchequer. His youngest child, Megan, who was the same age as Puffin, told me: 'I fell in love with the sweet, pixie-like boy next door. We became inseparable and kept running through the intercommunicating door from one house to the other, romped rather noisily up and down the stairs, and played hide and seek in the vast warren of rooms in the two houses.'

When she told me this at lunch many years later, I asked Megan, knowing that a quarrel had separated the two families, how long it was since she had last seen Puffin?

'Forty-seven years,' she said.

'Would you like to see him again?' I asked.

'It isn't possible,' she said; then glancing at the glasses of sherry the waiter had brought to the table, she added, laughingly: 'If they knew we were lunching together, they would have put hemlock in both our drinks.'

'Nonsense!' I said. 'Would you like to see him?'

'It isn't possible,' she said again.

Knowing Puffin as I did, I said confidently: 'I can arrange it . . . Shall I?'

'It would be wonderful. Do you *really* think you could?'

Two nights later, after a film board-meeting, Puffin and I talked of a number of things and then, quite casually, I mentioned that I had seen Megan. His face was lit with eager enquiry as he asked about her. I told him of my plan to bring them together. He put his two fists together against his left shoulder and tilted his head to one side – his gestures, more exaggerated than his mother's, always expressed a childlike joy. He said: 'I'd *adore* to see her again.'

He arrived at the restaurant with a small cellophane box of tiny roses and with it still in his hand, embraced her. They were both excitedly happy and talked during the meal of the many things they did together as children.

'Do you remember,' he asked, 'how we used to go up and down in that wheezy old lift, clattering the heavy gates to the annoyance of everyone?'

The noise of the lift, near enough to the Cabinet room, did not disturb the ministerial deliberations, because of the double doors to the Cabinet room to prevent the Ministers being overheard.

'And do you remember the day when the lift got stuck between two floors?' said Megan.

'Oh yes! It was wonderful!'

'I was terrified,' said Megan. 'I thought we would be left there for ever. Nobody seemed to care what happened to us.'

For some time nobody at No 10 was aware that anything had happened to them. Alarm came much later. The children were missed because they were no longer running about the house to the distraction of everyone. A search of the numerous rooms in the two houses and the garden made it obvious that the son of the Prime Minister and the daughter of the Chancellor of the Exchequer had vanished. Various members of the family and the staff ran out into the street and into Horse Guards Parade calling them by name. Then the awful fear began to spread that the children must have been kidnapped, possibly by the suffragettes who were embarrassingly active at that time. Then somebody who wanted the lift pressed the button and discovered that it was not working. The children were rescued, scolded, and sent off to bed.

'We *had* rattled the gates,' Puffin turned to me and said, 'but nobody heard us. After a time we gave it up.'

'When we found that they were in a state of panic,' Megan added, 'we just lay low. We were always being scolded and we felt this was one way of paying them back.'

Childhood memories held them both spellbound. At teatime the two children used to sit together at a table at No 11 – they said nothing about wearing bibs, though I daresay bibs were provided – and if Lloyd George happened to be at home he joined them and they sang Welsh hymns together, the Chancellor conducting with both hands and leading with his resonant Welsh voice.

'He tried to teach me Welsh,' Puffin said, 'but finally gave it up. I had to confine myself to just humming.'

# 3

# His Love of Music

PUFFIN'S INTEREST IN music was markedly apparent in his infancy and one was able in time to gauge from his reaction the kind of music that attracted him.

Margot encouraged it by playing the piano and soon perched him on her knee and guided his tiny fingers on the notes. He responded well and by the time he was five, although one could hardly say that they were able to play duets, he certainly gave the impression that he was contributing something to the music that was being produced by this co-operation. When he was a little older he played duets with his sister Elizabeth.

The tuition by his governess not only improved his playing, but also awakened a keen interest in the composers of the music he heard and played. By the time Puffin was ten he was able while staying at Antibes in the south of France, to give a short talk on composers at an after dinner soirée. His father was as impressed as the audience by what his son said about Bach, Mozart, Scarlatti, Beethoven, Wagner and Greig.

It was not his only 'lecture' on musical composers; there were a further half-dozen, most of them in London. Already at this early age Puffin was convinced that one day he too would be a composer; Mozart, as he knew, had begun early, but, aware that he lacked his precocious talent, Puffin was prepared to wait.

To his mother this seemed likely: they would have to wait and see how he developed. While she wondered in a diary entry what 'his proper niche will be', she never doubted that if he kept his health he would go far in life.

But his material success was not her main concern. In his growing years her advice and guidance exercised a powerful influence on his personality and his attitude to others. The precepts were set down by her at the time of his Confirmation and are quoted in her diary. She wanted her son to have compassion rather than pity; to have humility and tenderness, without which one could not help others; to have no intellectual arrogance or a dialectical skill that scores; to protect people's failings and not to laugh at them; and never to be afraid of saying what is right even if it is, or even if it is not, an epigram. To the end of his life all these admirable and far from common qualities were apparent in all he said and did.

* * *

Puffin was nine and a half when he went to his first boarding-school Summerfields in the summer term of 1912. Chosen because it was close to her riverside house at Oxford, Margot went most Saturday afternoons to see him and watch him running about without a hat on the playing-fields.

An early attachment developed between him and Steven Runciman whose father Walter (later Lord) Runciman was in the Asquith Cabinet. Steven Runciman is well known today for his brilliant three-volume *History of the Crusades*, *The Fall of Constantinople*, *Sicilian Vespers*, and other interesting historical books.

'We used to play piano duets together,' Steven told me. 'We liked best two of Moszkowski's duets – one Polish and the other Spanish. I played treble and Puffin did the more complicated bits.

'Exactly fifty years later, in the summer of 1966, Puffin decided that we should give a public recital of these two pieces. He mentioned this to Yehudi Menuhin, who agreed to include it in one of his school concerts.

'But nothing came of it, which was a great relief to me.' A severe motor accident prevented Puffin from playing the piano at the time.

Steven Runciman confirmed what Puffin had told me about not being very good at games. 'I enjoyed them,' Puffin said, 'but was hopelessly incompetent. Once when the school was decimated by German measles I played for the third eleven against the Dragons, scoring a duck.'

In Chapel he and Steven used to whisper comic poems of their own creation to each other and dissolve into helpless giggles, which did not always escape the master's notice.

'Margot came every other weekend and took Puffin and me out,' Steven went on. 'She arrived on one occasion wearing a harem skirt. The boys were startled and stared at her. Puffin was half-embarrassed and half-delighted: it had to be a blend of the two as his manners were impeccable and I have always felt that he was born with good manners.

'His father, who was devoted to Puffin, was at his best with children of Prep school age. He used to take time off from being Prime Minister to read up about operas and ask Puffin obscure questions about them. Though only thirteen at the time, Puffin was always able to give the correct answers.

'Margot was frightening, but much more exciting. She knew everybody, but she was no snob. Her devotion to Puffin made her feel that he was superior to all other children and she encouraged him – it was an affectionate encouragement – to feel that he was superior in intellect and in other ways. But Puffin was not influenced by it.

'I spent only one night with Puffin at No 10 Downing Street – in the summer of 1916. While wandering about the house we lost our way and found ourselves in the dining-room where the Prime Minister, Margot, and their distinguished guests were at dinner. I was very embarrassed for Puffin. He spluttered his apologies and we fled from the room.

'At school we shared a small garden and quarrelled endlessly about it. He wanted to terrace it. I wanted to put in a pool. In after years, every time we met, he would say suddenly: "Do you remember how terrible it was to share the garden with you?" I *hadn't* forgotten – and it took me days to forgive him for reminding me of it.' His clear, indelible memory was stirred by a passing remark or a smile and Puffin always clung to his old arguments quite tenaciously: his arguments were always prolonged, he would argue about a word or a note of music for four hours, but he was never rude.

Both boys went up for Public School scholarships, Steven Runciman for Eton, Puffin for Winchester. 'I was in a state of great nervous tension,' Puffin told me. 'I had gone to Summerfields rather late and I knew that if I failed I would not get a second chance. My father and mother told me again and again that it did not matter at all if I got a scholarship or not. But I was only too well aware that my father and two of my brothers had achieved it with oustanding success; and so I very much longed to keep up the family tradition.

'The first few papers were easy. I was a little worried about the Latin Prose paper, but I was pleased in the end with what I had done; but after placing the fair copy on the pile, I suddenly had a doubt. I looked at the rough copy I had in my pocket and noticed just one tiny error. My fair copy was still on the table; all I had to do was to alter just one letter in one word. But as I had theoretically handed it in, I felt it was wrong to make a correction. I just stood there looking at the paper and saw it in time being submerged by the papers handed in by others.

'I knew I had no hope now of getting a scholarship. Arriving home, I put on a brave face when I saw my father, but after I had said goodnight to my mother I sobbed myself to sleep. The next day we left London for the country. When the train stopped at Reading, the stationmaster handed a telegram to my mother. It read: "Cobb first. Anthony third."' He *had* got a scholarship.

'In honour of this,' his mother tells us, 'he was allowed to dine downstairs with us.' His health was proposed by his father and they all stood up to honour it. Puffin, delighted and blushing a little, expressed his thanks in a neat speech. Lord Morley, a member of Asquith's government, was staying at The Wharf that weekend and was pleased to have been 'a witness to this pretty scene'. After dinner Puffin played the piano for Lord Morley, who thought his playing was divine. In the preceding year the First World War had broken out.

For Margot the change from Summerfields to Winchester made visits to her son much more difficult. The distance was greater and she realised that she would not be able to see him quite so often. 'For aught I could tell, new and entertaining Winchester men might efface some of my influence with my little son . . . Had it not been for Elizabeth, I felt like hiring rooms near Winchester College to watch my boy and await events.'

Puffin's last Sunday before going to Winchester was spent at The Wharf. Margot had converted the barn into an additional residence. It had a large drawing-room with a piano and a bedroom for her upstairs. Puffin, who slept in the barn, was told that after dinner he could come in his pyjamas and join her and the other ladies while the men were in the dining-room. They were engaged in playing a game when Margot was called to the telephone and was told the shattering news that Raymond, Asquith's eldest son, who was in France with the Grenadier Guards, had been killed in the Battle of the Somme. He was thirty-seven, had been married for a very few years, and had three children.

When the others were told, Puffin left the game he was playing, went up to his mother and took her hand. She then went to tell her husband. A glance at her face made him realise what had happened: he put his hands over his face and followed her to an empty room where they sat together in silence.

# 4

# Out of Downing Street

'AT WINCHESTER,' HIS brothers told Puffin, 'there is no such thing as a boy. They are all men.' When he got there he found they really were men – 'all of them over six foot tall and with deep bass voices.'

Everything was different. Fresh friendships had to be formed. His closest friend, Steven Runciman, had won a scholarship to Eton.

At the weekend Margot arrived and insisted on seeing his bedroom to make sure that he was really comfortable. It was a shock to find that he was sleeping in a dormitory.

'Must Puffin,' she exclaimed, 'have twenty boys sharing his bedroom?'

Like his father and three of his brothers, Puffin had decided to read Classics when he went to Oxford; so it figured prominently in his school curriculum. Music ran it very close.

By now he had begun to hope that music might provide him with a career. Encouraged by the progress he was making, he had started composing some modest piano pieces which he handed shyly to his music master, hopeful for his commendation.

In his first week or two at the school somebody had written on the blackboard

*Hail to thee, blithe spirit,*
*Bird thou never wert!*

While the assembled class were whispering and trying to check their laughter, the door opened and the master, Mr Bird, entered. He saw their smiles, then glanced at the blackboard, and asked sharply: 'Who wrote that?'

The timid voice of Puffin was then heard saying: 'Please, sir, wasn't it Shelley?' The others found it impossible to control themselves now. But Mr Bird was very angry.

A few days before the end of his first half at Winchester, Puffin – indeed the whole school – learned from the newspapers that his father had resigned the Premiership and the family would have to vacate No 10 Downing Street at once for Lloyd George, the new Prime Minister.

Their own house in Cavendish Square had been let to Lady Cunard, who was in residence there. It was an appalling situation to face. The Asquiths had been living at No 10 for eight years and 241 days and were faced now with moving from it with all their clothes and books and papers, and such furniture and pictures as they had brought in – all in a matter of hours. Margot had no idea where they could go. The family of Asquith's first marriage were grown up, even Violet was married. But Elizabeth, who was twenty, and Puffin, aged fourteen, still lived at home and room had to be found somehow for a family of four. She mentioned this to Mrs George Keppel, who invited them all to live with her in her house at 16 Grosvenor Street, gave up her own bedroom and sitting-room and moved to an upper floor.

The Keppels had two daughters, Violet, a year or two over twenty, and Sonia, who was about eighteen months older than Puffin. Their mother Alice, who was married to a younger son of the Earl of Albemarle, was very beautiful with large turquoise eyes and light chestnut hair, keenly intelligent, witty, lively, and a close friend of King Edward VII. Her daughter Sonia remembers as a child the King's visits to their home for tea. 'In my life,' she says in her book *Edwardian Daughter*, 'Kingy filled the place of an accepted kind uncle. His advent always meant fun for me.' She was brought in after tea 'to say How d'you do to the King'. 'On such occasions he and I devised a fascinating game. With a fine disregard for the good condition of his trousers, he would lend me his leg, on which I used to start two bits of bread (butter side down), side by side. Then, bets of a penny each were made (my bet provided by Mamma) and the winning piece of bread and butter, depended, of course, on which was the more buttery. The excitement was intense while the contest was on. Sometimes he won. Sometimes I did.'

The Asquiths stayed with the Keppels all through the winter, visiting The Wharf at Sutton Courtenay near Oxford occasionally at weekends.

Shortly after Christmas, when Puffin had gone back to school Margot informed Alice Keppel that she was going to bring him home.

'Why? What has happened?'

'There's a case of meningitis at the school,' said Margot, 'and . . .'

'No, Margot dear, you can't bring him here. We have to think of Sonia. I'm sure you wouldn't want her to get it.'

Sonia told me much of this. It was through Puffin that I met her. He had a way of referring to his friends by their Christian names and taking it for granted that you knew them. 'You *don't* know

Sonia?' he said with aggrieved surprise. 'You *must* meet her'; and a lunch followed. Sonia married the Hon Roland Cubitt, the heir to Lord Ashcombe.

Almost the entire summer vacation was spent in the pleasant Tennant house in North Berwick. 'There were always gatherings there of relatives and friends,' says Anthony Havelock-Allan, who was at Summerfields with Puffin and was associated with him as producer on a number of films. 'They kept open house – there was an endless stream of visitors – uncles, aunts, cousins, friends. They used to assemble after the season had ended, after Ascot and Henley and Cowes and Goodwood. The atmosphere there was essentially Victorian. Some would leave after a while to go to one of the Continental spas or the South of France. It was the social world Margot was brought up in and was gay, intellectual, and most enjoyable. Puffin spent every summer there.'

Sylvester Gates, later Chairman of the Westminster Bank, was at Winchester with Puffin, and thought he was rather odd in some ways, but nobody laughed at him; his charm won them all over. 'It was a dismal period. The war was going on and on and took a heavy toll of the senior boys, who were killed within a few months of leaving school. We could see no future for us.

'Puff was made a prefect and eventually became one of the top prefects, which entitled him to wear no coat, but a waistcoat with long sleeves edged with velvet. He worked hard and won a prize for English verse and also a prize for German. A lot of his time was spent in the Music School and he was always composing songs.'

During Puffin's fourth year at Winchester, Richard Crossman, who was later a Cabinet Minister in Harold Wilson's government, arrived at the early age of twelve with a scholarship and became a fag of Puffin's.

'As fags, we had a very easy time. We had to provide tea,

prepare a great fire in the prefects' room and, as there was no running water in the school buildings, we had to fill water cans and carry them up the stairs before we went to bed, which the small boys did early.

'A can filled to the brim with water was rather heavy for a boy of twelve and once while carrying it up I fell down the stairs and was soaked and frightened, not knowing what my punishment would be.

'Puff came running out to the stairs. His only question was, "Are you hurt?" He picked me up, comforted me, then filled the can himself and took it upstairs.

'There were huge fires in the dormitories, in each of which there were beds for twelve or fourteen people. There were no bathrooms; we had to bath in tubs.'

Margot managed to get down to Winchester on most Saturdays and generally brought Elizabeth with her.

'The fags made the tea for the visitors and we stayed in the room watching and helping while they ate,' Dick Crossman told me. 'What was left uneaten was our perquisite. I kept my eye on some of the cakes, saying to myself, "I hope they won't eat that – and that." Very often they *did*, but quite often I got some of the delicious leftovers. The food in the college was very bad.

'On Saturday evenings the prefects would come up with food and drink and have parties in the dormitories. In college we had two groups – the Aesthetes and the Athletes. Puff, McDougall, and Eric Stepman were Aesthetes and their special fags belonged of course to their group. We had readings of plays, drawing on world literature – Shakespeare, Maeterlinck, Chekhov, who was very new at the time – we read in fact an astonishing amount of modern drama; the small boys took the female parts, I read the girl's part in Maeterlinck's *The Blue Bird*. We read poetry, Flecker's *Hassan*, and prose too, especially Dostoevsky. We were told in advance what we were going to read and worked really hard at them.

'I was tremendously influenced by Puffin – indeed all of us were. He never beat a fag nor would he allow any other Aesthete to beat us. But the Athletes not only beat their own fags but beat us too. Puff was very solicitous about us. He felt that we were made to suffer for the cause of Asquith and high literature. Because of his love of books he ran the school library.

'No one could have been more considerate of others. Margot brought him masses of food and he divided it equally in the dormitories. What I got was also equally divided.

'Puff had at that time a shrill high-pitched voice and his Adam's apple stuck out. In a sense he was a caricature. But we looked on him as a cheery red overlord because of his reddish-gold curly hair. He was sensitive, an epicure, snobbish only so far as books were concerned. I say again he had a profound influence on one. I think what drew *us* together was the fact that his father was very much a lawyer and my father was a Chancery judge: perhaps that was what made him be so sweet to me.'

I asked Crossman if Puffin dressed in school in the untidy way he dressed in the film world.

'The Aesthetes had a special way of dressing up' he said. 'They used to wear mauve shirts and flowing ties and took a delight in flaunting their get-up before the Athletes.'

# 5

# A Difficult Decision

In his last year at Winchester Anthony Asquith found he had to make a difficult decision. His intense love of music had increased with the passing years of childhood and youth. His musical studies continued: he added greatly to his ever-expanding knowledge of the great composers and their captivating operas, symphonies, and sonatas. He gave to the piano every moment he could spare and practised often for hours on end. Nor was composing neglected. Ambitiously he wrote the words and music of a song that had been taking shape in his head: he knew it was the best thing he had done and timidly asked his music master what he thought of it. That it would be accorded praise was beyond his modest hopes. But the verdict he received was sadly dampening. It was expressed as kindly as it could be. He was not told 'All this is really beyond you,' but that was what it meant. In effect he said: 'I know what music means to you. I've seen you work unremittingly at it all the time you've been here. Your playing has improved, but it is not above average.' He paused, then added: 'Whatever plans you make for the future, I think it only fair for me to say that you cannot rely on music to provide it.'

With his unfailing good manners, Puffin thanked him for his kind advice; but it took a long time for him to accept it. For months he clung to the long-cherished hope that music would provide the only career he wanted. There was nothing else he could turn to.... nothing that would give him the same satisfaction and joy.

On leaving Winchester he went to Balliol in Oxford, the college his father and three of his brothers had been to, and like them read Classics. But, unlike his father and his brothers, he was interested neither in politics nor law. He was a Liberal not merely because of family loyalty but because deep down and by conviction he was a radical and always ready to take up the cause of the underdog. It was apparent in everything he did throughout his life. But it did not prompt him to make politics his career.

He told me some years later that, while trying to decide on a career, he felt that the only thing apart from music that interested him was films. By then films had but recently emerged from the teething stage. Thomas Edison had always feared they would be a passing novelty and was strongly opposed to their being projected on to a screen. If the public peered into a box, one at a time, he could foresee a fairly long life for these moving pictures. But in defiance of his warning, screens were provided – at first only in music-halls where the five-minute picture on the screen was put on as the closing item so that those who had tired of the novelty could leave their seats, grab their hats, and go home. It had advanced since then, but the pictures were silent, the subtitles provided a monosyllabic indication of what was going on and the public had to rely on the exaggerated facial contortions on the screen for the dialogue. There was no certainty in 1920 that pictures would ever talk. They did not begin to do so until seven years later.

Going to the pictures now became Puffin's main diversion although he enjoyed playing bridge and often, like his mother, played for long hours: he also played golf at North Berwick with her and others. But the inarticulate figures on the cinema screen in 1920 with their ridiculous mouthing of anger and their unconvincing behaviour stirred his questing mind. All manner of developments and changes in visual storytelling should, he felt, be possible. They did not spring to his mind at once. He would have to see more films, see the ones he liked again and again. Ideas would begin to come then. It was a new and fascinating art form and he intended to develop it.

'At Oxford and even in London I spent all my spare time at the cinema. I kept going from one to the other. Some films I saw six or seven times and I began to realise how one could express emotion and mood with a camera; and what striking results could be obtained by effective lighting and well-designed sets. During my four years at Oxford I haunted the cinema, studying the technique and working out new effects. At last, I felt, I had found a career. I wish it could have been music, but –'; then with his engaging modesty he added, – 'but I had no real talent for a musical career.'

Jimmy Smith, grandson of W H Smith, First Lord of the Admiralty and Secretary for War in Lord Salisbury's government, was at Oxford with Puffin. 'One outcome of his visits to the cinema was that he fell in love with Pauline Frederick, the silent film star. I remember his going all the way from Oxford to Liverpool just to see a film in which she was starring. He spent the entire day in the cinema and sat through five performances of the film.'

Despite his expanding enthusiasm for films – he saw *The Golem*, *Caligari*, *Warning Shadows*, and *The Student of Prague* – his loyalty to music remained unaffected: he never missed the chance of sitting down to play the piano no matter where it was, whose it was, and whether he had been asked to play it. At the Russian embassy in London some years later Puffin, being escorted to the large reception-room where the guests were being announced, saw a piano in an anteroom and began to play it. He did not go to the party.

During a night journey by train from Paris to London in a *wagon-lit* shared with his mother, she 'looked up at the bunk above me to see how Anthony was sleeping and saw him writing on music paper. "What are you doing? Can't you sleep?" I said. "I am writing an unaccompanied chant to *Nunc Dimittus*," he answered.'

Nor were visits to concerts and the opera discarded. Apart from the joy they brought him, his mind was actively engaged in trying to link music – real music – with films. There must be, he felt, a substitute for the woman seated behind a large potted plant in a dark cinema tinkling something romantic when the young lover kisses the girl and thumping out noisy breathless notes when the mounted law officers are in pursuit of the gun-runners.

'A registered letter used to arrive for Puffin every morning,' Jimmy says, 'with his allowance for the day, and immediately he would set out for the shops and buy pullovers, ties, and other things for his friends. I've never known anyone as generous and kind and considerate as Puff. He was quite indifferent to what he wore himself and left it to the butler at The Wharf to go to Harrods and buy his clothes – anything would do – mostly grey flannels and, of course, a muffler.'

He had a very large number of friends. Lord David Cecil and Sylvester Gates were his closest companions. 'When they got together,' says Jimmy Smith, 'they would talk and talk to the exclusion of everything around them. We went to The Wharf almost every weekend. Maurice Bowra was another of his close friends. Puff had an unconscious sense of adventure. He couldn't ride at all, yet he would jump on to a horse and not care what happened.' Of course, his mother used to do that, but she rode extremely well.

'I first met him at Oxford,' says John Sutro. 'He was my original music critic on the new, resuscitated *Cherwell* magazine, of which I became editor; other contributors included Evelyn Waugh, Christopher Hollis and Harold Acton.'

Sylvester Gates said: 'It was a wonderful time to be at Oxford in those after-the-war years. There was a feeling of release and relief. With us were men who had come back from the war and were four years our senior.' Among these were Anthony Eden (now Lord Avon), L P Hartley, Robert Graves, Robert Nichols, Richard Hughes, and Edmund Blunden; of the women, Dorothy Sayers, Vera Brittain, and Winifred Holtby. Living in or near Oxford were W B Yeats, John Masefield, John Buchan, and, also fresh from the war, Lawrence of Arabia. We used to go to concerts, and talk – discuss many things, but not politics; and we did not aspire to join the Union.'

All were agreed that Puffin was unable to look after himself. The youngest child of an elderly father, fifty at the time of his birth, and a mother then in her thirty-ninth year, Puffin had been caressed and indulged. Surprisingly, it had not spoiled him, nor had it directed the focus of his thoughts on himself. In time his friends realised tht he was quite unaware of the need to look after himself. His first thought always was to do something for others.

# 6

# To Hollywood

In May 1919, while Puffin was still at Winchester, his sister, Elizabeth, married Prince Antoine Bibesco, a Rumanian diplomat. She was twenty-two, dark, and very pretty, he tall, good-looking and nearly twenty years older.

The attachment between Puffin and his sister had always been close and it was in no way affected by the marriage. They saw each other constantly while in the same town and made long journeys across Europe and the Atlantic to be together. And so when he set out for Hollywood on leaving Oxford, Puffin went first to Washington, where Antoine Bibesco was the Rumanian minister.

Felix Aylmer, who was appearing in Frederick Lonsdale's play, *The Last of Mrs Cheyney* at Washington prior to opening in New York, told me: 'The first time I met Puffin was when Elizabeth brought him to my dressing-room after the performance. I had known the family well, saw a lot of Margot and Elizabeth, but Puffin was at Oxford at that time.' The family had moved in

1920 from Cavendish Square to a cheaper but spacious and attractive house at 44 Bedford Square as Puffin's father was worried about money. It was in that year that Margot published the first volume of her autobiography. The second volume followed two years later.

'Margot and I,' Felix Aylmer added, 'went to the Everyman Theatre at Hampstead to see *The Painted Swan*, which was written by her daughter Elizabeth, and often went to a concert or to see films, occasionally accompanied by Elizabeth. Margot was not only amusing and extremely witty, but astonishingly energetic. When she was nearly seventy she vaulted over the dress circle rails in order to get in front of the crowd leaving the theatre, and on another occasion she seized me by the hand, dragged me across Shaftesbury Avenue with the traffic hooting at us and finally succeeded in getting a taxi in Cambridge Circus by practically strangling the driver. We got in and had to go back for Elizabeth who was waiting on the pavement outside the theatre.

'I saw Puffin and Elizabeth on just that one evening at Washington. Antoine Bibesco entertained us at dinner at the embassy and the next day Elizabeth and Puffin left for Hollywood where they were to be the guests of Mary Pickford and her husband, Douglas Fairbanks. Later, when Puffin was directing films in London, I appeared in quite a number of them.'

The journey to Hollywood was made by train in those pre-airline days. 'All trains,' Puffin noted, 'coming from the East are automatically met by reporters ready to pounce on visiting lions or, failing the larger fauna, even a mouse whose name might be remotely known to the public. Not knowing this, I was a little surprised when a young man, after a doubtful scrutiny of my old tweed jacket and rumpled grey flannels, asked me if I was the Honourable Anthony Asquith. I said I was and was immediately asked for my impressions of Los Angeles.'

At Mary Pickford's house he was greeted by an English butler. Lillian Gish, famous with her sister Dorothy Gish for their brilliant acting in *Broken Blossoms* and other films, takes up the story: 'I met Puffin for the first time,' she told me, 'when he came with his sister Elizabeth to stay with Mary Pickford and Doug Fairbanks at Pickfair, their home in Hollywood. I saw a lot of them while they were there, for I used to take over as hostess when Mary Pickford was busy filming at the studio.

'My first impression of Puffin was his remarkable likeness to the little statuette of Peter Pan. Only the pipe was missing and his hair seemed to defy gravity for it rose upwards in a mass of red-gold curls.

'His sister was so pretty. She is the only one I ever saw come down to dinner in a lovely nightgown over a slip and with a beautiful silk scarf. She looked an enchanting painting against the pale green background of Doug and Mary's dining-room walls. She was the image of innocence and the conversation was so witty and amusing.

'The remarkable thing about Puffin was his amazing knowledge about films. We thought in Hollywood that we knew it all. We knew about American movies, but here was this young man from England who could talk with authority about Swedish and German films, as well as American films – indeed about films made all over the world – the techniques of the various directors . . . how all the effects were obtained. He was really dedicated to films. It was his vocation – like the priesthood. He felt he had a call to make films – and he made them so very well. Many of them, like Bernard Shaw's *Pygmalion*, were classics.'

A great deal of his time, Puffin told me, was spent in the Fairbanks film studio watching Mary and Douglas at work. 'It was a unique opportunity. I made a close study of all the processes of film-making from camera work to cutting and editing. I asked endless questions, I'm afraid, and they were kind enough to guide me through every stage.'

At that time Charlie Chaplin lived in the next house to Pickfair. Puffin met him in Douglas Fairbanks' Turkish bath: Charlie was in the nude 'in soft focus and heavily gauzed by steam'. He got to know Charlie well, went often to his studio and learnt a great deal from him, Puffin told me.

Chaplin was making *The Circus* at the time and Puffin watched him with intense excitement. But he did not only listen: sometimes he argued. An early argument was over a scene in Dupont's film *Vaudeville*, which showed a jealous trapeze artist with murder in his heart, swinging over the audience. 'Dupont,' said Puffin talking of it later, 'did not show the scene objectively, but put his camera on the trapeze so that one had the feeling that one was in fact seeing through the eyes of the character concerned. Charlie thought this merely an irritating trick. To him any odd cinema angle, any transposition of a shot which was so striking as *to draw attention to itself*, was not expressive but merely a distraction. He mentioned that such devices took the attention of the audience away from what was all-important – the doings and feelings of the people. I remember I argued that, for example, if some one in a story was terrified, you could help the actor by not making him express terror with his face, but by making what he saw look terrifying. Of course we were both right about the really fundamental thing – the paramount importance of the human element.'

During the months he was there, Puffin met a number of other famous film directors, among them the great Ernst Lubitsch, 'whose English, though fluent and picturesque, was a little unorthodox,' and saw them at work in the Metro-Goldwyn-Mayer, Warner Brothers, and other studios. All this provided a very important training for his career.

His father, who accepted a peerage in the New Year's Honours in 1925 and became the Earl of Oxford and Asquith, followed his son's activities with, we are told, 'keen interest and some amusement'. In a letter to a friend Lord Oxford states: 'Puffin writes enthusiastically from Hollywood of the good time which he and Elizabeth are having in the centre of the film world. They are the guests of Douglas Fairbanks and Mary Pickford; Charlie Chaplin drops in to lunch; Lilian Gish hovers about in the offing; and (to Puffin the climax) he has had ten minutes with Pauline Frederick. *Que voulez vous?*'

Lilian Gish told me of some of their diversions. 'Puffin, Elizabeth, and Douglas Fairbanks used to set out before dawn every morning on horseback and ride over the mountain on the other side of which the butlers, who had been sent on ahead, were preparing breakfast for us. Douglas would not allow Mary Pickford and me to ride. He was afraid we might fall off the horse or have some sort of accident that would prevent us from carrying on with our film work. So we were made to walk. Of course we had to start earlier than the others and we got badly scratched coming through the sage brush in the dark. But it was a joy to see the dawn come up while we had our breakfast of bacon and eggs and coffee.'

Douglas's son, Douglas Fairbanks, jnr, who was fifteen at the time, tells me: 'Frankly I don't remember much about Puffin's stay there, except that he was thought by everyone to be extremely nice, although, in that particular setting, an eccentric character. We once went in a group to the Santa Monica fairground, most of which was built out on a pier into the Pacific, and I remember how keen he was on going on *all* the various roller-coasters and other contraptions.'

A flattering invitation to a reception, which Puffin felt it would be churlish to refuse, he himself described to me with some embarrassment. With no achievement at all to his credit, with nothing yet begun, let alone accomplished, he was invited to the Hollywood High School to meet the 'debating squad' of the school.

Having just graduated from Oxford, it seemed harmless enough. He arrived at the appointed time of eleven o'clock in the morning, was escorted down a long corridor, introduced to an elderly lady, and was asked to sit beside her in an enormous and very impressive chair, not unlike the Papal throne.

Wondering where the debating squad was, he was surprised to see the curtains rising and to find himself on a stage facing an audience of about 2,000, who rose instantly and began to sing the hymn of the Hollywood High School to the accompaniment of the organ. It went on interminably. When at last it was over, the head of the school came forward and announced: 'We are proud to have with us one whose work, I feel, will be remembered for ever.'

Asquith felt that the tribute was much too premature; then he noticed that the lady beside him was rising. She was cheered lustily and he learned that she was Carrie Jacobs Bond, the author of 'When You Come to the End of a Perfect Day'. The audience thereupon rose again, and, the organ accompanying, sang the entire song.

Mrs Carrie Jacobs Bond bowed when it ended and addressed them. Her talk was quite unconnected with either the school or her song. She spoke of kindness to animals, for three-quarters of an hour.

Realising with relief that he was to be no more than a spectator, though puzzled as to why he was placed on the stage at all and made to sit in such an imposing chair, Puffin suddenly became aware that his own name was being called. The Head was saying: 'Mr Asquith will now deliver his address.'

He spoke for less than a minute. Greatly embarrassed, he mumbled a few hurried words of apology, with a prayer through each word that the curtain would descend quickly.

# 7

## His Start in Films

EARLY IN 1926 after six months in Hollywood, Puffin returned to London to start his career in films. He already had one foot in the world of films in England, for, on leaving Oxford after getting Honours in Greats, he became a founder member of the Film Society.

It had been clear for some time to his family that he was departing from the path his father and his brothers had taken. Whatever regrets they may have had, it must have been obvious to them, as it was to his friends, that neither the law nor politics would have provided him with a satisfying career.

In films his intention was to be a writer-director. After trying his hand at an original screen story, he sent it to Bruce Woolfe, who was in charge of production at British Instructional, which had been making such war films as *Ypres*, *Mons*, and *Zeebrugge*. His story showed not only promise but an understanding of film requirements and Woolfe gave Puffin his first job. It was in fact just an apprenticeship. He was required to start at the bottom and do every kind of task, however menial, from making tea, assisting with the make-up of the players, carrying 'props' from one part of the set to another, and even taking on the arduous and dangerous work of stunt men. He took it all on readily, indeed eagerly. His father was amused when told of it and wondered what the future would bring.

His opportunity came later that same year, 1926. Somewhat ambitiously Bruce Woolfe embarked on making a film about the warrior queen, Boadicea. It was directed by Sinclair Hill, and Puffin not only collaborated on the script but acted as Sinclair Hill's personal assistant. In the list of credits Anthony Asquith's name appears as 'Property Master, Assistant Make-up Man, Assistant Cutter and Stunt Man'.

'I did everything in that production,' Puffin told me. 'I had to make up ancient Britons with woad and even did some acting.' He shut his eyes and giggled, then added: 'Lilian Hall-Davis, as Boadicea's daughter, had to career at great speed across the Sussex Downs in a chariot. It was felt that if the horses bolted and she was thrown from the chariot and broke her neck, it would be impossible to complete the film. So I put on a flowing blonde wig and billowing robes and sat perched high in the chariot while the horses tore across the field.

'Phyllis Neilson-Terry, who played Boadicea, had a great speech to make, in which she was haranguing the Ancient Britons. Although it was a silent film there were occasions when you had to *see* artists speaking. She said she couldn't do it without words. So I had to write a speech for her, which was a splendid Shakespearian paraphrase on the lines of Friends, Romans, Countrymen, but rather better!'

Wally Patch, a member of the cast, who played two roles – an NCO in the British as well as the Roman Army: they were in fact the same film 'extras' dressed in different uniforms – said: 'Tony

Asquith was a little wisp of a chap and we used to think he was a bit of a joke, but one day he got kicked in the groin by a horse, and picked himself up without a whimper. We got very attached to him after that. He was the friendliest person one could ever hope to meet. He was always hobnobbing with the workmen.

'I acted as stunt man too in that film. I had to fall off the drawbridge and in another scene fall out of a chariot. When Boadicea was taken captive I had to flog her on the orders of the Roman commander. I did it quite gently of course, but it looked very convincing.

'Two of Victor McLaglen's brothers, Cyril and Clifford, were in the cast. Cyril kept taking off the nuts on the wheels of the chariot so that the wheels would roll off when the chariot was going at full speed in order to make it all much more exciting. Tony Asquith was adventurous enough to take on anything, yet he looked rather like a jockey and so frail that one wanted to look after him.'

Acting, doing dangerous stunts, and assisting the director were not his only activities. He also helped the cameraman and worked in the cutting-room. 'At that time, as you know,' Puffin said, 'we had none of the wonderful machines that are such a tremendous help in the cutting-room. Handling yards and yards of negatives, all of which got out of hand and played little games – forming entanglements of knots and loops.' Recalling it, he gave his recurrent gulping laugh, which was really rather attractive. 'What a blessing the movieola is: it helps one to get things done in an orderly way in a fraction of the time.'

Cricklewood Studios, where Puffin was working, had been an aircraft factory during the First World War and had been bought and converted by Sir Oswald Stoll into a silent-film studio. The vast factory floor was used for shooting five films at the same time, each on a defined but unpartitioned section of the floor:

that was all right for close shots and medium close shots, but when a long shot was required the shooting of one of the other films in the adjoining section had to be stopped for a few minutes.

'There was a great hubub all the time. The noise was quite deafening,' said Victor Peers, who was at that time an assistant director. 'Orders were being given to the cameraman, the electricians working the lights, the men erecting or dismantling the sets – you could hardly hear yourself think. Of course the noise didn't matter in those days of silent pictures.'

A number of partitioned rooms at the back were used as offices; one was for cutting and editing films and could be darkened for loading the camera – the films were developed and processed in a laboratory on the premises. There were two artists' dressing-rooms, one for the men, the other for the women, and two wardrobe sections similarly divided; and finally a projection-room for the 'rushes', that is to say the films shot on the preceding day; and also a canteen.

'The film unit was small. We had a cameraman, an assistant director, a cutter or editor, if we were lucky we had a continuity girl; and sometimes one or two more who did everything that was required – worked as stagehands, helped to build sets, and even acted, walking on with the crowd of extras.

'It was my job as assistant director to engage "bit" players and "extras", who are now called "crowd artists". Every morning a large number of people, all of them looking for work, some seeking small acting parts in the film, others just walking on, would assemble at the door and clamour in loud voices to get taken on. I used to look them over – there was no need to audition them for their role in a silent film. If they looked right for the part, I engaged them and made a note of their address in my address book.

'I got paid £3 a week. We worked very long hours – there

were no trade unions to say how long we worked or what we should be paid. If I worked after seven o'clock in the evening, I got half a crown for a meal. At the end of the road from the studio, there was a sort of cabman's shelter where we could buy fish and chips. I paid sixpence for some chips and made a two-shilling profit.'

After Puffin had been with Bruce Woolfe for a while they put him on to a film called *Thou Fool*, 'they had titles like that in those days, which I was allowed to edit and even directed an extra shot for it. I remember the first shot I ever directed. It was taken from Chelsea Bridge and it was of Lotts Road Power Station. It was shot on a misty November afternoon. Stanley Rodwell shot it and it was an extremely beautiful shot I thought. Then I had another idea for a film. From a story of my own. With Jock Orton collaborating, we wrote *Shooting Stars* which Mr Woolfe, I never called him anything but Mr Woolfe even behind his back, let me co-direct with A V Bramble. It was a film I would very much like to remake. It was a film about the making of a film. And I really taught myself to *cut* while working on that film. Most of my first films after that I cut myself, with no assistant or any joiners. Everything had to be scrape, scrape – scraped with a little blade.'

It was a departure for Bruce Woolfe, who had been producing mainly documentary films, to make *Shooting Stars*, a fictional feature picture. It appeared to have been prompted by the remarkable impression Anthony Asquith had made on him in such a short time.

'Puffin's jump over our heads surprised and puzzled us,' Victor Peers said. 'While he was doing various odd jobs from making tea to assisting with the make-up of the artists, we thought he had come as an apprentice, to learn the job. To find him suddenly moved up several grades ahead of us was astonishing. He never gave the least indication that he had spent some months in Hollywood with foremost directors there and had watched them at work. When he began work on *Shooting Stars*, after having written the original story himself and was co-directing the film, it became obvious that he was really a professional in his handling of the job.'

It was a simple story about film stars – hence its punning title: and it should be remembered that it was written and shot nearly half a century ago. Asquith brought to its interpretation an inventive skill which gave it a fresh dimension. The subtitles, numerous in silent films, were scarcely used; by brilliant cross-cutting from one action to the next, he was able to indicate pictorially the moods and at times even the thoughts of the characters.

It delighted the public to see the story set in a film studio and to observe how the players were put through their paces in front of a camera. The story is centred on three people – a popular star of Western films (played by Brian Aherne); his beautiful wife (Annette Benson), the darling of cinemagoers because of her devotion to her husband in their private life; and a film comedian (Donald Calthorp). We find that in fact the wife is engaged in a clandestine love affair with the comedian. When her husband discovers this he decides to divorce her. But, eager though she is to marry her lover, she realises that divorce would shatter the carefully built up image of her loyalty and love for her husband. So she decides to kill him and inserts a real bullet in place of the dummy used by the villain in the film her husband is making. When the shot is fired, the bullet turns out to be a blank. The gun, required for another scene, goes off this time and kills the comedian. Following a breakdown in health after her divorce, the wife is no longer the public's darling. Her husband meanwhile has become a prominent film director and she gets work from time to time as a film extra in the crowd scenes in some of her husband's films, without his being even aware of her. One evening, after the others have left, she waits to have a word with him. Uneasy, nervous, alone with him at last, she asks him 'Will you want me any more?' Without looking up he shakes his head . . . and she goes slowly out of the studio.

The camera work, the skilful editing, and the brilliant portrayal of character brought Asquith success with his very first film. The Press was full of praise. They singled out the ingenious and unforgettable effects he employed. A quarter of a century later Roger Manvell wrote of it: 'The last scene in which the actress kneels to pray unrecognised in the vast church set which is being struck* while she is absorbed in thought and disintegrates around her – this is for me the most imaginative moment in the film.'

Rachel Low, daughter of the famous newspaper cartoonist Sir David Low, and author of the massive *History of Films*, also recalled moments in the film many years later. 'The most obvious signs of a break with British film-making practice are two dazzling pieces of quick cutting. These are the trick cyclist's fall on the cliff, and later, at the climax of the film, the comedian's death as he clowns high above the studio floor on a property chandelier. Rapid and impressionistic cutting is used in both cases to shock, horrify and daze the audience.'

British Instructional was so pleased with Anthony Asquith's fine film that they raised his salary to £4 a week.

He was now asked to make three films in the course of the coming twelve months. The first of these, again based on an original story by him, was *Underground*. He wrote the screenplay and directed the film entirely by himself this time, with complete authority to do it his own way.

Once again the story was simple. It tells of the love for Nell, a shop girl (Elissa Landi) by Bill (Brian Aherne), and of Bert, an

* Dismantled.

underground porter (Cyril McLaglen). After much conspiring and lying by Bert, a fight in the power station and an escape into an underground tunnel, Bert is finally trapped in an underground lift, and Bill and Nell are free to marry.

'When I made silent films,' Asquith said, 'I sometimes talked to my artists whilst they were performing. It all depends on the actor. Some liked being talked to. They were a different type of actor from those in films today, who have lines to learn. They didn't have any distraction, so they concentrated exclusively on performance. One would, of course, always talk to them under one's breath. In my second film, *Underground*, I had a wonderful actress, Norah Baring, who played Bert's mistress and looked rather like a Modigliani. She had a scene where she gets very bad news, and we decided that when you get bad news you don't feel it at first, you can't get it in focus. So we worked out some perfectly ordinary things for her to do. She folded up her sewing very carefully, adjusted the curtains, and picked up a flower-pot with intense concentration. As she turns from it she bumps into a dressmaker's dummy which was on springs. It rocks. She deliberately pushes it again, then came a sub-title, "Funny". From that we went to a big close-up. We see her come to herself and rush out hysterically.'

Some did not think *Underground* was as good as *Shooting Stars*. One critic said Asquith was too obsessed with weird effects. Others felt it lacked the touches of quiet humour noticeable in his earlier film, which became indeed a characteristic of all his future productions.

But the majority of the critics gave him unstinted praise: they praised his 'cleverness', the striking effects obtained by adopting new techniques. Asquith stood out because at that time there was only one other director who showed great promise – Alfred Hitchcock. A few years older than Asquith, Hitchcock was by now in his thirtieth year: his film *The Lodger* came out at the same time as Asquith's *Shooting Stars* and was a enthusiastically received by the critics and the public. In the following year his *The Ring* appeared at the same time as *Underground*; and for some years their careers ran parallel. But whereas Asquith was shy, extremely modest, and shunned publicity, Hitchcock was conscious of its value and received much more of the limelight.

While he was engaged on *Underground*, Puffin's father died. He was in his seventy-sixth year.

Two more silent films followed. In 1928 Bruce Woolfe arranged with a German film company, *Laenderfilm*, to make a joint Anglo-German production and sent Asquith to Germany to direct it. A novel by Elizabeth Russell, sister-in-law of Bertrand Russell and best known as the author of *Elizabeth and her German Garden*', was chosen. It was called *Princess Priscilla's Fortnight*; the film script was written by Asquith and it was renamed *The Runaway Princess*. As his German technical adviser and assistant director he had Frederick Wendhousen, although Asquith spoke German fluently. All the players were English. Part of the film was shot in Berlin, Asquith always liked to use natural backgrounds, and the rest of the shooting was carried out at Welwyn studios in England, to which they had moved from Cricklewood.

Having been taught to speak German as a child by his sister's German governess, he was able to translate, adapt the script, and direct the film in that language. The story was rather Ruritanian. Disapproving of her betrothal to the Crown Prince of Savona, whom she has never seen, the Princess runs away to London where she becomes aware that she is being followed by a handsome stranger. This gave Asquith the opportunity to shoot outdoor scenes in London for a background. When her money runs out she takes a job in a Bond Street shop and, while visiting one of the clients, she finds herself involved with a gang of forgers. The mysterious stranger comes to her rescue and turns out to be the Crown Prince. She falls in love with him, they return to her homeland and have a slap-up wedding. Mady Christians, a pretty blonde who played Priscilla, was given two songs, written in English especially for the film, and Asquith managed to put them on a sound track just before the film was shown to the public.

Asquith's last silent picture was *A Cottage on Dartmoor.* The first talkie *The Jazz Singer*, starring Al Jolson, had been made in Hollywood in the preceeding year and film-makers everywhere, having witnessed its sweeping success, soon began to acquire the new costly equipment, for it was obvious that audiences would no longer want to sit through the old-fashioned silent films; at the same time thousands of cinemas in America, in Europe, and in Britain began to adopt the necessary means of reproducing sound.

The film-making technique was, of course, very seriously affected. To get the lip movements of the characters on the screen to coincide with the words on the sound track, the film had to travel through the projector at a faster rate. Until then sixteen frames of the picture on the film had to pass through the projector every second in order to provide the movement of people, dogs, railway trains and fire-engines on the screen. This had now to be speeded up to twenty-four frames per second. The adjustment made an important improvement, for it eliminated completely the old jerky movements of the actors and we no longer saw men and women walking across the screen in quick shuffles, an unfortunate pace in a funeral procession.

Asquith and Hitchcock had already begun work on their new pictures, both of which were silent. Hitchcock's was called *Blackmail.* By the time their films were completed, each added one or more talking sequences before delivering their films for public showing.

Asquith's *A Cottage on Dartmoor*, based on a story written by Herbert Price, was made at Bruce Woolfe's new studio at Welwyn. Though aware that the invention of talkies placed him at a disadvantage, for the sound recording equipment was not yet obtainable in England, Asquith was far from discouraged. Ideas kept bubbling up. He introduced fresh techniques. 'In one scene I had a talkative bar boy talking to someone who doesn't want to be talked to and I had flashes of all the various things he is talking about. For example, I cut in about six frames of a cricket match, a flash of horseracing, and various different subjects he hit upon; the other person meanwhile was getting more and more restive, until I cut to a close-up of his lips moving and then cut in a shot of a hen clucking, as a sort of visual metaphor. And, at the end of the film, the hero, who is an escaped convict, goes back to the little cottage where the woman he loves lives with her husband – although the convict has had every opportunity of escaping. The warders, who think he is dangerous, are armed and I had him deliberately run back to the cottage knowing he would be killed.

'Well now it's quite easy to show a man running fast, you intercut up from his feet to his head and so on, but I wanted to give an ecstatic feeling, so I intercut those shots with like shots of waves seen from the bow of a ship, a cornfield swept by a gust of wind, waves breaking on the shore, and then foam running up the shining beach – of course there were no waves on the moor but it was like the wind going across grass. It was like saying he ran without leaving a footprint so light was his tread, and as he was shot and fell against the door I had a flash of a wave breaking against a rock. All these shots were part of a movement, they had a full flow. These were *visual* metaphors of urgent movement. Not symbols, metaphors. And as this movement was common to each shot the whole sequence made perfect visual sense. The impact on the emotions was made by this visual rhythmic flow.

No call was made on the intellect to work out the meaning, as is too often the case with symbolism. And I didn't use any subtitles to explain my meaning.'

The convict was a hairdresser named Joe, in a small town in Devon, in love with Sally his pretty manicurist, who was attracted to a young farmer. They go to the cinema together and Joe follows them. Cleverly, Asquith made the film they were watching a talkie and its brief dialogue has a bearing on the love story of the three in the cinema.

Next morning when the young farmer comes in to be shaved, Joe, having seen an engagement ring on Sally's finger, approaches the farmer with an open razor. Puffin made the camera take the place of the man in the chair, thus justifying the point he had made to Charlie Chaplin some years earlier in Hollywood.

Asquith's inventiveness received the highest praise from the Press. 'There are flashes of inspiration in the film,' said one newspaper. 'His admirers are convinced that Anthony Asquith will in the course of time make a great film.' Elizabeth Bowen, the novelist, praised his 'feeling for landscape'. Asquith himself said: 'I am fond of sky shots and also staircase scenes. I put them into *Underground* and *A Cottage on Dartmoor*. I like shots of reflections in mirrors, too. There were a number of both in the films I have mentioned. However, I do not want to overdo it.'

# 8

## His First Talking Picture

Bruce woolfe, the tall, benevolent father figure, who had encouraged Asquith since the very beginning and had given him such splendid opportunities to show what he could do, selected his first talkie film for him. It was Ernest Raymond's novel, *Tell England.* It appealed to Woolfe because it told the story of the British, Australian, and New Zealand troops landing at Gallipoli during the First World War and could thus be ranked with his other war films such as *Mons*, *Ypres*, and *Zeebrugge*.

Asquith, who was delighted with the assignment, prepared his first full-length talkie script with great care and set out for Malta with three cameramen and Geoffrey Barkas, whose experience in making war films was considerable. At Malta the landing and battle scenes were to be shot.

'For the war scenes,' Puffin told me, 'a number of large crates of "explosives" had been assembled. They contained only a black powder which, when ignited, suggested shell-bursts. I was standing by these crates, about to shoot a scene when the Governor arrived.

'At that moment, possibly through nervousness on seeing the Governor, someone threw away his cigarette and it fell into the crate nearest to me.' He underlined the memory with his hiccuping laugh.

'I was quite unaware that the cigarette had fallen into the crate beside me. There was an instantaneous shell-burst which blackened exactly one half of me. One side of my nose was white the other black. Half my mouth, half my chin, exactly half my clothes were given this harlequin effect. The Governor, Sir John DuCane, stared at me for a moment, then extended his hand to welcome me to Malta.'

'Two battleships, seven cruisers, and four destroyers were very kindly lent to us by the Royal Navy without any charge,' Charles Hillyer, who was with Asquith at Malta, told me. 'We found we were unable to shoot the landing scenes because the sun was in the wrong position for our purposes both in the morning and the evening. The Commander-in-Chief of the Mediterranean Fleet, Sir Alfred Chatfield (later Admiral of the Fleet Lord Chatfield), on seeing our difficulty told Anthony Asquith: "I am doing an exercise next week. I don't want to know what you do about it." We were thus able to pick just the right spot for the landings at Suvla Bay in Gallipoli. The spot we chose was Ghain Tuffatia. The Commander-in-Chief asked Asquith to come aboard the *Queen Elizabeth* and asked him: "How many marines do you want?" Asquith said, "Five hundred." They were provided. We used the mail-boat running from Syracuse to Malta as our landing-ship, the *River Clyde*; we ran it aground and three lighters were used, one in front of the other to provide a path from the *River Clyde* to the beach. The whole thing worked splendidly.

'The enemy, that is to say the "Turks", kept shelling the troops as they landed. The entire first wave of marines were "killed"; the whole of the second wave were also "killed"; and the third wave had to climb over the "dead" marines, piled in high heaps one on top of another. Only a handful landed "safely".

'When we had finished the scenes we discovered that seventy-six rifles belonging to the marines were missing. The Commander-in-Chief had to be informed. He said: "Don't worry about them." He sent down divers who retrieved the rifles from the seabed, where they had fallen when the marines were "killed". We were not allowed to pay the marines, but gave them two bottles of beer each – ludicrously inadequate for what they had done for us.'

Victor Peers, the sound editor, described the early microphones: 'They were large, heavy, black carbon mikes with a very thick lead to the recording apparatus. For the scene in which the Captain makes a speech we hid the ungainly mike in a fruit dish on the dining-table. At the end of his speech he said "I'd like one of those bananas", not realising that it would be recorded. We had to erase it, of course. Welwyn studio was built before sound came in and we had a sound-proof studio built especially for sound recording. It was not all that good, but it served our purpose.'

The story of *Tell England* is about two young men, close friends at school, who join the army on the outbreak of war in 1914 and eight months later take part in the landing at Gallipoli. Months of inactivity and then the terrible slaughter of war dimmed their enthusiasm. The more sensitive of the two, Edgar Doe, becomes edgy and quarrels with his friend Rupert Ray, an inarticulate young Englishman who is by now a captain. Doe has a nervous breakdown, but recovers when he is selected to lead a raiding-party on the Turkish trenches. Single-handed he succeeds in putting the Turkish trench mortar out of action, but is seriously wounded and dies. Shortly afterwards the British

Puffin Asquith and his mother; Lady Oxford and Asquith.

Another early study of Puffin with his mother.

Puffin Asquith drives a shot to green during a family game on the links of North Berwick, 1926, watched by Patrick Balfour (now Lord Kinross) and Peter Lubbock. (*Photo:* Courtesy of Baroness Elliot of Harwood)

Puffin's mother, Lady Oxford and Asquith, drives a ball at North Berwick, 1926. (*Photo:* Courtesy of Baroness Elliot of Harwood)

Puffin with his father H H Asquith then Lord Oxford and Asquith. (*Photo:* Courtesy of Baroness Elliot of Harwood)

Lady Oxford and Asquith walks ahead of the family golfing party on the links at North Berwick.

troops are withdrawn from Gallipoli. The entire exploit, inspired by Winston Churchill, had proved to be a failure.

A P Herbert (later Sir Alan Herbert) supplied additional dialogue, and Mary Field, who was later famous for her excellent children's films, was the editor. In the cast were Fay Compton (Edgar Doe's mother), and Wally Patch was the Sergeant Instructor.

'In one sequence,' says Asquith, 'I showed Doe's mother, Fay Compton, who has just seen her son off to the front. You see her coming into her house, talking to the housekeeper and going through her books, doing the most prosaic things imaginable. Then a neighbour comes in, forces herself on the mother, and tells her that "it's always hardest for those who are left behind" and the rest of those terrible old clichés, and you gradually close in on the mother's face and the other woman's voice disappears, and you hear the sound of soldiers marching, and newspaper boys calling the battle news; and suddenly the woman's voice is heard back in shot, and then her face pokes in, asking, "Don't you agree dear?" And the mother says, "Yes, yes absolutely."

'Then the woman starts off again, and again her voice fades, and over the mother's face we hear the slamming of train-doors, the guard's whistle, the train going out of the station, and again the woman's face breaks in and asks, "Well, what would you have done in my place, dear?" The mother gets up and tries to pull herself together and says "I . . . I . . ." and faints.

'The faint I did visually. A quick glimpse of the woman's hat, about six frames, cut very short, and the mother's face. And I had the sound of the faint on the track. It was what would now be called, *musique concrete*. A note on a string and then, as she falls, a very high note on a piccolo, and the sort of telephone-bell ringing you get in your ears if you are feeling ill. It was, in fact, a kind of sound metaphor of a faint.'

Critics had been waiting to see how Asquith would use sound. They were deeply impressed by the result. Some described it as the best film of the year. The *Evening News* said: '*Tell England* proves to be one of the two or three outstanding British talkies made so far. It is certainly a great achievement for young Mr Asquith, whose first talkie it is. It is a brilliant piece of work pictorially and contains many novel and impressive ideas in the use of sound. It is such a capable bit of work that it may well achieve greater success than the film *Journey's End* and some of the triumph of *All Quiet on the Western Front.*'

Paul Rotha, a distinguished movie-maker himself and always shrewd in his assessments, stated in *Celluloid, The Film of Today, 1931:* 'Broadly speaking, the brilliance of *Tell England* lies in the scenes of the two landings and in Doe's capture of the Turkish trench mortar . . . It is in these terrific spectacles that the combined talent of Geoffrey Barkas, an experienced director of war record films, and Anthony Asquith, an exponent of modern methods of cutting, puts on the screen something which has never been done before . . . The film grips our imagination . . . No war film yet produced has been more convincing than these scenes of landing, not even the often-mentioned sequence in Pudovkin's *End of St Petersburg* or the long shots of the French attack in Milestone's *All Quiet on the Western Front.*'

Asked how he felt about using sound, Asquith said: 'At first I, in common with some other directors, was unhappy about the introduction of sound. I considered that the silent film was a self-sufficient art form which had found its artistic feet, but it was not the only form, and I now realise that the visual and the oral are indispensable elements of the cinema . . . A new technique has had to be found which synthesises the two mediums.'

The title of the picture was taken from the inscription on Doe's grave –

*Tell England ye who pass this monument,*
*We died for her and here we rest content.*

Asquith used music sparingly and always most effectively; he rarely wrote any incidental music himself; he always spent hours discussing with the composer the music he required. And he was equally sparing with the use of sound: many directors in those early days made talkies that were a riot of sound. His were not. Alfred Hitchcock also reacted against the current trend. He said: 'Talk is the essential propulsion of the stage play, but is only an aid in the case of the film. The ideal of the film is to present its story.'

# 9

# British Films Fight for Survival

HAVING BEGUN AS an apprentice with Bruce Woolfe at £2 10s a week, Asquith got small rises after *Shooting Stars* and *Underground*. By that time his salary had been nearly doubled and after the sweeping success of *A Cottage on Dartmoor* he got a great deal more. But even so the figure was not large. British films were going through a very difficult time. American films began to flood the English market while Britain was involved in the 1914-18 War, which the United States did not enter until 1917. Too much ground was lost by British film-makers during those years and they considered themselves lucky if one British feature film a year managed to get a showing on the screens. American film-makers, with an enormous market on their own doorstep, were able to recover their costs at home and consequently to sell their films in Britain for far less money than the British producers.

This strangle-hold was killing the British film industry and a campaign was launched to induce the government to do something to save it. In 1927 the Cinematograph Film Act was passed, which required the film-renters' organisation, as well as the film exhibitors, that is to say the cinema owners, to book and show a percentage of British films, rising from the low starting level of 5 per cent to 20 per cent in 1935. It was not enough. It provided a modest outlet but it also did a great deal of harm to the film industry, because quite a number of producers, with an eye only on getting a quick return, began to make 'quickies', low budget films about gangsters and murders, with a scratch team of actors and actresses and no rehearsals, which were completed in a week and were sold for very little money. These were used to meet the quota of British films required under the new Act; as the films were worthless they were generally shown on the screen while women with mops and buckets were busy cleaning the cinemas before the public were admitted.

For the most part it was documentary and instructional films that had the best chance of being shown on the British screen. They were short and were put on as buffers to precede or follow the American feature film. But British feature films were also being made by Asquith and Hitchcock and others.

Welwyn studio, built just before talkies came in had one very large stage about 250 feet long, equipped for sound-recording. There was still no film trade union and the crew, consisting of only six technicians, worked for very long hours. Asquith arrived very early in the morning by the workmen's train and often didn't take the last train back to London but spent the night at the studio editing the sections of film shot during the day and assembling the sequences of the days preceding. He identified himself completely with the workmen, even dressed like them.

'He wore old flannel bags, a faded brown jacket and, when it was very cold, a big coat with leather patches,' says Muriel Baker, who took over as continuity girl on *Tell England* for a time.

'One evening he suddenly remembered that he had to be a

a social dinner in Mayfair and dashed off, wondering if the train would get him to London in time. When I asked him the next morning about it, he said: "The train got me there only just in time, but" – and he started to laugh – "the butler looked at me as he opened the door and said solemnly 'His lordship is not in.' I told him my name and said I'd been asked to dinner. But he looked me up and down and shut the door." I daresay Anthony Asquith was very angry to find himself shut out after his breathless dash to town. But he seemed to enjoy the memory of what had happened as he recounted it to me.'

Neither what he wore nor what he ate meant anything to him, as I know. He lived largely a cerebral life. 'We all found him very friendly, charming and considerate;' Muriel went on, 'in fact there was no distinction whatsoever between him and any of the studio crew. But he was personally unapproachable; one was conscious of a barrier that could not be penetrated. I would say that the drawbridge which could have led to a *close* friendship was never let down.'

Not long after the shooting of *Tell England* had been completed about half of the permanent staff engaged on the film were sacked. It was in the summer of 1931, the year the Wall Street crash of 1929 hit Britain. 'I was one of those sacked,' says Muriel, 'and with recession everywhere I didn't know where to go. I had been in the script department at Welwyn for eighteen months and I was getting £2 10s a week. It was all I had and out of it I had to pay my rent, buy my food, get to the studio by bus and train and cope with such personal needs as arose. You can imagine how upset I was.

'One morning, seeing me look dejected, Anthony Asquith asked: "Can I help you?" I didn't know what to say. "Could I lend you some money?" he said. I still didn't answer. "Or is there any other way?" he went on. In the end I told him I needed another job and he wrote a lovely letter saying all sorts of nice, kind things. Gainsborough studios at Shepherds Bush took me on at once. It was an open letter and I used it for years afterwards. It always worked.'

In between writing and vetting scripts on the top floor at Lime Grove ('Hitchcock had a room near mine') Muriel in moments of slackness wrote two plays for the theatre. Not long afterwards she married Sydney Box, who was also writing scripts at the time and they went into film production together with impressive success. After the break-up of the marriage she married Lord Gardiner, who was Lord Chancellor for almost six years in Harold Wilson's Government.

If he got home early enough, Puffin Asquith was able to join in the various diversions his mother provided in her house in Bedford Square. Often she went to the theatre or the cinema, sometimes if her daughter Elizabeth Bibesco happened to be in London, they went together. But from time to time she entertained. There was generally music. Celebrated pianists, violinists and cellists were invited and on a summer evening when the windows were open, crowds gathered outside in the square to listen.

Artur Rubinstein, the pianist, who knew the family since the early days of the First World War, told me that whenever he played in London, Margot asked him to go round after the concert. 'On one occasion, when I arrived I found she had the entire Diaghilev Ballet there and they were all leaping about the large drawing-room, Margot leaping about the room with them. It was most enjoyable. Sometimes I played to the guests.

'I remember when Margot came to the Wigmore Hall to hear me play. I was young, just getting known, and thrilled to find the Hall packed. Their appreciation of my playing was most enthusiastic. When the concert finished, I got a big ovation. I came out and bowed once or twice. The cheering went on and on and I felt that I must go out again and give them an encore. I was turning over in my mind what I should play when quite suddenly the cheering and the cries of "Bis! Bis! Encore!" stopped. There was silence save for the shuffling of feet.

'I beckoned to the manager and asked him what had happened. He said: "The audience is going home." I was puzzled. "But they were calling for me to come back and play to them." He raised his hands. "The hall is now quite empty."

'I wondered if somebody had called out "Fire!" This seemed like sabotage. In the past when I played badly, really badly, a few friends always stayed in their seats. I said to the manager: "I didn't think I played badly today." He replied: "You were very good. Their applause was rapturous. They wouldn't stop until a woman in the front row rose and said to them – 'Go home! Didn't you get enough for your money? Mr Rubinstein is very tired. Do you want to kill him? So go home and give him a chance to get some rest.' I have no idea," the manager added, "who she was." I said: "I know." It was Margot. I had seen her sitting in the front row.'

While Puffin was an undergraduate at Oxford, Artur Rubinstein used to see him sometimes at The Wharf at weekends. 'Our friendship developed then. He was the youngest member of the family, and a little shy. His mother, Margot, was very brilliant; his sister, Elizabeth, was musical, she loved music; but I found that Puffin was incredibly keen on music. The only one who really knew about music and was studying it seriously. I felt certain he would be a musician, I would not have believed that it would be the movies.'

During Rubinstein's visits to Bedford Square, if Puffin got back early enough from the film studio, they would get into a corner together and talk. 'His deep interest in music gave us so much to talk about. What contributed most to the strengthening of the link between us was my realisation that Puffin was not only a *receiver*, just listening to music and enjoying it, but an *inspirer*; it made me play so very much better. You have no idea how much collaboration there is between the musician and the public. They can be discouraging or inspiring. I felt I got more inspiration when Puffin was around. I had no interest in anyone else. I really enjoyed being with him. He lived for music.'

I asked Artur Rubinstein if he had thought of Puffin being a composer. 'No,' he said. 'Not a composer. He didn't have it in him. I did a lot of composing when I was young – songs, concertos, sonatas . . . but I discovered, fortunately soon enough, that I didn't have the talent. Puffin didn't have the talent for composing. He would have been a very good, an outstanding Doctor of Music – a Professor: he had as much knowledge as a musical encyclopedia.'

'Could you see him as a conductor?' I asked.

He smiled. 'A conductor is like a film director and I must confess that I never could imagine Puffin being a film director. I spent thirteen years in Hollywood and knew many film directors – Ernst Lubitsch, Cukor, Mankiewitz, John Ford, Selznick, John Houston, and lots of others. I collaborated with some of them and wrote music for their films. They all had *hardness* in them. They had to dominate other people. They knew what they wanted and they could enforce their will, often on more than a hundred people. But Puffin was so delicate, so utterly shy, I could never imagine him giving orders to anyone. If he had inherited one little part of his mother he would have had that quality.

'Yet he directed some very good films. I was enchanted by them. I remember *The Young Lovers*. It was very good indeed. I especially liked his use of the music from *Swan Lake*. It was absolutely right. *Swan Lake* always moves me and I congratulated him on using it with such wonderful effect.

'Before the Second World War, Margot, Puffin, and I went to Spain together. I know Spain like my pocket.' His eyes were alight with laughter. 'I saved their lives, I think.

'We were in Seville and I took them to a cabaret after Easter week. During the whole of that week everything is closed, just everything, but the town begins to wake up and live again on the Saturday night before Easter Sunday. The restaurants, the theatres, cabarets, young singers and dancers make their début, we have flamenco – everything is in full swing: a resurrection of gaiety.

'I took a box at the cabaret. There were six of us in it, for in addition to Margot, Puffin, and myself, we had Madame d'Elanger, Sir William Jowett, who was later Lord Chancellor in Attlee's government, and his very beautiful wife Lesley, who had a passion for music. Margot was wearing a *décolleté* dress, showing nothing, for she had nothing to show. Puffin sat on the floor beside her.

'To my surprise and horror I saw Margot put into her mouth a big cigarette. The audience noticed it and were shocked. The people of Seville are very hard and outspoken. They objected. There was a roar of criticism. "Shame!" they shouted. "How can she do such a thing?"

'Margot thought it was a roar of recognition and appreciation. She smiled and twiddled her fingers to indicate her pleasure and her gratitude. Puffin just sat quietly leaning against his mother's legs.

'In Spain every gesture with the hand means something and gestures with the fingers are regarded as obscene. The crowd began to rush to the box.

'I realized that something would have to be done *quickly*. We had no bodyguards. Fortunately I knew the way to the stage from the box and I hurried them away from the fury of the crowd. Some of us would have got hurt if I hadn't got them away in time.'

# 10

# His First Ballet Film

MUCH MORE AMBITIOUS than Asquith's first talkie, was his second which followed almost immediately afterwards, in 1931. Called *Dance Pretty Lady*, it was based on *Carnival*, Compton Mackenzie's excellent novel of Oxford; the title had to be changed because it had already been used by the famous actor-director, Matheson Long, for a play in which he had been touring.

Compton Mackenzie says British Instructional had told him that the film was going to be handled by a young director of talent, namely Anthony Asquith, and Puffin went to Eilean Aigas, an island off the west coast of Scotland where Compton Mackenzie was living at the time. 'I was delighted to see him and after discussing the film with him I felt all would be well.'

The film script was written by Asquith, who engaged an impressive cast which included Flora Robson, Hermione Gingold, Sybil Thorndike, and Lewis Casson's daughter, Anne Casson, Rene Ray, Sunday Wilshin, and the Marie Rambert Corps de Ballet, with Frederick Ashton as choreographer and technical adviser on the ballet sequences.

Set in the Edwardian age, it tells the story of a ballet-dancer named Jenny who is in love with Maurice, an artist who is young and rich and wants her to be his mistress. She refuses, goes through a phase of acute unhappiness, and, when, after a time, he agrees to marry her, she declines because she feels it would not be a success. Maurice goes away. She begins to realise her folly, waits vainly for his return, and eventually becomes the mistress of Maurice's friend, Danby. It ends with Maurice realising that he was the cause of what she has done. He forgives her and all ends happily.

Summarised, it seems rather trite, but on the screen the atmosphere of gaslit London, the sequences in the theatre and the very lovely ballet scenes were talked of for years as the most delightful ever seen in a film. It was for Asquith a unique opportunity to use music effectively. Writing in *Footnotes to the Ballet* of the initial ballet scene, Asquith said: 'It was the performance of a classical ballet to the music of *Lac des Cygnes*' – his first use of *Swan Lake* – 'and Frederick Ashton designed for it an exquisite fragment of *ensemble* in the classical manner. The dramatic point of the scene was that on the ending of the dance the heroine, who is a member of the *corps de ballet*, and the hero, who is sitting in a stage-box, see each other for the first time and fall in love. For this reason I did not use any close-ups until that moment, for a close-up is the most emphatic kind of shot there is. The ballet scene itself was purely lyrical, and my object was to translate it into film terms. It was a kind of metaphor preparing, as by anticipation, for the love of the two main characters. I therefore treated it quite straightforwardly as a ballet scene, but in a way only possible in sound films.'

Compton Mackenzie had early doubts about the film. 'I recall,' he says, 'walking round the island with Puffin and prophesying that it would not be a success, let alone a great success.' John

Grierson, a pioneer of the British documentary film and an honoured member of the film industry in Britain and abroad, did not share Compton Mackenzie's disappointment. *Dance Little Lady*, he said, 'is a very lovely account of yet another exercise in infidelity. The sets, the camera work, the cutting, are superb. Movement is laced together with the feeling for movement which only half a dozen directors in the world could match. The observations of character and incident are sometimes devilishly clever. There is altogether enough in *Dance Pretty Lady* to give you a most fascinating time. Asquith, with or without knowing it, is going to match Rene Clair quite easily in a couple of years. He has a sense of movement. He has at least equal intelligence.' He then weighs up the assets of Asquith and Hitchcock – most film writers were doing that at the time. 'They are opposites,' Grierson said. 'Hitchcock has had successes in one rather limited field, but he has all the training in the school-of-life background which Asquith lacks. But Asquith has the academic schooling, the little knowledge of this and that in music and painting and aesthetic which Hitchcock has had to grab on the side. He has more taste in the old, rather empty sense of the word. He knows more in his head and less in his solar plexus.'

# II

# Uneasy Years

SIX UNEASY YEARS followed. Shortly after *Dance Pretty Lady*, British Instructional, for which Asquith had made four silent films and two talkies, was taken over by British International Pictures which had studios at Elstree, and both Asquith, and shortly afterwards Bruce Woolfe too, left. He spent part of the summer at North Berwick, playing golf which he enjoyed though some of those he played with didn't think he was very good at it; and of course bridge at which he was extremely good. 'He had an astonishing memory,' Jimmy Smith told me. 'He remembered every card that was out. He sat at the top table, I didn't, nor for that matter did his mother.'

'There were two pianos at Glenconner,' Lady Elliot told me, 'and I used to play Bach, Mozart, Brahms on two pianos with Puff, starting sometimes at seven o'clock in the morning before breakfast, so that we could devote the rest of the day to golf and going to the Edinburgh Festival in the evening.'

At the end of the summer, Michael Balcon of Gainsborough

Pictures at Islington engaged Asquith as script-writer and director. His first assignment was disappointing. Balcon had arranged to adapt a German musical comedy and asked Asquith, because he knew German and had had made *The Runaway Princess* in Germany and England, to write the screenplay. Both the English and the German versions of the film, which was called *Marry Me*, were directed by Wilhelm Thiele. The English cast included the well-known German actress Renate Müller, George Robey, Ian Hunter, Maurice Evans, and Harry Green. Asquith said later: 'I had really nothing to do with this film except a little work on the translation and adaptation.'

In the following year he was given a film to direct, but for the first time in the seven years he had been making films he was not asked to write the script. Nor was the story very promising. Called *The Lucky Number*, it was about a famous footballer, adored by thousands of fans, whose girl has just left him. Hurt, he decides to go to France for a holiday. On his return he meets a girl in a funfair sideshow. He takes her out, discovers after a drink or two at the pub that he has lost his wallet, and asks the publican if he will accept a French lottery ticket. The man agrees and the next day it proves to be the winning ticket. Every subterfuge is used by the footballer and his girl to get the ticket back and in the end they succeed – but discover that the man who organised the lottery has run off with the money. But love provides a happy ending.

Shot at Gainsborough Studio at Islington and on location, it had a talented cast. Clifford Mollison played the footballer, Gordon Harker the publican, Joan Wyndham the girl, and among the others were Frank Pettingell, Esmé Percy, and Hay Petrie, all three destined for stardom on stage and screen.

'We did the sound recording for the football scenes at the West Ham ground.' says Charlie Wheeler, the sound-recorder.

ıffin Asquith filming Norah ıring for his film *A Cottage on ıartmoor* at Welwyn in 1929. (*Paul ·pper Photo*)

ıffin examines his film negative: 31. (*Paul Popper Photo*)

ıcked away in a corner of a film ıdio, Puffin Asquith always played : piano while awaiting readiness set and artistes.

Puffin distributed leaflets for his fil union case. (*National Film Archive*)

The film team of Puffin Asquith, Anatole ("Tolly") de Grunwald and Terence Rattigan confer on a film set. (*Note Puffin's boiler suit and navvy's belt.* He is sitting on the wooden horse 'Epifania' which Sophia Loren gave him.)

Association of Cine Technicians' General Secretary George Elvin presents an illuminated address to Puffin Asquith in recognition of his services to the film union. (*ACTT*)

'When we arrived with our apparatus we were told to go away. It all seemed new and frightening to them. We went behind a building and put the microphone on the top of four poles tied one above the other, which was all that could be seen from the ground and was in fact not noticed.

'Among the best scenes Tony Asquith shot was one of a group of kids, who enjoyed being with him – he loved children, as you know – and another outside a pub where a barrel organ was being played. Tony worked all night for a whole week on the editing, restoring some of the comedy that had been cut out. Thousands of little bits of film that had been cut out, all of them unnumbered, had to be put together. But Tony got what he wanted. It was a delightful film.'

Basil Wright, a brilliant documentary film-maker himself, wrote of it in the *Cinema Quarterly:* 'The main thing about the film is that it is mainly Asquith, and Asquith at last fully fledged. There is a firmness of touch about the main sequences of *The Lucky Number* which his previous productions lacked. I recommend for special attention the pub scenes. They are witty, authentic and beautifully directed and cut. Gordon Harker has never been in better hands, and there is a superb Yorkshireman (Frank Pettingell) whom Asquith, in incredibly few feet, gets blindly, disgustingly, obscenely, but above all gorgeously, drunk. This is the best sequence in the film. Note too the use of musical comment. In addition to some very competent use of natural sound, Asquith has succeeded in insinuating some extremely witty musical remarks which emerge – again beautifully timed – at unexpected but wholly appropriate moments.'

For his next film, *Forever England*, based on C S Forester's famous book *Brown on Resolution*, Michael Balcon chose Walter Forde as director and assigned to Asquith the direction of the second unit, that is to say the shooting only of exteriors on location. In a sense it was a demotion.

We see a British cruiser attack a heavily-gunned German commerce raider. John Mills, who plays Brown, spots the German ship making for a safe estuary to carry out repairs and swims to a high rock to try and stop them.

'We went to Cornwall,' Charles Hillyer told me, 'and searched everywhere for a site that would serve our purpose. We walked up and down rough tracks for hours. Asquith kept stopping and talking to himself as to whether this – or perhaps that – would serve. Eventually we saw ahead of us a rock in the middle of a bay. Asquith said: "If we put a camera here at this angle it will look all right on the screen. Nobody will know that it isn't a land-locked harbour."

'We set up the camera and the crew were busy getting the various sound and other apparatus ready, when an angry farmer carrying a gun and accompanied by a horde of fierce dogs turned up. Asquith seemed to be completely unaware of the barking dogs that were trying to get at his legs, but went straight up to the farmer and apologised for the intrusion. The farmer said: 'Who the hell are you?' "I'm making a film and I'd like to . . ." Asquith began.

'"Oh no, you don't," the farmer interrupted angrily. "I want your name and I'll see that the people like you don't come trespassing on my land." He fumbled in his pocket for pencil and paper.

'Asquith gave him his name, a little uneasily.

'"Are you Lady Oxford's son?" the farmer asked.

'With some shyness and not knowing what the farmer might do next, Asquith said: "Yes."

'A broad smile spread across the man's face. He put out his hand and seized Asquith's. "I am proud to meet you, sir. Just carry on – and let me know if I can help in any way."

John Mills, with a rifle and two cartridge belts on the top of the rock, begins firing on the Germans.

'I was astounded,' John told me, 'to see Puffin, a frail little man, scaling the steep rock with no rope, no climbing gear, and, even more important, no fear. His physical courage was quite astounding.

'His outdoor location scenes, of which there were a great many, really *made* the picture.' Many of the film critics were of the same opinion.

John Mill's wife, Mary Hayley Bell, author and playwright, added: 'We invited Puffin to John's birthday party at our home in London. He didn't come. He'd had a car smash. The party was nearly over when he arrived, his face covered with blood and his arms laden with gifts for both Johnny and me.'

No one who knew Puffin would ever agree to travel in a car he was driving. They knew he was a dangerous driver. Those who were offered a lift would wave him away frantically. An elderly Irish woman he knew quickly turned away and made the sign of the cross.

After *Forever England,* Asquith left Gainsborough. Michael Balcon, asked about it later, said: 'We already had several well-known directors, Walter Forde, Alfred Hitchcock, Anatole Litvak, Victor Saville, and others and I suppose they had the first choice of subjects. Apart from them there were others who, on looking back, I feel did not possess the same talents as Asquith.'

# 12

# A Meeting With Proust

APART FROM HIS mother, Puffin's closest attachment was to his sister, Elizabeth. Though nearly six years his senior, she shared his intense love of music, played duets with him on the piano, went to concerts and ballets with him, generally accompanied by their mother, read the same poets in French and English and German, had the same quick wit, quite unlike their mother's which was sharp and cutting and could be very hurtful.

Often Elizabeth came to London and stayed at Bedford Square with the family; at other times Puffin, either alone or with his mother, went to Madrid and stayed at the Rumanian Embassy where Antoine Bibesco was for some years the minister. Best of all Puffin liked going to stay with them in Paris. Antoine and Elizabeth Bibesco had, and their daughter Priscilla still has, a very beautiful house in the centre of Paris. It is on the Quai Bourbon at the tip of the Isle St Louis on the River Seine, facing Notre Dame Cathedral. Marcel Proust, author of the seven-volume *À la Recherche du Temps Perdu*, was a close friend of

Antoine's, who later edited the letters he received from Proust and published them in a volume entitled *Lettres à Bibesco*, which has since been translated into English.

After reading the early volumes of *À la Recherche* (only five of the seven were published in Proust's lifetime), Puffin looked forward most eagerly to meeting him; but it was not easy for him to get away in the middle of a school term just to see Proust in Paris. Not until he was at Oxford did the opportunity occur. Part of the summer vacation in 1922 was spent with Elizabeth and Antoine in their lovely house which Proust described as 'Byzantine' because of the preponderance of gold leaf in the decoration of the drawing room.

Telling me of it some years afterwards, Puffin said: 'We went to an opera – Elizabeth, Antoine and I – and Marcel Proust was to join us afterwards for supper. I can't tell you how excited I was' – while saying it his thin lips began to nibble the air. 'We waited for a while and then ordered supper, thinking he would not mind if we began without him. But he didn't come. Just imagine how acute my disappointment was. Would there be another chance of seeing him? It couldn't be during that stay in Paris as I had to return to England on the following day.

'On returning to 45 Quai Bourbon – it must have been after two in the morning – I put the whole thing out of my mind, terribly disappointed of course, but there was no point in dwelling on it. I said goodnight, went to my room which was alongside theirs, and went to bed.

'I was in a deep, deep sleep when I heard someone knocking on my door and voices in Elizabeth and Antoine's adjoining room. One was an unfamiliar voice. I opened the door and saw that Proust was there. Still in my pyjamas but wildly excited, I went up to him. We shook hands and talked until after four o'clock He looked very frail and had a sickly pallor, for he always spent most of the day in bed in a darkened room. It was my only meeting with him, for he died about three months later.'

It was an unforgettable encounter. Occasionally, when I was with Puffin at his home in Thurloe Square, looking at one of the books on his shelf about Proust (he had a number written by Princess Marthe Bibesco, a relative of Antoine's) he would refer rather briefly to that evening and early morning at 45 Quai Bourbon in Paris and with a slight gesture with his expressive hands he would indicate yet again how much he would have loved to have got to know Proust.

On leaving Michael Balcon after *Forever England*, Puffin settled down to write about Covent Garden with the intention of using it for his next film. Months were spent on research. But two interruptions prevented him from completing it.

The first was an offer to make a film about Schubert. No composer meant more to him; whenever one saw him seated at the piano it was always something by Schubert that he was playing – one of his songs or perhaps one of his valses. But I find it difficult to believe that the film he was invited to make would really have appealed to him: the use of Schubert's music, yes; but the story, one wonders – he certainly was in no position to make any alteration or even a minor adjustment in the story.

The film was in fact a Viennese production and Asquith was co-director of only the English version, for which Benn Levy, the playwright, wrote the script. Puffin went to Vienna and worked there with Willy Forst, who produced and directed the German version. Asquith retained the two principal German stars – Hans Yaray, who played Schubert, and Marta Eggerth, who played Caroline Esterhazy, with whom Schubert was in love. He was her music teacher and she was deeply attracted to him, but was prevented by her family from marrying out of her social circle. Disgusted, Schubert tore out the final pages of his new symphony – hence the title of the film *Unfinished Symphony*. In the cast was Beryl Laverick, now Mrs Reginald Maudling: only fifteen at the time, she was escorted by her mother to Vienna.

Asquith enjoyed working in Vienna and hearing Schubert's music played by the Vienna Philharmonic Orchestra and sung by the Vienna Opera Choir and the Vienna Boys' Choir. But the story, he realised, was novelettish and historically inaccurate. But it was well received by the public because it was so handsomely mounted and so tastefully handled.

The other interruption was an invitation from Alexander Korda, the Hungarian film producer who was building at Denham, near London, the largest film studio in Britain. *Moscow Nights* was the title of the film Asquith was asked to direct. Based on a story by Pierre Benoit, the French novelist, it had already been filmed in France where it had a successful run as *Les Nuits de Moscou*. Asquith collaborated on the English script and directed the English version of the film.

It was a wartime story about a pretty but poor Russian girl, Natasha (played by Penelope Dudley Ward), who is engaged to a rich contractor, Brioukow (Harry Baur appearing for the first time in an English film). A young officer, Captain Ignatov (Laurence Olivier), has been wounded and is brought to the hospital where Natasha is a nurse. They fall in love with each other. Her middle-aged fiancé and the young officer quarrel, but Natasha insists on being loyal to Brioukow. In his distress Ignatov loses heavily at the gaming-tables but is helped by Madame Sabline (Athene Seyler), who is discovered to be a German spy. Ignatov, suspected of being her accomplice, is arrested, but is saved by Brioukow, who, being aware of Natasha's great love for the young man, sacrifices his own happiness for hers.

Though the story was rather commonplace, the film benefited from its distinguished cast. Laurence Olivier's acting established him as an outstanding film actor. Asquith was handicapped by the fact that it was just a remake of a French film and Korda, absorbed in building his mammoth studio at Denham, began the shooting at Worton Hall studio and transferred it to Denham while it was still in production and finally sold it as part of a package deal to General Film Distributors.

Greatly upset by all this, Asquith left Korda and decided to try his hand at independent production. Temporarily he joined Max Schach, but the British film industry ran into a financial crisis just then and Asquith made no films for two years.

# 13

# President of ACT

THE PURPOSE OF the Film Society, of which Anthony Asquith was a founder member, was to look at and make a study of the latest and most interesting films made in Europe. The key personalities in the organisation were Ivor Montagu, Sidney Bernstein (now a life Peer), Iris Barry, and Thorold Dickinson. One of the members, Harold Elvin, pedalled all over Europe on his bicycle, bought seats at cinemas in Paris, Berlin, Rome, Moscow, Stockholm, and elsewhere, and wrote reports on the films worth getting and screening. The films shown, generally at the New Gallery Cinema in Regent Street or the Tivoli in the Strand, included *Die Dreigroschenoper*, Pabst's film version of Brecht's play with the bitter, nostalgic music of Kurt Weill; *Ekstase*, a most impressive film made in Prague; the German *Mädchen in Uniform*; Sasha Guitry's *Roman d'un Tricheur*; and many Soviet Russian films by Eisenstein and others.

The cost of Harold Elvin's trips was inexpensive; his bicycle needed no refilling with petrol, nor was his shoe-leather damaged.

His cinema seats were paid for as well as his bed and meals. But as he enjoyed the trips anyhow, he sought no personal remuneration.

This combination of cinema-lovers who established the Film Society and the eccentric bicycle pedalling Harold Elvin led to a new development. Many of the film technicians belonging to the upper echelons felt that, whilst looking at these films was instructive and diverting, it would be of immense advantage to form an association for meeting and exchanging views on technical advances and problems. Others, while welcoming this, wanted to go a stage further and establish a trade union which would be concerned with economic as well as cultural matters. Prominent members of the Film Society, including Thorold Dickinson, Sidney Cole, and Ivor Montagu, favoured this course.

A start was made and quite a number of members were enrolled. But, regrettably, the trade union aspect was overlooked and the organisation, called the Association of Cine Technicians, became a snob association of top film technicans. This was contrary to the intention of the pioneers and a vital change was planned in the running of the organisation.

Thorold Dickinson recalls that he and like-minded colleagues had a talk with Harold Elvin, who was then in the art department of British and Dominion Film Studios, and asked him if he knew of someone who could take on the job of secretary. He mentioned his brother George, who was honourary secretary of the British Workers' Sports Association and had roots in the trade union movement: his father was general secretary of the National Union of Clerks (which is now the Clerical and Administrative Workers' Union) and was later president of the Trade Union Congress.

George Elvin was approached, agreed to take it on and was

with the ACT (now the ACTT) as general secretary for forty years. He hardly knew what he was taking on and, but for the £5 lent to him by Thorold Dickinson and repaid in Paris twenty-five years later, he would never have got past the liftman in charge of the building where ACT had only one room on the top floor overlooking Piccadilly Circus. ACT had at the time eighty-eight members of whom only eight were fully paid up; the debts outstanding amounted to several hundred pounds. A hard fight was begun to build up a strong and viable organisation and transform the disillusioned into enthusiastic members.

Parallel with this endeavour there was a film crisis which had a shattering effect on British film production. Of the 10,000 persons engaged in the industry in 1936, as many as 80 per cent were unemployed. Many studios were idle or only partly engaged in production.

The Quota Act passed in 1927 to operate for a period of ten years was to come up for review in 1937 and ACT was resolved that, the old quota and its conditions having failed to help the British film industry, its members should fight hard to eliminate the shortcomings of the earlier Act.

'We needed somebody to lead us into battle,' Thorold Dickinson told me. 'I had returned from West Africa where I had directed a film called *The High Command.* Lucy Mannheim, the well-known German actress who starred in it, phoned and asked me to lunch with her at her place in St John's Wood. "Is there anyone you would especially like me to invite?" she asked. I promptly said "Anthony Asquith," and we met for the first time there.

'After lunch he and I shared a taxi. By the time we reached Oxford Circus I said: "Will you become president of ACT?" After a brief pause he asked if he could think it over, and that night he informed me on the phone that he would be delighted to accept.

'At the next meeting of the Council – I was a vice-president of ACT at the time – I pointed out that the film industry had gone through a terrible year and that unless the technicians did something about it we could not survive. ACT would have to point out to the Board of Trade the dangers that faced the industry. We would in fact have to do much more than that – we must tackle the ministers in the government – go and see them in their offices and tell them what must be done if they wanted the British film industry to survive.

'They were all eager for action. Someone asked: "Are you going to do the lobbying?" I said: "Yes. I'll certainly help, but the man who is best fitted for the task is Anthony Asquith. As the son of a former Prime Minister . . ."

'There was a confusion of voices as everybody tried to speak at the same time. "No one better," said one voice. "Will he take it on?" asked another. When I told them that I had sounded him out and he was prepared to be president of ACT if they wanted him to, there was delighted and unanimous endorsement. He became president in May 1937 and served ACT, as you know, until his death.'

George Elvin who succeeded him in 1968 as president said, 'He was the first British film director to join a trade union – not for what he could get out of it, but for what he could put into it, in fact to help other members.'

'Our first task,' Thorold went on, 'was to fight for the survival of the British film industry. Not only was Anthony Asquith most energetic and resourceful, for he knew most of the ministers – or, if he didn't they at any rate knew who he was; but his mother, Margot, plunged into the fray too. She used to invite members of the government – Neville Chamberlain was Prime Minister at the time – to lunch at her house at 44 Bedford Square. The President of the Board of Trade, Oliver Stanley, was there and Walter Elliot,* and oh! a lot of them at different times – and she had her son Anthony, and George Elvin and me and some others members of ACT there to meet the ministers and explain how the film crisis could be overcome. More than that, if the ministers weren't prepared to accept our arguments, she went for them, denounced them for not having the sense to see how important films were to the country, for they did not just entertain, they educated the public and showed the world what Britain was able to do. She was a stalwart fighter – a crusader in fact – and we owed a great deal to her.'

When the first Quota Act was passed ten years earlier many in the political and business world declared that if the film industry had not become a viable economic proposition by 1938 then it deserved no further protection.

'Tony Asquith saw Randolph Churchill, who was writing at that time for the *Evening Standard*,' Thorold Dickinson added, 'and gave him all the details about our critical position, together with diagrams indicating clearly the state of the British film industry because of the continued domination of our cinema screens by American competition. Randolph wrote a splendid article for the *Evening Standard*, but it was thrown out by the management. "If ACT wants their case put before the public we must charge them advertising rates." It was ludicrous to expect *us* to pay a great deal of money to try and save the entire British film industry. We hadn't any money anyway. What the paper did was to analyse in an editorial article all our arguments and turn them against the film technicians. Actually it did a lot of good. The public got to know what exactly was wrong.

'Then ACT discovered that the new Quota Act was going into Committee at the House of Commons. We rented a meeting-room in the Strand and informed all our members about it.

* He was married to Puffin's Aunt K.

They turned out in strength and poured into the committee-room in the House. The approaches to the room were crammed, the stairs were crammed. The members of the Parliamentary Committee found they couldn't get in. We then marched up Whitehall and on to our meeting-room in the Strand to work out the next stage of our campaign. Anthony Asquith worked very hard – we all did and the improved terms of the new Quota Act enabled us to survive the American invasion.'

At the annual general meeting of ACT in 1938, Anthony Asquith, delivering his first address as President, said: 'Unsatisfactory as the new Films Act is in many ways, it would have been very much worse but for the efforts of ACT and other interested unions. I am convinced that but for the long continuous pressure from us many of the improvements on the old Act would never have been obtained. They were not in the 1927 Act – they *are* in the present Act.'

# 14

# *Pygmalion* — His First Great Film

In that same year Asquith began work on his most important film so far, *Pygmalion*. Only two of Bernard Shaw's plays – *How He Lied to Her Husband*, a short plays tarring Edmund Gwenn, and *Arms and the Man*, with Barry Jones and Maurice Colbourne – had been filmed, both in the early 1930s and neither of them was of any real consequence as a film.

*Pygmalion* was quite another matter. Even Shaw, who was always reluctant to have his plays filmed because he would not tolerate any tampering with his dialogue, was excited. He had been persuaded by Gabriel Pascal, a Hungarian film producer, who gave Shaw the solemn promise that not a word would be altered. Asquith was selected to direct it and also collaborated in the writing of the film script, but Shaw always had the last word. Some additional scenes were required for the screen and, after some persuasion, Shaw wrote them – and it was to Shaw that Hollywood awarded an Oscar for the *film script*.

Leslie Howard, who played Professor Higgins, was associate

director of the film. Wendy Hiller, with whose acting in the Shaw Festival at Malvern GBS had been greatly impressed, was given the role of Eliza Doolittle. The cast was large and included Wilfrid Lawson as Eliza's father, Marie Lohr (Higgins's mother), Esmé Percy, Violet Vanburgh, Iris Hoey, Irene Brown, Ivor Bernard, Kate Cutler, Cathleen Nesbitt, and Stephen Murray. The film was edited by David Lean, whose later successes as director of Noel Coward's *In Which We Serve* and *Brief Encounter*, *The Bridge on the River Kwai*, *Lawrence of Arabia*, *Dr Zhivago* and *Ryan's Daughter* made him world-famous. Arthur Honegger, the French-Swiss composer, wrote the music. Gaby Pascal insisted on hearing the whole of it. 'For myself I am delighted, he told David Lean, 'but the director does not like the *boom boom boom* of the brass. He wants something sweet on a violin' – not a true interpretation of what Asquith said.

'Leslie Howard was wonderful,' said Anthony Asquith. 'He'd come on the set, have a quiet walk through in rehearsal and then he could repeat a shot again and again – even his eyelashes would be in the same place at any given moment, yet his performance was never mechanical. He had the most wonderfully controlled technique I have ever seen.

'I think *Pygmalion* was Wendy Hiller's first film. Before we started shooting I had an interview with Shaw about the ballroom scene, which was quite splendid. We decided, quite rightly, that you must show Eliza and her triumph at the ball, which isn't in the play at all. I was delegated to go and see Shaw, to sell him the idea, so that he'd write the scene, and I hoped I could sketch out the sort of thing I thought should happen.

'I had lunch with Shaw and his wife. Shaw was in splendid form, all through lunch we talked about nothing but music, which was his great passion and mine, and after lunch he sat at the piano and demonstrated how all six parts of the sextet from

*Lucia* should be sung; and I had got nowhere near the point of my visit.

'When finally I broached the subject Shaw thought the idea was out of the question, but Mrs Shaw came to my rescue. She commanded him to listen to what I had to say. By this time I was trembling with nerves, but I asked him to let me read to him the kind of thing I had in mind, the kind of thing which we thought might, just *might*, happen in the scene. "Of course, naturally, we would want you, Mr Shaw, to write the actual scene," and very reluctantly and impatiently he said all right and I began reading. There was one phrase where I said "Eliza comes up the stairs with the frozen calm of the sleepwalker", and that pleased him, and he kept repeating the phrase "frozen calm of the sleepwalker", and from that moment on he was settled, hooked. So I will take that much credit for the extra scene.

'Of course the *My Fair Lady* show is based on the film. "The Rain in Spain", for example, that's not in the play. We had an expert on phonetics as adviser on the film, and there were two montage sequences of Eliza learning, first of all how to pronounce, and then how to behave. In the first one I asked for a sentence she could practice on the "a" sound and the expert produced "The Rain in Spain stays mainly on the plain", and the complementary sentence of her dropping her "h's" was by me, which is "In Hampshire and Hereford, hurricanes hardly ever happen".

'And I put in one other thing which is not in the play. I once saw Mrs Patrick Campbell, who was the original Eliza, in a revival of the play and in the tea-party scene I remembered two words which she had put in. The text read "My aunt died of influenza so they say, but it is my belief they done the old woman in." Mrs Campbell said: "but it is my belief, *as how* they done the old woman in." Her accent was perfect, but not her grammar. I remembered the "as how" which lifted the whole thing. Shaw spotted it, but he let it stay.'

Before the shooting of the film a publicity lunch was given at Pinewood studios, at which Shaw was the guest of honour. When he was called on to make a speech, he rose to his great height, raised a glass of water (he was a teetotaller) and said: 'Ladies and gentlemen, the toast is Shaw!' and sat down. It got a great laugh, followed by applause.

Everywhere the film was shown its reception was rapturous and the box office takings were enormous. Wendy Hiller's brilliant interpretation of Eliza raised her to instantaneous stardom. And Asquith himself, after a rough passage for some years, was placed by the critics in the foremost rank of British directors for his delicate touch and skilful handling of the amusing and satirical sequences. Telegrams poured in from Hollywood with offers to direct films there. But he refused them all. He preferred to make films about England and the English way of life in all its varied moods ranging from challenging cheekiness to comedy.

His decision was right, for a few months later a door opened which provided him with a long and most successful association with a new writer, Terence Rattigan, whose play *French Without Tears* was to be Asquith's next film assignment.

Wendy Hiller told me: 'I was extremely lucky to have Puffin as the director of *Pygmalion*. I was very shy and frightened; he was most kind and patient. He encouraged me to play the role instinctively, which gave me great confidence. Anyone else might have forced me to interpret the part differently and it would have confused me. Puffin had great artistic taste and impeccable good manners. There was nothing vulgar or cheap about him.

'Gabriel Pascal was quite different. He was on the set all the time while we were shooting and kept on interfering. He was an awful nuisance – after a time I refused to talk to Pascal or to take any guidance from him.

'We had only a week's rehearsal and then eight weeks of shooting, taking in two Sundays to get it finished in time.

'At first it was a little baffling to find Puffin with his unique background and upbringing, the way he spoke and played the piano, and of course his fine manners, looking the way he did: he dressed like one of the electricians – if anything was less well groomed. But no one could have been more considerate. I remember I had a very bad toothache while we were shooting the ballroom scene. He was really wonderful. He noticed that I was in pain, fussed over me and did everything he could to help, and solved it in just one more take. Somehow he even managed to get on with Pascal – a lot of tact was required for that. They talked and argued far into the night.

'When the film was finished Puffin asked me to appear later in some of his other films and, although I wasn't able to, he always sent me flowers.'

'It was a great game to work for Pascal,' said Asquith, 'especially if you learned how to do it. One time David Lean and I were at the cutting stage of *Pygmalion* and we showed a reel of it to Gaby who asked for some impossible cut, but by this time we knew him. We'd say, "Right you are. In half an hour we'll show it to you." Then we'd go and have a leisurely cup of coffee and show him the same reel again, not having touched a single frame of it; and this time it was, according to Gaby, *p-a-r-f-a-i-t*. But although there were times when he would ask you for something quite absurd, the next time it could be something absolutely splendid and constructive.'

Bernard Shaw told me when I saw him shortly before his death that Leslie Howard was not the right man to play Higgins because he could *never* have bent Eliza to his will. When I asked whom he had in mind, Shaw replied: 'Charles Laughton' and pooh-poohed my remark that the film would have lost the tenderness

Leslie Howard supplied. 'It was not a tender part,' he said. 'It was *not* a love story.' While the film was being made Shaw wrote to Pascal: 'It is amazing how hopelessly wrong Leslie is. However, the public will like him and probably want him to marry Eliza, which is just what I don't want.'

The sweeping success of *Pygmalion* made Asquith one of the highest-paid film directors in Britain. But money meant nothing to him – he spent it whether he had it or not, always on others, never on himself. His mother had no sense of money values either. She almost always lost money at bridge and found that the enormous income bequeathed to her by her father Sir Charles Tennant was constantly being strained. In the thirties, shortly before the war, Margot got a Polish refugee named Peter Ruckle, who later changed his name to Russell, to keep an eye on her accounts and indicate how much she could or could not spend. After Margot's death, Peter Russell was bequeathed to Puffin who, she realised, needed a hard taskmaster to control the money he received.

By now the working hours in the film studios had been defined by the trade unions and the management, and nobody any longer worked all night, except Anthony Asquith and one or two other directors, but they worked generally at home on plans for the next day's shooting. With his films now being made mostly in studios at Shepherd's Bush and Islington, it was possible for Puffin to do something with his evenings. Usually he dined with Charles Hillyer or one of the other technicians at the Café de l'Europe in Leicester Square and walked home from there to 44 Bedford Square. 'During that walk, Asquith was waylaid by a number of down-at-heel scroungers – they knew him because he always gave them money,' Charles Hillyer told me.

'If he got home in time he and his mother would take me, or Victor Peers, or whoever happened to be with him, to the opera or a concert. He always looked upon his fellow-workers as his friends – and most enjoyable evenings they were too.'

When not filming he would go away for a few days in the summer, usually to North Berwick where he enjoyed playing golf; or spend a few days with his sister, Elizabeth, in Paris. Quite often he went to film societies at Liverpool or Ipswich to talk about 'Building a Film Star', 'Directing for the Screen', and so on. In *Pygmalion*, he explained, he made the visual provide the accompaniment to Shaw's excellent dialogue. 'Perpetual cuts backwards and forwards from one speaker to another would be intolerably jerky. When Professor Higgins decides to take on the bet to turn the flower-girl into a duchess, he strides about the room dynamically and the camera follows his movements with the minimum of cuts. But when he sits down and there is a brisk argument between him and the housekeeper, with the girl and Pickering intervening, we have the other kind of movement – quick staccato, with the eye in partnership with the ear.'

Work on the filming of Terence Rattigan's play *French Without Tears* began early in 1939. The shadow of a devastating war with Hitler hovered over Europe, getting more menacing every hour. The radios bellowed the Fuhrer's loud-lunged threats, on the newsreels we saw his storm troopers marching to the Czechoslovak frontier, the massed flight of Nazi planes, the thunderous advance of tanks – the screen spared us nothing.

A film production company called Two Cities had been formed by a flamboyant Italian named Fillipo del Guidice who brought a swarm of his fellow countrymen with him and took on the making of the Rattigan film at Shepperton. Anatole de Grunwald, a member of an exalted pre-Revolution Russian family, wrote the film script in collaboration with Terence Rattigan: these two with Puffin made in the succeeding years many fine films together.

Terence Rattigan, in his middle twenties and strikingly handsome, was expected after Harrow and Oxford to follow his father into the diplomatic service. But, like Puffin, he turned his back on family expectations.

The setting of his *French Without Tears* was Professor Maingot's 'cramming' establishment in the South of France. Ray Milland, destined to attain stardom in Hollywood not long afterwards, played the leading role. The arrival of the pretty flirtatious sister of one of the students provides delightful complications, which are added to by the sudden appearance of a naval commander who has come for a crash cramming-course in French for an impending examination.

'I remember on *French Without Tears*,' said Asquith, 'we had a sort of carnival scene with a chain of dancers going round one way and another chain of dancers going in the opposite direction. Jack Hidyard, our cameraman, shot it brilliantly. As they pass, the end of one chain grabs the end of the other chain and immediately you go in the opposite direction.

'Jack had his camera on a rostrum right in the middle and they went round him. He had to move jolly quickly I can tell you. At the moment the end man of one chain grabbed the end of the other, Jack changed direction with them. It was absolutely flawless. It was so brilliant that no one believes it isn't cut, which I suppose is the quintessence of good camera work.

'Another thing we did was the scene on the bicycles, which nowadays we would automatically do with back projection. Actually it was done on the circular road at Shepperton. It was also direct recording, with the dialogue going on all the time, and we didn't post sync' an inch. It was a very complicated shot for timing; someone would come into the shot and say something, then gradually fall back to let another cycle come in position. We carefully rehearsed it and Jack got it in the first take.'

Asquith's brilliant, light-hearted handling of this amusing comedy added greatly to his reputation.

Graham Greene, soon to be famous as a novelist and playwright, reviewing the picture in the *Spectator*, stated: '*French Without Tears* is a TRIUMPH for Mr Anthony Asquith. After the first ten minutes his witty direction and firm handling of the cast (Mr Ray Milland has never acted so well as this before) conquer the too British sexuality of Mr Rattigan's farce. There is always something shocking about British levity; the greedy exhilaration of these blithe young men when they learn that another fellow's girl is to join them at the establishment where they are learning French, the scramble over her luggage, the light-hearted badinage and the watery and libidinous eye – that national mixture of prudery and excitement – would be unbearable if it were not for Mr Asquith's civilised direction (unlike most adaptations from stage plays it is the padding that is memorable). The situation is saved, too, by the Navy; Mr Rattigan must be given credit for the sketch of a stiff, shy commander who finds himself dumped down from his ship into this adolescent kindergarten, and Mr Roland Culver for a brilliant performance as the commander.'

# 15

# The War Years

*French Without Tears* was completed immediately before the outbreak of the Second World War and there was some doubt whether any films would be shown in cinemas or any public places in wartime with the country plunged in darkness and under imminent attack by enemy bombers.

'I went to the Ministry of Information,' Thorold Dickinson told me, 'and saw Sir Joseph Ball who was in charge of the Films division and discussed the position of the film industry with him. "You have nothing to worry about at all," he said, "because we are closing down all cinemas and so there will be no film industry."

'I was horrified. "No cinemas! No theatres!" I exclaimed. "Theatres," he replied, "will be open only in the middle of the day – not after dark. Cinemas will not be open at all."

'Nothing more inconceivable or indeed nonsensical could have been given out as official policy. I said: "But you will need cinemas. They are vitally important for purposes of propaganda – to keep the public fully informed of what is happening – for raising morale. There are all sorts of things that the public will have to be told – about rationing, fire-fighting, coal supplies, conserving one's water supply, and so on. And then there is the very important need to show short documentary films about recruiting for the services and for the coal-mines and for training those who volunteer to help – men as well as women . . ."

'He interrupted. "It's a Cabinet decision," he said. I went at once to see Anthony Asquith, and his mother lost no time in inviting a number of Cabinet Ministers and Members of Parliament as well as myself, George Elvin, and other ACT members to 44 Bedford Square. She denounced the Government. Films were vitally important not only for the people in Britain, but for keeping foreign countries, especially neutral countries, informed about what we were doing. Her attack was devastating: it galvanised the Government into action. Sir Joseph Ball was replaced by Sir Kenneth Clark, who was Director of the National Gallery and Surveyor of the King's Pictures and has since been made a life peer. He reversed the earlier decision and we were able to continue to make films and show them in cinemas all over the country.'

The number of films made in Great Britain fell. Over a hundred in the year 1939, the total in 1941 was sixty-five and in the following year only forty-six. Even the number of foreign films shown in Britain dropped from 535 in 1939 to 364 in 1946. Though some of the feature films made in Britain had a war setting – Noel Coward's *In Which We Serve* for example; *The First of the Few*; *San Demetrio*; and *The Way to the Stars*, directed by Anthony Asquith, most of the documentary films dealt directly with the war effort – *Target for Tonight*; *Coastal Command*; *Desert Victory*; *Fires were Started*; *Western Approaches*: in the six war years more than 700 documentary films were about the war.

Asquith made two short documentaries – *Channel Incident*

about the evacuation from Dunkirk, with Peggy Ashcroft, Gordon Harker, and Robert Newton; and *Rush Hour*, a short, witty comedy about British workers during the rush hour with Joan Sterndale-Bennet and Muriel George – both for the Ministry of Information.

The first of Asquith's longer feature films was *Quiet Wedding* which he was asked to make for Paramount who had distributed *French Without Tears*. Based on the play by Esther McCracken and scripted by Anatole de Grunwald and Terence Rattigan, it presented most amusingly the attempt of a young couple (Margaret Lockwood and Derek Farr) to be married quietly, but their efforts are disrupted by interfering relatives, local busybodies, and others. On the night before the wedding Aunt Mary advises the bridegroom to kidnap the bride: they are arrested for dangerous driving and are locked up in a police-station; but are bailed out by the family and get to the church in time.

It was highly praised by the critics for Asquith's inventive handling of the satire and the 'richly human qualities' of the film. It had an enormous success in Britain as well as in the United States.

Following this, Puffin joined Gainsborough Pictures, which had recently been bought by Rank, with Edward Black as Producer and Maurice Ostrer as Executive Producer. Of the four films he was given to direct, the first was *Cottage to Let* – a Nazi spy story. Once again Anatole de Grunweld had a hand in the scripting but not with Terence Rattigan, who by this time had joined the Royal Air Force. In the cast were John Mills, Leslie Banks, Michael Wilding, Alastair Sim, Catherine Lacey, Jeanne de Casalis, George Cole playing a boy evacuee, and Wally Patch, who was with Asquith in his very first film, *Boadicea*. Most of the film was made in the studio, but the climax provided a number of exciting thrills in the bazaar when the boy evacuee unmasked

John Mills as the Nazi spy in a tent of distorting mirrors. It cannot be ranked, however, among Asquith's best films.

Immediately after completing this film, Asquith went on to his next, *Uncensored*, for the script of which he persuaded the Air Ministry to grant Terence Rattigan a short spell of leave. It dealt with the Nazi occupation of Belgium and the starting of an underground newspaper called *Le Libre Belge* to fight the propaganda the enemy was putting out. Like *Cottage to Let* and an earlier film, *Freedom Radio*, which Asquith made just before his two short documentaries, it spotlighted certain Nazi activities and the valour of those who risked their lives to combat them. Clive Brook, Diana Wynyard, Bernard Miles, and Clifford Evans were in *Freedom Radio*; Eric Portman, Phyllis Calvert, Peter Glenville, Irene Handl, Felix Aylmer, and Phyllis Monkman played in *Uncensored*.

Later in the war he made two further short documentaries – *Two Fathers* – for the Ministry of Information, telling of a Frenchman's daughter who works with the Maquis against the Germans and the Englishman's son who is in the RAF and has had to bail out ('There are many,' says the Frenchman significantly, 'who will help a British airman in France'); and *Welcome to Britain* made for the US Office of War Information and shown to American troops in Britain – a kind of guide telling them what to do and what not to do. Burgess Meredith, Bob Hope, and Beatrice Lillie were in the cast of this film.

Though not made for either the British or the Russian Ministry of Information, *The Demi-Paradise*, about a Soviet marine engineer's visit to England with a new type of propeller he has invented, could well have served to inform our newly-found Russian allies about the ways of the English. The script was written by Anatole de Grunwald, a pre-Soviet Russian, and he was also the producer. The company sponsoring it was Two Cities, for which Asquith made *French Without Tears*. Laurence Olivier, who eight years earlier played the role of a Russian in Asquith's *Moscow Nights*, was the Soviet marine engineer in this film. Margaret Rutherford, who was to give many fine performances in Asquith's future pictures, now made her second appearance in a film of his; Joyce Grenfell, Miles Malleson, Felix Aylmer, and Wilfred Hyde White were also in the cast.

Laurence Olivier's performance was described as dazzling and yet a real and sympathetic portrayal of the bewildered Russian – it put him, said Dilys Powell, for the first time in the top flight of British film actors. Asquith's skilful direction also received the highest acclamation. 'The section describing the visit of the Russian to this country is the best part, the nearest thing to English René Clair,' wrote William Whitebait. Dilys Powell, referring to Asquith's brilliant handling of the sequences, says: 'The film drew a picture, ironic and yet at the same time affectionate, of English foibles. The visitor encounters all the surface idiosyncrasies of a reserved people: the unwelcoming landlady, the silent railway travellers, the apparent casualness and coldness and suspicion of the average Englishman towards the foreigner. The Russian is chilled and discouraged until, with the entry of his country into the war against Germany, the genuine warmth and friendliness underlying British reserve come into play. *The Demi-Paradise* had numerous touches of pictorial satire.'

Felix Aylmer, who played the role of a wealthy eccentric shipowner and grandfather of Ann (Penelope Dudley Ward), has Ivan (Laurence Olivier) for the weekend at his country house. 'Puffin,' Felix told me, 'had numerous little touches in the film to represent England in wartime. He managed, for instance, to get Beatrice Harrison to play the 'cello to the nightingales for the film. There were some nightingales where I live and the recording was made near there in a part of the Surrey woods.'

Carmen Dillon, who was assistant art director on the film, mentioned a spot of bother while *The Demi-Paradise* was being made. 'Maisky, the Russian ambassador, complained that he had not been shown the script. "Who is this fellow from Latvia called de Grunwald? He is making fun of the Russians."' De Grunwald's family was in fact Russian: the *de* was prefixed to the surname by many members of the Russian aristocracy during the eighteenth and nineteenth centuries.

The script was sent again to the Russian Embassy. There was criticism of a few of the scenes, which were eventually modified. Meanwhile there was conflict between the local works committee at the studio and Asquith, who promptly resigned as President of ACT. But at the Annual General Meeting he was re-elected unanimously.

One afternoon not very long ago, when Laurence Olivier talked to me about Puffin Asquith, he said: 'We enjoyed a very intimate friendship, an intimate personal friendship, entirely without any passion. It was really an extraordinary, most enjoyable friendship.

'The first film of his in which I appeared was, as you know, *Moscow Nights*. It was a transcript of a very successful French film with the French actor, Harry Baur, in the character part and Penelope Dudley Ward, making her first appearance as an actress, in the role played by Annabella in the French film.

'Puffin was a very polite, extremely gentle creature. He spoke very quickly but not more quickly than he was thinking. He was witty. He made you laugh and he laughed at your jokes. But you felt there was a strong layer of nervousness there. He seemed to be in very much awe of Alexander Korda, who produced the film. On one occasion while we were on the set right in the middle of a shot being taken, some production manager came up and put his hand gently on Puffin's shoulder and said very softly: "Mr

Korda wants to see you." Puffin leapt up as if someone had shot him, turned very quickly, hit a lamp, and, as it fell, turned and apologised to it and left the set in a great hurry with the film in the camera still rolling. That sounds as if he was a coward. He wasn't. The most you could ascribe to him was anxiety to please.

'By the time I made my next film, *The Demi-Paradise*, with him I was in a position to be allowed to work on the script with Anatole de Grunwald and Puffin Asquith. Quite frankly it was a propaganda film. I daresay it was unnecessary propaganda. The purpose of the propaganda was to make the English love the Russians who had just come into the war. Again I had Penelope Dudley Ward as my leading lady, and all sorts of famous English character actors and actresses – Margaret Rutherford, Felix Aylmer, etc, etc.

'And again we had a marvellous time making the picture. And here again one was conscious of his strange, seeming mixture of reserve and yet – I wouldn't call it kitten claws, for there was always some admirable strength somewhere . . . and fondness . . . and charm . . . and wit . . . and delight . . . delight.'

There were at times long gaps between their meetings but, Larry added: 'The feeling of friendship never changed. It was as though we had been together only a day or two before. He very sweetly introduced me to a famous work called *Choreartium* by Leonide Massine at Covent Garden. It was a splendid work – a pure, abstract dance – no story, just dancing, to Brahms' No 4 Symphony of course. And he added to the charm of the evening by sending me all the records of this piece.'

To Puffin he attributes something to which Puffin did not actively contribute. 'It was towards the end of the war, just before I made *Henry V*. We hadn't seen each other for some time and met by chance at the Ministry of Information in the hall as we were leaving. We shared a taxi when we left as it was difficult to get one during the war.

'He asked me about my ideas for *Henry V*. I poured them out to him and in doing so I found that I owed him something. While I kept telling him of my ideas he was a sort of cushion and suddenly there was a little bit of magic. He didn't say anything, I just hit upon the idea. First of all I thought that at the end of the film *Henry V* the chorus should appear, and that up to that time there should be an off-screen commentary. I thought what fun it would be at the end of the film to see *who* Henry V was and *where* he was and to discover that you were in fact in an Elizabethan theatre. No sooner had I said this and Puffin was wagging his head in furious agreement and enthusiasm I said suddenly: "Of course I've got it. I must start in the playhouse." Puffin approved very thoroughly. I remember that conversation and remember feeling always that it was Puffin I was talking to when I received this wonderful gift. I never lost the feeling of friendship – it never changed.'

* * *

Another war film made by Asquith was *We Dive at Dawn* with John Mills playing a naval lieutenant and Eric Portman as a leading seaman.

Despite its story this was really a documentary film. Some of the sequences, such as the sighting and pursuit of the German battleship, were exciting, but Dilys Powell summed it up very neatly when she said: 'Anthony Asquith sometimes gave the impression that he was working against the grain; his story of life in a submarine, efficient though it was in a cold way, lacked the warmth of life.'

The last of his four films for Gainsborough Pictures was *Fanny by Gaslight*, based on a recent novel by Michael Sadleir, which was a bestseller. It starred James Mason, who made a great impression on his audience as the evil Lord Manderstoke; and Phyllis Calvert who played Fanny, the daughter of a West End publican, who also ran a dissolute Victorian night haunt. It was a little too novelettish and Asquith was brave enough to try his hand at a rather crude melodrama. 'Anthony Asquith has obviously taken immense pains with his backgrounds of low public-houses and stately English homes,' said *The Times*, 'but atmosphere is not enough, and emotion is seldom there to illumine it. The film is persistent in its suggestion that it is the product of some forgotten bestseller of the deliberate, gaslit 1880s.'

'uffin confers with an artiste during location filming for *Dance, Pretty Lady*. (*British Instructional* *'ilms Limited*)

udrey White with Puffin Asquith and author R J Minney—an 'off-set' shot taken at Pinewood.

Viewing Rattigan's memorable cricketing film, *The Final Test*, are: Top Row (l to r) Puffin Asquith, A Gover, Helen Cranston (film editor); R J Minney (producer). Bottom Row (l to r) Jim Laker, Alec Bedser, actor Jack Warner, Godfrey Evans.

A Mediterranean alfresco scene as Puffin Asquith rehearses a shot for *The Yellow Rolls Royce*.

Elizabeth Taylor and Louis Jourdar rehearse a scene for *The VIPs* unde Puffin Asquith's direction.

# 16

# *The Way to the Stars* – His Finest War Film

A FILM ABOUT the British and American air forces in Britain, *The Way to the Stars*, was based on a story written by Terence Rattigan and scripted by him and Anatole de Grunwald, who, as the producer, engaged Asquith to direct it.

By the time everything was set in motion for shooting the film at an air base in Yorkshire it was apparent that the war was likely to be over before the film was shown. 'We eventually decided,' Terence Rattigan told me, 'to begin the picture with a shot of a bare derelict field and say on the sound track "This *was* an airfield", and flash back to the story of what really happened there.'

Asquith, who also worked on the script, as directors do, made the camera wander over the derelict airfield, picking out the down-at-heel, empty living-quarters, the wash-houses with the fading scribbles on the walls, the empty buildings around, and the torn flapping posters on the walls. It was a brilliant touch and most effectively moving. This method was adopted later by many film directors, and especially in *Twelve o'clock High*, which was made in America four years later.

The cast of British and American players included Michael Redgrave, John Mills, Rosamund John, Renee Acherson, Stanley Holloway, Bonar Colleano, Trevor Howard, Joyce Carey, Jean Simmons (as a singer – it was her very first film part), and David Tomlinson. The chief American character in the film, Johnny Hollis, was played by Douglas Montgomery and the film was consequently called in America *Johnny in the Clouds.*

Michael Redgrave, married in the film to Rosamund John, manageress of the Golden Lion, is killed in action, and his widow is comforted by Johnny, who in turn is killed. New young pilots keep arriving and the substory develops. John Mills, in love with Renee Asherson, feels it is wrong and most unfair for pilots to marry. He tells Renee this, but is made to see things differently by Rosamund who has suffered two shattering blows. Bald though this may sound, the life at the station, the many little incidents concerning the various members of the large community constantly in danger (Asquith's character studies were always excellent), the initial mistrust between the British and the Americans which develops eventually into understanding and warm friendship, makes *The Way to the Stars* an outstanding war film. A poem, entitled 'For Johnny', by John Pudney,* provides the picture with an added emotional quality:

*For Johnny*

*Do not despair*
*For Johnny-head-in-air;*
*He sleeps as sound*
*As Johnny underground.*

* First published in *Dispersal Point*, 1942.

*Fetch out no shroud*
*For Johnny-in-the-cloud;*
*And keep your tears*
*For him in after years.*

*Better by far*
*For Johnny-the-bright-star,*
*To keep your head,*
*And see his children fed.*

John Mills recites it as he walks, with the camera on him all the time in a long tracking shot. Asquith, walking beside the camera with his eyes on John Mills, walked straight into a wall and of course apologised to it.

'Puffin, as a director,' said John Mills, 'was a marvellous audience. His enthusiasm was quite fantastic. There were times during the shooting when he was so deeply moved that one could see the tears pouring down his cheek.' Puffin would have called that 'Floods'. I once heard him tell a young actress, very gently and kindly, how to try doing her part a little differently. 'Just this once more,' he said sweetly. Realising that she had done it wrong and was being very considerately corrected, she dissolved into tears. He comforted her. 'Let's leave it now,' he said and led her off the set to spare her any embarrassing glances. Slipping his arm through mine on his return, he said: 'Floods! Floods, my dear! We'll try it again a little later on.'

'The film acquires nostalgic overtones from a skilled repetition of thought and scene,' Edgar Anstey said in the *Spectator*, 'and by the judicious employment of poetry by John Pudney. But most memorable is Anthony Asquith's creation of a typical British and American flying man. Perhaps only Michael Redgrave as the moody poet attempts an untypical characterisation (and true to type may be misleading in this ritualistic world of air combat), but John Mills, Douglas Montgomery and particularly Bonar Colleano (who played Johnny's American friend, Joe) do throw light on the kind of young men who have been flying the Blenheims and the Fortresses.'

Released a few weeks after the war ended in Europe, the film received the *Daily Mail* National Film Award for 1945 and was later top of the ballot organised by Sidney Bernstein (now Lord Bernstein) of Granada Theatre for the best British or American film since V-Day.

The origin of *The Way to the Stars*, Terry Rattigan told me, was a documentary film. 'Willie Wyler – Major Willie Wyler at the time – was over here to make a film called *The Spirit of St Louis*. I was assigned to it as an RAF Flying Officer, with an American Lieutenant, who was also a writer, to work out a story of an airfield. That was the germ of the idea of Anglo-American co-operation. Willie Wyler made his film. It had nothing to do with an airfield, but with the crew. When it was finished he got his medal and went back to Hollywood and so did the American writer.

'Tolly de Grunwald rescued the material and got del Guidice sufficiently interested to set it up. Puffin directed it marvellously well at Catterick. It was made during the winter of 1944 and it was fairly obvious that the war would be over before long and the ending we had for the film wouldn't be of any use. It was not until after the film was completed that we shot a bare field and used it for the opening shot of *The Way to the Stars*.

'We had our script conferences in my chambers at Albany. At the time, as you remember, the German doodle-bugs kept coming over and while talking about the script Tolly and I listened for them with half an ear. We had decided – Tolly and I – that at the cutting out of the buzzing of the bomb we would make for the passage: it was the only possible place to seek some sort of shelter. Albany was a rather old building.

'Puffin kept walking up and down the room, talking rapidly as always and incessantly. We heard the buzz-bomb, but he obviously was quite unconscious that there was any sound other than his own voice. The bomb came closer and closer and then suddenly we heard the cut-off. Tolly and I dashed into the passage, knowing that within seconds the bomb would drop and explode. I quickly threw myself on the floor and Tolly fell on top of me – or perhaps it was the other way round. After the explosion – the bomb fortunately missed our building – we came back. Puffin was still walking up and down the room. On seeing us coming through the door, he realised that we hadn't been listening to what he had been saying. "This is no time for games," he said. "We are supposed to be getting on with the script of *The Way to the Stars*."

'The strange thing about Puffin is,' Terry went on, 'that nothing could ever frighten him. He had absolutely no fear. His courage was really marvellous. He would have done anything in the war if it was necessary and even if it wasn't. He took all sorts of dangerous risks in order to get authenticity for his pictures. And he expected others to do the same.

'In *The Way to the Stars* there was a good deal of flying, of course, and Puffin was apt to say: "I wish they would fly closer together. Why are they so far apart?" When he was told that it would be a bit dangerous, he said: "It *can't* be dangerous if they aren't actually *touching*."

'Puffin was in the Home Guard during the war. I don't know what he did in the Home Guard and I don't think he knew either. But he never got out of the uniform or the Home Guard boots. He used to come and see me day after day and sometimes night after night at Albany, and those boots used to make a most terrible clatter going up the stone stairs. He made even the Home

Guard uniform look worse than it was. It made him look like an old tramp.

'One evening the man at the gate rang me up and said: "Excuse me, Sir, there's a person down here who says he's Anthony Asquith but I can see that he's not, so I've sent him about his business." I was horrified. "Oh my God!" I said. "What have you done? It *is* Anthony Asquith." At that moment Anthony Asquith rang me from a call-box. He was furious. "I don't understand what they're doing. They've turned me out."

'I said: "Puffin, you see the point is there are a lot of deserters about" – in fact there were quite a number trying to hide in odd corners round Albany.

' "I don't look like a deserter," he said angrily.

' "To him you must have looked like one. I'm awfully sorry, Puff. Do come along. I'll talk to the porter and see that it is put right"'.

# 17

# A Long But Victorious Fight

THE WAR BROUGHT a number of changes in Puffin's life. When the bombing became heavy and buildings were shattered or set on fire, Margot, now nearing eighty, decided that she would have a better chance of a night's sleep if she moved into the Savoy Hotel: the danger did not matter to her any more than to her son, but, as a lifelong sufferer from insomnia, she was resolved to try and get as much sleep as she could. So she moved to the Savoy and took Puffin with her, though they still spent a certain amount of time at 44 Bedford Square.

Her daughter Elizabeth had been with her husband at his home in Bucharest since the early months of the war, unable to return to England until it was over. Margot's excitement, and Puffin's too, may well be imagined in those early months of 1945 which brought the certainty of their meeting ever nearer. But before hostilities ended Elizabeth died and Margot survived her by a very few months. The two blows coming in such quick succession made it difficult for Puffin to realise what a terrible change had come into his life. He was alone now, with close on a hundred relatives and an even larger number of friends. But these two meant much, much more to him than all the rest.

Some think it was at about this time that he took to drinking rather heavily. Sylvester Gates says he did not drink at all at Oxford and does not know of his taking more than an occasional drink until 1939. The only thing Puffin did to excess was smoke, one never saw him without a cigarette between his lips.

During the war he seemed to be drinking much more heavily. It is difficult to indicate its cause. A few attribute it to heredity, quoting references by Sir Douglas Haig (later Earl Haig) and by Winston Churchill to his father's rather heavy drinking. Lady Cynthia Asquith, Puffin's sister-in-law, states in her *Diaries* that Margot had an obsession about drink: she had received anonymous letters about her husband when he was Prime Minister. 'There must be,' said Margot, 'some terrible temptation in the family.' A malicious jest about Puffin's father went the rounds at that time. It was said that on the only night when Asquith returned from the House of Commons to No 10 Downing Street quite sober his dog bit him.

That Puffin was trying to fight it was obvious. While at Catterick he often went to Joe's Café. It was just a small pull-up for long-distance lorry-drivers in the wide village street which was once the Great North Road. There were no alcoholic drinks only tea and coffee and light refreshments. Joe, who ran the café, had been a regimental sergeant-major. Stocky in build and about forty years old, he lived with his wife, Rita, and their (at that time) two young children, Paul and Peter. Behind the café where the lorry-drivers sat and ate and talked, was the modest parlour; upstairs were the bedrooms. To Puffin it was a refuge, a place to escape to. The friendship that began in that last year of the war was maintained until the end of his life, nearly a quarter of a century later. Joe became an important influence in his life. He was protective, warm-hearted, close, considerate: the atmosphere there was restful, and Puffin never drank. Always, when not busy making films, Puffin would dash up to Catterick to spend a few days with Joe and his family, living as they did. Like them he would get up at five o'clock in the morning and serve the coffee and sandwiches to the lorry-drivers who had spent the long dark night wearily on the road. He loved getting on a bicycle and going on the newspaper round, pushing the morning papers through the letter boxes. He would brook no argument: if Joe and his family could do it, so would he.

When the shooting of *The Way to the Stars* ended at Catterick, Puffin gave a party at Joe's Café for the film unit. It was not confined to them; the transport drivers, the village girls and local families, even the jockeys and grooms at Catterick for the race-meetings were invited. To them all he was just 'Tony'. A few years later when Puffin and I made Rattigan's *The Final Test* together various letters were brought to me to deal with as producer. One of them, which had been opened by the secretarial staff, was addressed to Puffin, but as he was busy on the set, it was handed to me. Scribbled on a sheet torn out of a child's school exercise-book, it had pinned to it a clipping from the *Evening News* about *The Final Test* with a picture of 'The Hon Anthony Asquith'. The letter began: 'My Lord – I am writing you because I have seen your lordship's double at Catterick. He works at a pull-up café there and serves sandwiches and tea and I thought your honour would be interested to know this.'

His ability to give up drinking while at Joe's Café at Catterick seems to indicate that, quite apart from other contributory causes, he was subjected to heavy pressures in his normal daily life. It was not money, for he was by now doing extremely well as a film director with still greater opportunities awaiting him. His mother finally left Bedford Square and took him to Kensington. After her death he went to 27 Thurloe Square, opposite the Brompton Oratory, and all the furniture and pictures left him by Margot were moved there. Peter Russell, who had been handling her finances, moved into an upper floor and took over the managing of his money.

Restlessness had always been a marked characteristic of Puffin's behaviour. He was never still. He used to walk up and down a room, gesticulate extravagantly as he talked, join his hands together and place them against his cheek, touch your shoulder then withdraw his hand and for some moments he appeared to be moving his lips before speaking, as though he was nibbling the words he was about to utter. Then, suddenly, out they would come very rapidly. His ideas kept bubbling up. His brain was incessantly active and at times gave the impression that it was overtaxed. He worked off his restlessness by playing golf (badly), or bridge (always brilliantly, with his brain very alert), or canasta, and at times Racing Demon, or Black Jacks, just to be doing something. When he went to bed it was usually with a muscial score, or occasionally poetry, or perhaps Jane Austen – he read the six novels again and again, and loved *Emma* best.

Paul Dehn, poet, film critic, and film scriptwriter (his script, *Seven Days to Noon*, won the Hollywood Academy Award, and he also wrote the scripts for Asquith's Glyndebourne film *On Such a Night*, and his *Orders to Kill*) discussed with me the tensions to which Puffin was subjected. 'It is greatly to his strength of will,' Paul said, 'that he was able to keep so firm a control over the inherited tendency to drink. It was not until he was forty that it began to get the better of him and even then there were long spells when he didn't drink at all, as, for example, at Joe's Café. I felt that drink helped him to damp down his restlessness and rest his overtaxed brain.'

Music did that too: he used to find peace when he played the piano. In every film contract he signed there was a clause stating that a piano must be supplied for his use, not only in the studio where he worked but also in his hotel bedroom while he was on location.

This drinking phase – by no means drinking continuously, for he kept fighting and went for days without drinking anything stronger than a coca cola – lasted for six years or so, at the end of which, by undergoing a most drastic and unpleasant cure, he won through and drank nothing alcoholic for the last seventeen years of his life.

But during those six difficult years Puffin did in fact make three films of Terence Rattigan's plays: *While the Sun Shines*, *The Winslow Boy*, and *The Browning Version*. Terry told me of the anxiety he and Tolly de Grunwald went through, uncertain whether Puffin would be in a fit state to direct.

'Tolly de Grunwald, Puffin and I had been asked by Alexander Korda to lunch with him at the Berkeley. I had a phone call from Tolly that morning suggesting that we should meet before lunch and decide what we should do about Puffin's drinking, because the last time we had lunch with Puffin his head was in the soup and Korda said: "Even that he does with so much grace."

'Tolly and I met at 12.30 at the Ritz, just across the road from the Berkeley. We sat down, ordered two dry martinis and looked at each other wondering which of us would start talking. Tolly began: "Now *you* are his best friend." I shirked it: "No, *you* are," I said. "Well, whoever it is," he replied, "we must say to Puffin: 'You *must* stop this. It is ruining your career.'" I said I quite agreed with him, but it was really an embarrassing moment and we ordered more martinis while we debated what should be done.

'Suddenly we saw that it was well after 1.15, the time we ought to have been at the Berkeley for lunch. The waiter had kept on refilling our glasses and it was a little unnerving to dash across the roaring traffic in Piccadilly. We staggered into the Berkeley only to find a stone-cold sober Puffin, saying, "Where have you been? Why are you late? And you are both drunk!" '

The cure was ghastly. The doctor he went to, Dr Dent, gave Puffin injections to make him get sick and forced him to take his normal alcoholic drink again and again in quick succession. He was sick ceaselessly and kept on apologising to the doctor. After three weeks or so of this he was cured. He drank nothing but coca colas for the rest of his life.

'When he came to spend a week-end with us,' Simon Hodgson, husband of his niece, Priscilla, said, 'and we were pouring out drinks for the other guests, I would say to Puff: "Will you have a coca cola?" He never failed to smile. His lips made a nibbling movement and he said: "It is so kind of you to give me a choice." '

# 18

# The Rattigan Films

ASQUITH'S ASSOCIATION WITH Terence Rattigan and Anatole de Grunwald, which began with *French Without Tears*, was to continue for nearly thirty years: his last two films *The VIPs* and *The Yellow Rolls-Royce* were written by Rattigan and produced by de Grunwald.

Seated on a very hot summer afternoon in his luxurious suite at Claridges in London, with the windows wide open to let in some air and the busy traffic trying to drown what he was saying, Rattigan talked of his long and happy association with Anthony Asquith.

'I first met Puffin in 1939 when he was about to make a film of *French Without Tears*. I wasn't expected then to work on the film myself. He had an enormous reputation, of course, and I was delighted he was going to direct it. We met at a dinner party and he made a beeline for me. I couldn't believe that this man was already a veteran in films. The positively enchanting, delightful character he seemed to be was wild with enthusiasm about what he was going to do, while I thought it was just another film to him. He also seemed to be wildly enthusiastic about meeting me, who was after all just another author. I couldn't believe this was the great Anthony Asquith and frankly at that moment I more or less fell for him – fell for his personality, fell for his charm, fell for his enthusiasm and for his eagerness, for his way of life.

'Then I came to work for him, which I did not know I was going to do. While working for him I found that all the first impressions I had of him were marvellously borne out. Working with Puffin was an absolute joy because instantly we discovered we had a lot of private jokes, some of which Tolly entered into and some of which were at his expense, but always kindly – always kindly. I chiefly remember that those few weeks of my introduction into films were weeks of giggling and laughing, and at the same time weeks of rewriting a not very good film script, which, however, turned out to be a good one; mostly through Puffin's inspiration.

'This led to a friendship which lasted until his death, an unwavering friendship. I don't remember having a single row with him. We worked together on an enormous number of films. I remember a lot of disagreements about how scenes should be shot or not shot, but no umbrage was taken on either side – there was always the same air of gaiety and fun, always making work a pleasure. In fact it became true to say that he was the only director I wanted to work with.

'Our private jokes were endless. I remember when we were writing the script for *Quiet Wedding* in 1940. Paul Soskin, who was producing it for Paramount, was a very nice man, but we both slightly dreaded working for him, chiefly because his knowledge of English was a little uncertain. We had a marvellous girl to take down our dictation – I say marvellous because she could make order out of chaos, for Puffin talked an awful lot and I am no slouch myself at talking either.

'We would say: "Dallas enters left. Sits down. Camera comes into closer shot . . . then into close-up. Oh God, why have we to do this bloody script for this man Soskin!" And that's the way the script was typed and sent on to Soskin.

'He was always asking us to write little short cameo scenes, which he called "*comeos*". Puffin interpreted it as meaning a small scene which should put the audience into a coma.'

Asquith's first post-war film, *While the Sun Shines*, based on the Terence Rattigan play which Asquith had directed on the stage, was made in 1947, two years after *The Way to the Stars*. It was a highly successful farce about a young earl (Ronald Howard) who has joined the Navy as an ordinary seaman, coming home on leave in 1944. While on his way to his flat in Albany he sees an American officer (Bonar Colleano) drunk on the pavement and takes him to the flat for the night. In the morning, while the earl is keeping an appointment with the selection board, his fiancée, Lady Elizabeth (Barbara White), is mistaken by the American for Mabel Crum (Brenda Bruce), the earl's former girl friend. A flirtation begins, but is interrupted by a French officer, who also falls for Lady Elizabeth. The earl returns and everything is happily sorted out by Mabel Crum, whom the American delightedly accepts.

It had a distinguished cast – Cyril Maude played the old Admiral; Margaret Rutherford (her third time in an Asquith film); Ronald Squire; Miles Malleson; Joyce Grenfell; Wilfred Hyde White; Clive Morton; O B Clarence and Cecil Trouncer. The play was very closely adhered to, and as a result there were very few touches that were arrestingly Asquith, for he had already put them into the stage production. In that, Michael Wilding played the earl. 'He was used to films and not to the straight theatre,' Rattigan told me, 'and had rather a longer part than Hamlet. He floundered a bit during rehearsals. I remember once when he got to the door, he hesitated, then turned to Puffin and said: "I . . . er . . . er . . . how do I go off, Mr Asquith?" Puffin went up to him and said: "Oh, my dear. I am the last person you should ask." '

Richard Winnington reviewing the film in the *News Chronicle*, wrote: 'There are brief delightful moments when one recognises the hand of Asquith, but they are all too few and too brief. The cast is wholesome and competent and there are many familiar faces of good actors lurking in the background, opening doors and standing on stairways.'

This was followed by the filming of yet another play by Rattigan, *The Winslow Boy*. Once again Rattigan wrote the script in collaboration with Anatole de Grunwald, and Asquith had for the first time that very distinguished cameraman, Freddie Young, whose later work on David Lean's *Lawrence of Arabia*, *Dr Zhivago*, *Ryan's Daughter* and *The Battle of Britain* won the plaudits of the world.

Freddie, like all the people Asquith worked with, became his friend. While in Dingle, in County Kerry in the south-west corner of Eire, where David Lean was shooting *Ryan's Daughter* and waiting for the placid Atlantic waters to blow up into a raging storm (it didn't – David had to take the entire cast and the film unit to South Africa for the storm scenes), Freddie Young with a grey beard and looking very like Ernest Hemingway, talked to me over dinner about Anthony Asquith.

'*The Winslow Boy*,' he said, 'was the only picture on which I worked with Puffin. He knew my first wife, Marjorie Gaffney, for many years. She was first assistant director on some of his films and also on Hitchcock's and Victor Saville's. It was through her that I got to know him and we became very close friends. He

fin absorbed while shooting a studio scene.
*ational Film Archive*)

Puffin Asquith addresses a film trade union meeting outside the Kodak building at Hemel Hempstead in 1962. (*Paul Popper Photo*)

fin (second from right) is presented with an oil painting of himself by the film technicians' le union, the ACT (now the ACTT). (*Photo: ACTT*)

A surprise birthday party for Puffin during the filming of *The Final Test.* He is seen standing (centre right) holding a brandy glass surrounded by members of the cast and film crew.

A celebration for the Coming-of-Age of the Association of Cine Technicians. Puffin, as President, is given the 'key of the door'. Presenting the key is George Elvin, then General Secretary, now President. Next to him stands the distinguished film director, later Professor, Thorold Dickinson. (*Terence Wilson and Partners Limited*)

used to come to our parties and often stayed with us at weekends. Without a doubt he was the kindest and most considerate person I have ever met. Our two adopted children loved him: he was godfather to Barbara, and got my son, Michael, through the Winchester examination and later got him the *entrée* into the merchant navy. When my wife Marjorie died after a long and agonising illness, he comforted us and later when I married Joan, who was assistant editor on *Lord Jim* (we met in Hong Kong), Puffin became her friend and as close to us as he had always been.

'He played with the children as one of them – games such as monopoly, spelling bees, dominoes, charades: he often altered the rules to make things even more complicated, but at the same time more hilarious. And we played darts in our converted barn. At bridge he was very, very good. A delightful conversationalist, he never sat down while he talked but walked up and down the room expounding his views on every subject; and then suddenly he would stop and apologise for monopolising the conversation. His physical restlessness and his highly sensitive, nervous mind drove him on beyond his strength and he had to get away at intervals to recover.'

Terry Rattigan based *The Winslow Boy* on the famous Archer-Shee case about which there had been so much in the newspapers. Ronnie Winslow, a young naval cadet, is accused of stealing a five shilling postal order from one of the other cadets and is expelled from the Royal Naval College at Osborne. His father (Sir Cedric Hardwicke) is convinced that his son is innocent and takes the battle into the law courts. The most distinguished KC in the country (played by Robert Donat) is engaged to defend the boy's honour. The repercussions are many. Ronnie's brother leaves Oxford because of the embarrassment it has caused and his sister Catherine (Margaret Leighton) has her engagement broken off. In the end Ronnie's innocence is established and Catherine marries the distinguished KC. Others in the enormous cast were Marie Lohr, Frank Lawton, Basil Radford, Lewis Casson, Stanley Holloway, Cyril Ritchard, Jack Watling, Kathleen Harrison, and Wilfred Hyde White.

The *Sunday Times* rated it as 'one of the best films of the year, with a background, incidentally, beautifully precise as to period, class and place – the Wimbledon of bank managers and retired colonels and the House of Commons of Mr Asquith's father.' America's *Time* magazine was not as enthusiastic. 'Sir Cedric Hardwicke gives a moving performance as the father who courts bankruptcy to redeem his son's honour and Margaret Leighton matches it as the daughter who loses her stuffy fiancé when the case plunges the family into notoriety. Neil North ably fills the title role. With the help of British dependables in lesser parts, the stars give the film a lustre that shines only fleetingly in the script.'

Wilfred Hyde White, who was in many films made by Puffin, told me: 'He used to call for me in his car in the mornings and take me to the studio. At the end of the day he would pull up at the studio gate and offer lifts to anyone who happened to be there. On one occasion so many got into his car that there was no room for Puffin. "What about you?" I asked. "I'll pick up a bus," he said.

'Once when we happened to be alone in the car he asked where I would like to be dropped. I said I was dining with a friend at the Hungaria and asked him to join me. "I can't come like this," he said. "I'll go home and change." We waited some time for him and finally began dinner.

'Presently the doorman came up and said that my guest had arrived, but he wasn't properly dressed. He still had on the boiler-suit and had just put on a shabby jacket. I persuaded the man at the door to let him in. Just as his soup was about to be served, the man at the next table having finished eating, rose and pushed back his chair, which collided with the arm of the waiter and the soup was all over Puffin. Puffin was quite unperturbed. He apologised to both the diner and the waiter.'

Asquith's film first nights were always an event. It was almost the only time he gave up his boiler-suit, which was in effect his shabby old Home Guard uniform, and put on a dinner jacket and black tie, always remembering to display in the outer top pocket the handkerchief Mary Pickford had given him when he stayed with her in Hollywood. It was a delicate, most attractive diaphanous handkerchief, which as the years passed began to decompose, but he kept it in that pocket – a happy link with the past, which he no longer dared to send to the laundry.

On those first nights Joe and his wife Rita would come up from their café at Catterick (both dressed for the occasion, of course) and would dine quietly with him before going on to the cinema and then, after the film, join him and his other guests at supper. To spare them the long journey back to Yorkshire, he put them up for the night at his house in Thurloe Square, where Puffin's housekeeper, Mrs Julia Stowe had prepared a room for them. As their children grew older, the two boys came too, and later still their daughter, Rita, who wasn't born when *The Way to the Stars* was made.

Mrs Stowe lived in the basement with her husband, and together they looked after Puffin. The room Puffin used most was his study which was on the ground floor at the far end of the long hall. Everything was higgledy-piggledy in there. There was a very fine photograph of himself aged twelve, but looking very small for his years, seated beside his mother and looking at a picture book with her. The room was much too overcrowded to see exactly what it contained. There were some attractive *objets d'art*, alongside cheap metal and glass ashtrays and various odds and ends that one picked up at a fairground, which no doubt had been given to him by one of the juniors on the film set or perhaps by one of the lorry-drivers who had pulled up at Catterick. He kept them all. There were also piles of scripts that had been sent him, music sheets, newspapers – he bought all the newspapers every day, carried them about under his arm, but never read them. Quite often while working in the study he fell asleep and spent the night there.

The large dining-room on the ground floor and the drawing-room on the floor above had the furniture and pictures his mother had left him. Some of the paintings were interesting, especially one of some soldiers drilling, which, when sold after his death, fetched about £28,000. His bedroom was on the floor above that – not at all comfortable; the bedroom floor was uncarpeted save for a small strip of black carpet, three foot by two, the rest being just bare boards. The narrow single bed was uninviting, but he never gave a thought to comfort. The bathroom-cum-lavatory was half way down the stairs and he generally walked down to it in the dark.

Quite often he would invite some friends to come round and play bridge. A coal fire would be lit in the drawing-room. Actors, actresses, school and college friends, anyone who loved bridge was asked to come. Later he had Omar Sharif, a brilliant bridge player who thought Puffin well up to the top standard, Paul Massie, Richard Eastman, and others. Often they played far into the night.

When he was alone, Puffin generally went down to the kitchen and sat with Mrs Stowe and her husband to watch television. They were his friends and he was deeply grieved when they were knocked down at the crossroads and taken to hospital, where Puffin went every day to see them. Their place was eventually taken by a young Irish couple, Mary and John Brierley, who were with him for the rest of his life.

# 19

# He Finds The Tenth Muse

A FRESH CRISIS in the British film industry delayed the production of Asquith's next film by two years. The prosperity brought to the industry during the war continued until 1947, after which it was faced by a grave shortage of money. The cinemas were once again showing large numbers of imported American films and while the cinema-owners did well, the film producers suffered.

A new Quota Act was brought in and Harold Wilson, the young thirty-one year old President of the Board of Trade, set up the National Film Finance Corporation to provide money for the production of British films. The advantages were considerable and finance is still supplied by the corporation for film production.

The crisis had caused unemployment on a very large scale. Thousands of members of the Association of Cine-Technicians were out of work. At a meeting of the General Council it was decided that a film production company, to be called ACT Films

Ltd, should be formed for making films and thus providing work for the unemployed, who would be taken on in rotation, so that each in turn should be given a job. Anthony Asquith was elected chairman and about a dozen of us were appointed directors. It was to be non-profit-making.

It came into operation in the summer of 1950 and the first film produced was *Green Grow the Rushes*. The stars were Richard Burton (his first starring role) and Honor Blackman. Quite a number of films were made, and are still being made, and hundreds of members who had been affected by the crisis were able to use their technical skill and earn a living.

Puffin's next picture was *The Woman in Question* – a thriller about a young woman who had been murdered. Dirk Bogarde acting in an Asquith film for the first time, told me: 'It was not a very distinguished film. In it were Jean Kent and Susan Shaw and a new fellow who had been discovered by Puffin called Duncan Macrae, a quite marvellous actor, now alas dead. Puffin I think didn't want me; he had an American actor in mind, but the film was made for Rank, and he was forced to have a contract actor – me. He was *always* polite, but not wildly enthusiastic.

'I was utterly terrified of him, for no reason of his, simply because of my own realisation that I was not what he wanted. I did my very best – was attentive, willing, desperately anxious to win his approbation as a screen actor. About five weeks into shooting he came up to me after the lunch break, cigarette dangling from his lips, hair streaked with nicotine, the old faded boiler-suit and the scratched leather belt, the worn red and white spotted scarf round his neck. He said: "I really think it's all coming along terribly well . . . and you are really very good . . . I like the accent enormously." I said something like "Thank you, Mr Asquith", and he smiled, removed his cigarette, and said, "My name is Puffin, you know. Because of my nose."

'It was to be a happy film from there on. Somewhere along the line, and I don't know where myself, he had found that I was doing what he *wanted* . . . or was able to do what he wanted. Sometimes he would make me play a scene three, five or eight different ways, always with a gentle ironic smile. He told me that it amused him to see how rapidly I could "shift gears", as he called it, and give a completely dissimilar performance. It was hard to do but stood me in marvellous stead in the time to come. That was the first lesson Puff taught me. Total concentration at all times, and an elasticity of ideas. "I always think that one should have lots of different hats in the bag," he used to say . . . "You can't do much with just one." '

Of the film Dilys Powell wrote: '*The Woman in Question* has a good basic idea . . . with some lively situations, but it is far from being the perfect medium for the director of *Pygmalion* and *French Without Tears* . . . There is some good acting and in this case that certainly means good direction . . . Anthony Asquith has done with his material all that is asked of him. I wish only that more had been asked.' Paul Dehn said: 'Fair acting and good direction redeem the mediocre script which falls a shade gracelessly between the two stools of psychology and detection.'

His next film, *The Browning Version*, was one of his great pictures. It was a Rattigan play, scripted by Rattigan for the screen. The leading role of the schoolmaster who is forced to retire because of ill health was played by Michael Redgrave: he won the award for acting at the Cannes Film Festival; the award for the best screen play was given to Terence Rattigan. Jean Kent was Michael Regrave's wife in the film.

As usual, unlike the directors who place on their films a recognisable mark which one might call their signature, Puffin was self-effacing. 'Anthony Asquith's aim as a director seems to have been,' says Penelope Houston of *The Browning Version*, 'to obtrude his personality as little as possible.' William Whitebait, endorses this: 'So unobtrusive is Asquith's direction that we are hardly aware of his part in the collaboration until the final shot of the sunny quadrangle with speech-day groups, a couple of figures running and some bars of Beethoven: until this point we have been denied the release of music.' Terence Rattigan amplified it: 'He had a superb instinct, impeccable taste and always gave distinction to the films he made. That is what told us it was Asquith's work.'

Its art form was more important to him than his signature. The film was to him the latest of the muses – the Tenth Muse, he called it, engaged in climbing Parnassus to join the famous Nine. 'Looking back over her short life,' he wrote, 'the Tenth Muse could without immodesty congratulate herself. Though respectably born in a laboratory, her early life had been spent in the squalid surroundings of flea-circus and freak show. Her first advances to her sisters had been greeted with outraged ridicule. She a Muse! She, the unnatural offspring of an unholy alliance contracted between the magic-lantern and the novelette! But she had persevered: she had worked hard at improving herself, and now, at last, her sisters occasionally nodded to her or even smiled, if still a little patronisingly. She was not quite one of the circle, but her existence was recognised.'

Some years later he stood back to examine the progress the Muse had made. 'Technique is after all nothing mysterious,' he wrote in *The Cinema*; 'it is merely the answer to the question "How?" – "How shall I put this particular scene on the screen?" There may obviously be a hundred and one ways of approaching a scene. It will be different with different directors, but as long as a director treats the scene as unique and particular and not as a specimen of a genius, his answer to the question "How?" has a chance of success.

'This is not to say there are no aspects of technique that can be learnt. To become a good pianist you must first practice scales, and, as Aristotle said: "To become a virtuous man you must first practice morality." The more arrows the director has for his bow the more likely is he to hit the target. It is no use having the scene perfectly visualised in your mind if you have no idea what the lens of the camera will show or how one shot in the scene will combine with another, but it is just as bad to have all the tricks at your fingertips and misapply them as a camouflage for lack of visualisation . . .

'The permutations and combinations of image and sound are infinite, but nevertheless the nature of the medium remains in essence unchanged, because the imagination of the audience is still stimulated by only two senses, sight and hearing. However much our Muse's make-up may be improved, however dazzlingly her wardrobe may be enriched, her flesh and bones will still be the same. And the colour range will not avail her, her draperies will go for nothing if she wears them without a sense of fitness. Her sisters will certainly not be more ready to acknowledge her if she comes down to breakfast made up for the Opera in a mink coat and diamond tiara.'

# 20

# Edith Evans, Margaret Rutherford and Michael Redgrave

PUFFIN'S NEXT FILM, Oscar Wilde's *The Importance of Being Earnest*, was his first picture in colour. Its scintillant cast included Michael Redgrave (recently in *The Browning Version*); Edith Evans as Lady Bracknell; Margaret Rutherford as Miss Prism; Michael Denison; Miles Malleson; Joan Greenwood; Dorothy Tutin, who was then a new young actress; Walter Hudd; and Richard Wattis. The film script was written by Asquith himself. Carmen Dillon, art director on so many of his films, was responsible for the delightful sets in this too.

'As *The Importance of Being Earnest*', said Anthony Asquith, 'is absolutely an artificial comedy of the theatre, I started the film with two people coming into a stage-box in a theatre: they look at their programmes and you see the film through their eyes.

'It is a wonderful play – in my opinion the only good play Wilde wrote. It isn't witty – well, it's sometimes witty, but it's frightfully funny, which is a much more difficult thing to be. It's pure nonsense. There aren't many epigrams in it, which makes it much better. For instance when Lady Bracknell says: "Pardon me, you are *not* engaged to anyone. When you do become engaged to someone I, or your father, should his health permit him, will inform you of the fact." That phrase "should his health permit him" is very funny in that context.

'Although I was fairly sparing with the big individual close-ups, I was tempted in the scene where Edith Evans' voice goes up three octaves on a single syllable when she says the word "handb-a-g". On films, as you know, voices haven't to be raised to reach the back of the gallery. We take care of that and actors and actresses keep their voices right down. In the case of Lady Bracknell, however, it was different: she is a monster anyway and she is more than lifesize, and certainly Edith *is* lifesize. I didn't try to modify her performance in any way, because it seemed to me to be splendid.'

Most people find Edith Evans with her delightful three-tier voice an absolute joy to listen to and watch. The words in this film that linger in one's mind are 'In a per-*am*-bu- (then on a higher level) -later'. When the film was sold for exhibition in America, Puffin was told that the word 'perambulator' would not be understood there. It would have to be altered to 'baby-carriage'. He approached Edith Evans and explained it to her in his normal, very polite, gentle manner, but she firmly refused to substitute the new word. Persuasion failed. For some weeks Puffin was very worried. He asked her if she would just record that single word 'baby-carriage' it would be enough: it would be quite easy to replace 'perambulator' with it on the sound track. 'Will you?' he asked, looking at her very pathetically. He had brought a tape-recorder and held the microphone out to her. But she shook her head.

'Do you expect me, a Dame of the Most Noble Order of the British Empire, to change . . . to alter *our* good English word *perambulator* to baby-carriage. I positively *decline* to do it.'

Puffin raised his hands, wriggled a little, then touched her shoulder gently. 'You have given me the word. It's on the tape and I can use it, but I shan't do it unless you consent.'

She smiled. 'Under protest–and only under protest–do I consent.'

She told me how she enjoyed working with him. 'I loved his old world courtesy. He always gave you a rose when he came to dinner – in fact he was always giving one gifts – beautiful books with lovely large pages' – she pointed to one, a book about roses, standing on an easel to display its fascinating pictures. 'I knew his aunt Nancy Crathorne well' – she was Sir Charles Tennant's youngest daughter by his second marriage and only a year or so younger than Puffin. 'I used to go to her home in Yorkshire. She was responsible for the restoration of the Georgian theatre at Richmond and I used to give readings from the stage. I was sad when I learned of her death.'

This was Edith Evans' only appearance in an Asquith film; but for Margaret Rutherford it was her fourth – *The Demi-Paradise*, *While the Sun Shines*, and some years earlier *Quiet Wedding*, and she was to appear in another later. 'I would like to say how very inadequate I feel to talk about my friendship and admiration and gratitude for all Puffin has done for me. When I was given the role of Rowena Ventnor in *The Demi-Paradise* I was also appearing in a stage play and kept dashing to and fro from the theatre to the studio, which made me very, very tired. He did everything possible to help me – sympathy, understanding . . . he got me in the mood to do justice to my part. I had to make a grand entrance as Queen in the village pageant. I was nervous and uneasy. He asked me to wait, then disappeared for a moment and returned with a glass of whisky. "Swallow this," he said. He was gentle and comforting – gave me tremendous courage. I went on, still a little nervous, but they say my entrance was most effective: that was due entirely to him.

'I remember a party Puffin gave when the film was completed. It was in a basement restaurant near Covent Garden. The entire studio crew was there as well as the Press, and Roy Plumley was broadcasting the party, describing the guests as they arrived. In the course of the evening one of the film unit, a make-up girl, I think, was asked to do a turn. She began to sing "When Irish Eyes are Smiling". Puffin felt she was not getting enough attention. Too many people were talking. So he stepped into the middle of the room and held up his hand. There was quiet and he stood there with his hand up until she had finished singing. It was typical of his thoughtfulness and his determination that the girl, who had been asked to sing, should not be ignored and hurt.'

Margaret's husband, James Stringer Davis, said: 'After the shooting of *The Importance of Being Earnest*, it was found necessary to retake one of the scenes. Margaret was at the time busy on another film called *Castle in the Air*. They sent a car for her. While we were travelling from one studio to the other I wondered how on earth she was going to make the transition from being a grand Scottish lady to Miss Prism. When we arrived Margaret had to dress and be made up as Miss Prism and went on for the retake of the garden scene in *The Importance*. The transition was startling – all in an hour or two. I was astonished!'

With Michael Redgrave this was his third picture with Anthony Asquith. 'I don't remember exactly,' he said, 'where I first met Puffin; possibly when I was an undergraduate at Cambridge, because I was a keen follower of *avant garde* cinema at that time and he was considered a very leading young light. I remember very well *The Cottage on Dartmoor* and *Underground* and though they were melodramas they were told in a fresh and exciting way. I think that the prerequisite of a film director is to be able to tell the story through the camera lens and *that* Puffin could do superbly. It is impossible for anybody who knew

Puffin to escape the word "charm". One loved even his extreme mannerisms, like his habit of ducking his head on one side, rather like a bird, and clasping his hands and saying with a sweet smile "Oh, thank you! Do you think you could? Oh, that would be so good, I think that would be fine."

'It would be so easy to parody that charming *persona* of his. I have heard it done. In fact I have done it myself. I remember when he was directing *The Way to the Stars* and we were on location at Catterick. In one of the scenes there were several takes. I didn't have a great deal to do in that. It was a group scene. "Is that all right?" I asked. "Am I doing enough or am I doing too much?" He put his head on one side and his hands together as though he was praying. "I am so sorry," he said. "I wasn't looking. You see, a cow came into the next field at that moment and it made a beautiful composition." I often teased him about it afterwards. I don't think he liked that. It implied that he did not look after his actors. But that was not true.'

Michael Redgrave then talked of his scenes in *The Browning Version* in which he played the ageing schoolmaster Crocker-Harris. 'I remember particularly the scene,' he said, 'in which Crocker-Harris, the villain-hero of the play, has to digest the fact that he is known as the Himmler of the Lower Fifth. The set for that scene – the classroom – was a very big one with only two people in it.

'Puffin said: "Where do you feel like going? Where would you like to be for that bit?" And I said: "I would like to walk away from the camera, with my back to it – away – away to the end of the long classroom, take in the names carved on the walls, the initials and so on. Then come back again and come into close-up." I wanted to do this great circumambulation in this scene for my very long speech.

'Puffin said: "Fine! Fine!" But the sound people said, "We are going to pick up quite a lot of noise from the arc lights as the distance between the player and the camera gets longer and longer." One doesn't hear so much about arc noises these days. I don't know why it is, but it's just as well.

' "I can either do it your way," said Puffin, "and put the sound on afterwards – or I can follow you with the camera." I said: "No. I will dub what I am saying afterwards." Not many directors, especially of Puffin's magnitude, would say to the actor: "Where would you like to go? What would you like to do?" and be able to accommodate the actor's wishes with his own concept of how it should be done. He could afford to give one those bits of latitude. He was so humble and truly modest as really good artists usually are *au fond*.'

He next spoke of the making of *The Importance of Being Earnest*. 'I remember especially the arrangements Puffin made for Lady Bracknell's first entrance. Very carefully he explained to Edith that chalk marks had been made on the floor to indicate where she should stand when she came in, with a corresponding mark for the camera; then she should move on a certain word while speaking her line, on to the second chalk mark . . . and so on.

'It had been worked out and rehearsed very thoroughly for the camera movements and the artist's movements. It worked splendidly at the rehearsal. But Edith, who is her own mistress, would almost invariably come through the door saying: "Ah, Mr Worthing!", or whatever her line was, and go right past the first chalk mark and straight on to the second one.

'Puffin with his . . . er . . . I cannot avoid using the words "elfin charm", said: "Dear Dame Edith. If you go straight on to the second mark the camera isn't with you any more." And Edith said: "Well, I don't know what it is about me but I always feel the camera should come to *me* instead of me go to the *camera*." I shall never forget Puffin crumpling up with laughter, because he understood the actor's side extraordinarily well. He gave the minimum of direction. He was, among directors, like Adrian Bolt among conductors, the movement of whose stick was scarcely perceptible sometimes, yet Puffin always knew exactly what he wanted. His taste was of the best and usually he got the best responses from the actors.'

# 21

# *The Final Test*

AFTER *Green Grow the Rushes* had been completed and delivered for exhibition in the cinemas, the board of ACT Films met to discuss the making of future films. From the chair Anthony Asquith announced that he would like to direct the next feature film. It was a generous and indeed a courageous offer, for he was committed to other film projects and would obviously have to get leave to make one for ACT Films. Nor could he have been paid anything like the sum he usually received. But he was prepared to waive that. 'This is more important,' he said. 'It will help members of the Association who are out of work.' The board was excited and grateful, but made it clear that he would have to accept a fee, because 'the labourer is worthy of his hire.' We laughed and endorsed the project unanimously.

Asquith's choice fell on a recent television play by Terence Rattigan abaout a famous but ageing cricketer playing in his last Test Match. It was suggested that I should produce it and we went together to discuss it with Terry, who agreed at once and insisted on giving it to us without any payment. I told him what we had already told Puffin and in the end he agreed to accept whatever we could offer. It was a small sum, as Asquith's fee and mine were too.

Called *The Final Test* and scripted by Rattigan, it showed in the opening sequence the arrival of an American senator, who had come to study and report on the financial crisis Britain was facing. At Waterloo station he is confronted by disturbing newspaper posters – 'Can England survive?' . . . 'Will Disaster be Avoided?' . . . 'There is no hope!' He asks the driver of his waiting taxi: 'Are things as serious as that?' 'Yes, guv,' says the cabby 'things is pretty grim.' The senator says: 'That's what I've come here for.' He is told to jump in and is taken off to the Oval where the Final Test is being played. For this we got the entire England Eleven, with Len Hutton as captain, Denis Compton, Godfrey Evans, Alec Bedser, Jim Laker, Cyril Washbrook and the others. Jack Warner played the ageing cricketer. His son, a budding poet, instead of going to see his father play his last game, goes off on a visit to the rather eccentric poet-playwright (played by Robert Morley), who is too interested in watching the match on television to be bothered to come out and see his youthful visitor. When he discovers who the boy is, he is furious. 'Your father playing . . . I tried to get a ticket . . .' The boy has a ticket and they go off together to the match. It was touching at the end when the ageing cricketer was out for a duck.

The players' dressing-room with its balcony was rebuilt in Pinewood Studio, as the Oval authorities refused to allow us to do any shooting there. It was such a faithful reproduction, that on entering it each member of the England cricket team walked up to his own peg and hung his clothes there. On the day they were to appear for the first time before the film cameras, the Press arrived early and in vast numbers. There were about a hundred and twenty of them. The stage on which the shooting was to be done that morning was so packed that it was impossible for the film technicians to move about and do their work.

Asquith looked at me and raised his hands in despair. Something obviously had to be done. I stood on a chair and spoke to the Press. I told them that they would all be given a chance not only to see the shooting but to talk to the cricketers. I also invited them to stay for lunch. They cheered. I then asked them if they would be so kind as to clear the stage for the time being and let the technicians begin the shooting. 'The cricketers are not actors by profession and they are a little nervous at the moment.'

The Press was most co-operative. They withdrew and we got ready for the first shot. The cameras were focused on the balcony where Jack Warner, as the ageing cricketer, was seated, looking depressed and worried as he watched the first bats come out on to the pitch.

Len Hutton, as captain of the team, comes out on the balcony, notes his disconsolate state, and tries to reassure him. 'You have nothing to worry about. You are just as good as ever you were.' Those were the first words Len was required to say. He was nervous. He looked all round the stage; and though it had been cleared of the Press, he did not quite recover his composure.

Asquith tried to reassure him. 'This is just a rehearsal, Len,' he said. 'Let's do it once or twice – without the cameras and the sound.' Len tried. He felt he had to act. His words sounded a little artificial. He was asked to try again, and once again it was not right. Puffin came up to me and I went with him to Len. I said: 'All this, we can see, is a great strain for you, Len. You are trying to *act*. Just try and be as natural as possible. Put on a Yorkshire accent . . . The public would love that. They expect it of you.'

He tried again. After about an hour we felt we would have to put off that shot until the next morning. But he was not on call the next morning. He had to catch a midday train to Pudsey.

We had another word with him. 'A car will call for you at eight o'clock tomorrow morning to bring you here. We'll get the shot right I'm certain,' I said. 'Just keep on saying to yourself: 'You have nothing to worry about. You are just as good as ever you were.' He fell silent and after a moment said: 'But what about my train to Yorkshire? I have to be there tomorrow afternoon.'

'We shall see that you get your train,' I assured him.

The shot took less than three minutes the next morning. It was perfect. Some months later, when he was being honoured at a Savoy dinner as the 'Sportsman of the Year', he referred in the course of his speech to his uneasiness while preparing for that shot. 'I had a restless night,' he said. 'I kept turning and tossing, until finally my wife slapped me on the bottom and said: "What on earth's the matter with you? You keep telling me 'You have nothing to worry about. You are just as good as ever you were.'"

'I can understand Len's nervousness,' Puffin told me. Then, after a wriggling, gulping laugh, he said: 'I suppose I must look like the Dauphin of France – all the Dauphins look alike, don't they? I imagine that is why Gabriel Pascal asked me to play the part of the Dauphin in Shaw's *St Joan* opposite Greta Garbo. I remembered this when I watched poor Len struggling to get out his words.'

We got the shooting done in excellent time. Asquith, well aware of the tremendous additional cost if there were delays on the set, hardly ever went beyond schedule on any of his films. Occasionally he even beat the schedule by a day or two.

An interesting little touch was introduced by Asquith in the rather eccentric playwright's bedroom scene. With a great deal of lip-nibbling and his hiccupping laugh, he revealed to me the plan he had in mind. 'I suggest we spread books and magazines all over the bed after Robert Morley has got into it.' As I looked a little puzzled, he explained. 'That was my mother's practice,' he said. 'Her bed was completely covered by books and papers and whenever she turned in her sleep some of the books came clattering down and woke her up.' I said: 'I know she used to write letters in bed. I had three letters from her, all of them written in pencil, covering many pages and marked 3 am.' 'Yes, she always wrote her letters in bed. She did that because she didn't sleep very well.' I don't think Robert Morley liked it but it was done.

The Press hailed the film with most gratifying enthusiasm. *The Times* said: 'The ultimate feeling left by *The Final Test* is one of deep admiration for the consummate cleverness of Mr Terence Rattigan as a playwright . . . Mr Rattigan, who is a good cricketer himself, has so contrived that in the ninety minutes the film takes to run, character, emotion, humour and the essence of the game itself shall all have their innings, and in this he is greatly helped by the director Mr Asquith.'

In *Time & Tide*, that well-known critic Fred Majdalanay said: 'It is seldom that the fraternity and severe sorority of critics are as unanimously friendly. It is difficult to think of anyone who will not like this film.'

Surprisingly, even in America, where not much interest in cricket is normally shown, the film was well received. *Time* magazine wrote: 'Actor Morley, looked like a debauched panda, earns most of the laughs, but does not have it all to himself.'

*The Final Test* was at the Continental cinema and later at the Coronet in New York for nearly six months; and it still keeps on appearing on television there.

In the following summer, on Sunday, 5th July 1953 to be exact, Sir Anthony Tichborne asked Terence Rattigan if *The Final Test* would accept his challenge to play a charity cricket match against his team of locals at Arlesford in Hampshire. Terry phoned me. I said I would get as many of the England eleven as I could, but his suggestion that as producer of the film I should captain the team, I turned down flat: it had been discovered during my schooldays that my only role on the cricket field could be possibly as umpire. Terry, who had played for Harrow against Eton, was the obvious choice. Anthony Tichborne captained the other side. Puffin, who played cricket no better than he played golf, insisted on joining the team and, changing his boiler suit for a pair of borrowed grey flannels, he actually did better than some of the others. Of the England eleven there were Denis Compton and Godfrey Evans. Alec and Eric Bedser were to be there but a benefit match had been arranged for them that day in which Len Hutton played. Others in *The Final Test* team were Alf Gover, who advised and trained the actors in the film eleven; Michael Denison, who had played cricket at Harrow and was Algernon in *The Importance of Being Earnest*; Richard Attenborough; Stanley Holloway; and six members of *The Final Test* cast – Jack Warner, Richard Wattis, Richard Bebb, Ray Jackson (Jack Warner's son in the film), Stanley Maxted (the American senator), and George Relph, who was umpire in the film. Brenda Bruce, who played the barmaid, and Adrienne Allen, who played Jack Warner's sister, were there too and so was Adrianne's daughter, Anna Massey.

In a large marquee in the garden, Lady Tichborne entertained her guests to a six-course lunch. We did not linger over coffee, for the play was to start at two o'clock. As we approached the cricket ground we saw the spectators arrive in an endless stream of cars. Those who lived in Arlesford and in the nearby villages were already standing four deep round the grounds.

Money was collected from the spectators by pretty young girls, programmes were sold, the distinguished cricketers were badgered for their autographs, each one of them signing the programme every time a shilling was dropped into the collecting-box. Rattigan, Asquith, Michael Denison and occasionally I too sold our signatures. The Red Cross is said to have benefited by about £3,000. *The Final Test* team, with its star cricketers, beat the villagers . . . hold your breath – they were in fact beaten by the villagers, by a small margin of three runs.

Speaking of the match afterwards, Michael Denison told me: 'I was Terry Rattigan's fag at Harrow, but I never knew him very well. He invited me to come down for the match. I hadn't played for seventeen years, but brought my white flannels only because I was told to. I was startled after lunch when I stepped out into the lovely warm sunshine, to be told: "You are going in first." "This isn't fair," I said. Then I saw Denis Compton coming out to join me. That partnership made 50 runs, of which I made 18.'

He talked then about his first meeting with Asquith. 'I adored *The Importance of Being Earnest* when I saw Edith Evans and John Gielgud in it on the stage and had a pipe-dream that one day I might appear in a film version of it. A few years later, as the play was nearing the public domain and would soon be free of copyright, I went to see Robert Clark of the Associated British Picture Corporation. He was quite thrilled and registered the title as a forthcoming ABPC production. John Gielgud was asked to play in it, he refused and the registration right was surrendered to the Rank organisation on the condition that I should be in the film.

'I was asked to lunch by Puffin and felt rather like unwanted luggage and was prepared to cut and run. But an immediate *rapport* was established: it was in fact one of the happiest professional experiences of my life, although Puffin was, in a sense, blackmailed into having me. One delightful experience I recall was the shooting done in a railway train during a journey to Bunbury. We had a hamper with us and Puffin insisted that it should be opened. "All in good time," said the assistant director, "we aren't quite ready yet." "We *are*," said Puffin. "I want Michael to open it – it's his birthday." How he found out I don't know. I opened it and found it was full of bottles of champagne. Glasses were filled and a toast was drunk to me. A typical piece of Puffinism.

'His technique as a director was gentle and courteous, but one had the feeling that underneath this he knew exactly what to do. He had done his homework and had worked out the entire shooting plan. Yet he was accessible to the actors' point of view. He listened attentively, but if the actor's motive was selfish, he came down at once like a ton of bricks.'

While *The Final Test* was being made Puffin insisted on calling for me in his car. I pointed out that it would take him two miles out of his way. 'There is no point,' he said, 'in going to the same place at the same time in two separate cars. Ernie won't mind the extra mile or two.' Ernie, his chauffeur, now approaching seventy, had been Margot's coachman; he hated motor-cars and accepted the job out of loyalty and the realisation that it was not really safe for Puffin to drive a car.

So every morning at about seven o'clock (for we had to be at Pinewood Studio before eight) the Daimler pulled up at my front door with Puffin seated in front alongside Ernie – he had always sat there and possibly thought Ernie would feel slighted if he sat elsewhere. By the time the car came for me Puffin had completed about half *The Times* crossword. He always timed himself and one morning was able to give a whoop of joy because he had finished it for the first time in exactly seven minutes. Then he was ready to converse, sometimes with me, sometimes with Ernie. Occasionally he sat with his head against the back of the seat and slept till we got to the studio. He was always able to take a cat-nap and always apologised when he woke up.

'I had a delightful week-end,' he told me one Monday morning. 'I spent it at Oxford with David and Rachel' – he meant Lord David Cecil and his wife. 'You know David, of course . . . Oh, you *must* meet him.' Then he started to giggle and wriggle and gesticulate in the front seat.

'David,' he said, 'always cleans his shoes on a Saturday morning. He assembles them around him, puts on a green baize apron and sits on the kitchen floor, with the shoes all round him.'

'Last Saturday' – interruption caused by his hiccupping laugh – 'last Saturday, there was a ring at the front doorbell. David got up and went to the door with his left hand in a shoe and a polishing pad in his right hand.

'The man at the door – somebody trying to sell a Hoover I imagine – looked him up and down, rested his eyes on the green baize apron, and asked: "Is your mistress in?" David – (laughter) – David said: "Sorry. Married! Two children!" and shut the door.'

At the end of the day's shooting, Puffin always went among the technicians on the studio floor, asking 'Can I give you a lift home?' and usually five or six of us were somehow packed into the large Daimler. Each was dropped at his or her home.

About eighteen months later, Harold Wilson, whose interest in cricket is inexhaustible, seeing me at some public function, said: 'I've seen *The Final Test* five times. The last time was in Cornwall. I travelled twenty-five miles through the pouring rain to see it again. I can recite the whole of it to you.' I, who had seen it about fifty times while the film was being put together, am quite unable to recite more than a very few bits of it.

# 22

# His Covent Garden and Glyndebourne Films

*The Final Test* was the eighth film Puffin had worked on with Terence Rattigan. Terry's next, *The Sound Barrier*, was directed by David Lean, who had earlier edited two films by Puffin – *Pygmalion* and *French Without Tears*.

Terence Rattigan did not select David Lean as his director. The project was the child of David Lean's brain. Tremendously impressed by an RAF display at Farnborough, David embarked on a considerable amount of research to see how a film could be constructed on the sound barrier. He talked to the designers of the planes, then to the manufacturers and the test pilots, and flew in the planes himself. His research when completed filled 120 pages, and with it under his arm he went to see Alexander Korda.

Korda thought the idea a very good one. Rattigan was selected to write the script and David Lean, obviously since that was the whole purpose of his research, directed it. When Asquith heard of this, he burst into tears, David Lean told me, but nevertheless wished David success, which the film, starring Ann Todd, Ralph Richardson and Dinah Sheridan, certainly attained.

But Asquith's next film rather suggests that he hadn't quite got over *The Sound Barrier*. Based on the novel *The Net*, by John Pudney, it showed a group of international scientists working at a research station on aircraft capable of flying more than 2,000 miles an hour, far faster than those in David Lean's film and reaching far greater heights. It had Phyllis Calvert, Robert Beatty and Herbert Lom in the cast. Puffin was fortunate in getting as his technical adviser Air Marshal Sir Peter Wykeham, who was then commanding a fighter station in Suffolk.

'Puffin,' he told me, 'did not seem to be quite happy how to tackle the film – should it be a thriller, a psychological film, or a technical narrative like *The Sound Barrier*? I sat down with him and we did a lot of rewriting. Puffin kept walking up and down the room, then going out of the room and walking along the corridor into another part of the house. For a time his voice was far away and inaudible; then gradually it came nearer and nearer. Back in the room he would suddenly sit down at the piano for a while. On one occasion he looked up and said with delight: "I have just composed a hymn." Even when the film was on the floor at Pinewood he kept on rewriting. It was out of his normal run: technicalities kept on intruding, they could not be avoided.

'He got three fierce Alsatians to be used in the film as guard-dogs for the 2,000 miles an hour new aeroplane. Their owner held the leash very firmly. Puffin said: "They seem to be quite tame." "When you raise your arm above your head – that's their signal," she said. Puffin raised both arms at once . . . The dogs barked, reared wildly, broke loose from their owner, knocked over the studio lights. It took twenty minutes to restore order.'

The film was not a success, but it helped to get Asquith's acute disappointment over *The Sound Barrier* out of his system.

He made a rapid and brilliant recovery a few months later when he embarked on making a film which won him many coveted awards, British and international. *The Young Lovers* is about a girl and a boy – she is Russian, he is in American intelligence. At Covent Garden, watching the *Swan Lake* ballet, they meet and fall in love and a problem immediately confronts them because they are from different sides of the Iron Curtain.

'I have waited three years to make this picture.' Puffin said. 'I prerecorded a piece of music in order to get a certain rhythm in the film. This was for the very opening of the picture. The scene for which it was required was shot silent. I wanted the eyes of the boy and girl to meet for the first time at the *pas de deux* of the second act of *Swan Lake*. To achieve this I had the music played back to make sound and vision coincide. It worked perfectly.'

Odile Versois not only looked pretty but acted most movingly as the Russian girl in love; David Knight, new to the English screen, played the American lover. David Kossof was the girl's father. Anthony Havelock-Allan, who had worked with Puffin on earlier films, produced this.

The British Film Academy Award for the best screen play was conferred on its scriptwriters, George Tabori and Robin Estridge. The British Film Critics Circle made a special award to Anthony Asquith for his direction; and the film was selected for showing at the Edinburgh Film Festival. The praise from the Press was unstinting. The *Daily Express* said: 'Agonisingly moving. A film triumph.' *The Times* comment was: 'The film remains firm in its refusal to become a matter of spies and secret papers; it is throughout, save for a few brief minutes, a thing of the mind, the spirit, and the emotions. Mr Asquith, who is not afraid of going slowly, exploring the unhappiness and isolation of the girl and then finding their parallel in the experiences of the young man, handles his characters with what might be described as an elegant and civilised compassion.'

His next was a short film entitled *On Such a Night*, devoted to an evening of music at Glyndebourne. A young American, played by David Knight of *The Young Lovers*, goes to see Mozart's *The Marriage of Figaro*. The script was written by Paul Dehn; Benjamin Frankel, who had composed the music for Puffin's films *The Importance of Being Earnest* and *The Final Test*, helped with a selection of excerpts from Mozart's opera, but the entire production was under the approving eye of Carl Ebert, the musical director of Glyndebourne, one of whose greatest triumphs was in fact *The Marriage of Figaro*.

The sound-recordings were made during rehearsals at Glyndebourne; the scenes on the stage were photographed during a special performance. Oliver Messel designed the sets. We see the young American the next morning standing on a hillside and admiring the beauty of the South Downs. *The Times* verdict was: '*On Such a Night* manages to commemorate Glyndebourne in a way which is at once lyrical and light-hearted.'

Music, with an emphasis on ballet, was given even further delightful outlets by Puffin. Working yet again with Anthony Havelock-Allan as producer he made some fascinating, breath-taking films in colour at Covent Garden of Margot Fonteyn and Rudolf Nureyev for television. They included *Romeo and Juliet* and *Swan Lake* and reached a very wide public in America and most of the countries of Europe.

He was invited to produce Bizet's opera *Carmen* on the stage at Covent Garden. Although he had never undertaken a project of this kind before, he embarked on it without diffidence, but with enthusiasm and complete confidence. It involved him in much more work than he had anticipated and confronted him with a number of unexpected problems, but he battled on bravely. He talked of it to me, always without any apprehension. But the crowd scenes, never easy on the screen with multiple cameras to help you, were found to be far less manageable on the stage for one unfamiliar with operatic production. Tyrone Guthrie, as a kind friend, came to the rescue and all was well, but he most generously insisted that Puffin alone should receive the credit as he had worked so gallantly for so many weary weeks and had in fact accomplished it.

Puffin's closest link was always with those who were connected with music. Three weekends out of four were spent with Ben Frankel and his wife, Anna, at their charming home at Rodmel, a few miles from Glyndebourne. 'He adored operas,' Ben told me, 'and often went again and again to see the same opera – and, if it was new to him, he would read the musical score the night before in bed.' And, as I remember, on the morning after a visit he would be up early, playing records of what he had heard or possibly what he was going to hear at Glyndebourne that evening.

'He invited Tony Havelock-Allan to lunch with us one Saturday', Ben said, 'and half way through lunch invited him to come to Glyndebourne with us. Tony said he had no ticket and was unlikely to get one at the last minute. "I can get you one," said Puffin. "Besides," said Tony, "I haven't brought my evening clothes . . ." "My dear," said Puffin. "All that doesn't really matter. You will find that almost everyone there is in white flannel trousers."' Havelock-Allan was surprised, but finally consented.

'Puffin went dressed not in his usual boiler-suit, but, as a great concession, he put on a pair of corduroy trousers and a rough, rather shabby sports jacket. During the interval, as the audience walked out into the lovely gardens, the ladies looking so very *soignée*, the men in dinner jackets with gardenias on the lapels, Tony Havelock-Allan, deeply embarrassed and refusing to go out and join them as he was, said: "Isn't it a joy to see so many white flannel trousers?"

'One opera Puffin was most keen on was *Ariadne auf Naxof.*

We went to one or two ballets in London and quite a lot of concerts.'

Ben Frankel invited Puffin to stay with him and Anna at Salzburg for the Festival. 'He arrived with John Betjeman by air. They appear to have had a lot of fun together during the flight – Puffin, as you know, was like that, full of private jokes and laughs.

'We were staying on the Gaisberg, the big mountain overlooking the town. Throughout the two weeks he was there he was very gay and playful. Quite unexpectedly, while we were out walking, he would stand on one leg with a flower held above his head. These were his diversional antics. But most of all he enjoyed going to the music festivals. He was tremendously impressed by Pfitzner's *Palestrina*; but he was very critical of Gottfried von Einem's *Der Prozess*, which is based on Kafka's story *The Trial*. He bought the score and read it in bed.'

For many years, long before Diana met and later married Yehudi Menuhin, Puffin was a close friend of hers. After the marriage, he got to know Yehudi well and it was one of his many private jokes to say that he and I were 'gossips', because we were both godfathers of Yehudi's and Diana's first child: and although I corrected him by pointing out that I wasn't one of the godfathers (his assumption was based on my earlier association with Yehudi on a film I was making) the joke was trotted out every time the Menuhins were referred to in our conversation: Puffin always chuckled when he said it; in his philosophy a private joke could not be abandoned.

Yehudi gave me a very shrewd appraisal of Puffin's knowledge, understanding and love of music one afternoon when Diana, he and I talked over tea at their home in Highgate.

'What was wonderful about Puffin was that he loved music without having to exploit it personally. In other words his love was of the purest kind and it meant that everything about him was sensitive to music in a way that was almost more than that of the ordinary musician, who has to listen to a work with an eye on his performance or to the work's suitability and to the work's complexity.

'Everything about Puffin was refreshing because he was that *ideal* music-lover, the amateur to whom music meant more than it means almost to anybody else. His knowledge of music was incredible. Every note he heard left its imprint on his heart, on his sensibility. Nothing, I imagine, did he ever forget. He was so deeply musical that I'm sure behind every word he spoke, behind every thought he expressed, there was some music. He coloured everything with it, and I think that if he heard any sounds other than music he would transform those sounds into music if he could and if he couldn't, he would reject the sounds. Life had to be harmonious for him, or it had to have an expressive quality in terms of an art that could ennoble, but if something resisted ennobling, if it was so crude that it couldn't be ennobled, he would try to avoid it – avoid, I feel, rather than reject.'

We talked for a time about his elfin qualities. Yehudi said: 'He was an extraordinary wistful character and one always seemed to be awakening him from some dream. Whenever he spoke it was out of some very deep vision – or dream – or thought that took him far away. He brought the far away, as it were, to bear on the present. He wasn't of the present. When Puffin was in the room or Puffin was speaking he brought some other time dimension into the room and into the conversation – that was his contribution. He was probably fulfilling himself in a way utterly different from his background. He did not belong to the ordinary world; he felt out of his element in it, that is why he kept transforming his world – and other people's – into something else. In that sense he was a kind of alchemist. That gave him the quality that everyone adored. It made no difference for him who the person was; he looked upon people as he did upon music, as a source of interest, of fascination, an object of compassion.'

I asked Yehudi if he thought human beings were in a sense notes of music to Puffin. Did they by their movements and by their talk form some sort of melody in his mind? 'Yes,' Yehudi replied. 'He used them in that way in his imagination. An indication of this is in the films he made. I would say that the nearest he could come to music was in the creative art of the film, which he transformed as much into the creative art it has become as anybody else.'

# 23

# The Question of Marriage

DIANA MENUHIN'S MEMORIES of Puffin cover a long span of years and are much more personal. It was thought at one time because their friendship was so close and they delighted in being together that Puffin might marry Diana.

Quite early in his life his mother had wondered what sort of girl he would be interested in when he grew up; twice in her *Autobiography* she referred to it. The first time was when Puffin was not yet twelve. 'We were sitting by the sea,' she wrote, 'watching the gulls hovering over the Firth' – being August they were in North Berwick – 'and, after reading my letters, I asked him what sort of a wife he would like to have.

' "Well, mother," he said thoughtfully, "she must be medium high, pale complexion, dark gold hair, black eyes. She must have free movements and not walk like modern girls. She must not have an anaemic nature, as I don't want a bloodless wife, and she must be witty, sweet and musical. If I can't get this girl, I will have a short well-proportioned wife; black hair, violet eyes or green, like Kakoo's" – she was the Marchioness of Granby – "Spanish colouring as against red. Nature fiery, almost passionate, but of course her temper must be quickly over. Mother, how shall I know her children from mine?" '

The second entry was made in December 1917, when Puffin was fifteen. 'I look around me to see what child of which friend is left to become the wife of my son, Anthony; and I wonder whether she will be virtuous, loving and good-looking as my other daughters-in-law . . . In consequence of our unpopularity in Peebleshire, I had no opportunity of meeting other young people in their homes; and I knew no family except my own. The wealth of art and music, the luxury of flowers and colour, the stretches of wild country both in Scotland and High Leicestershire, which had made up my life till I married, had not qualified me to understand children reared in different circumstances. I would not perhaps have noticed many trifles in my step-family, had I not been so much made of, overloved and independent before my marriage.'

A number of the things Puffin mentioned as necessary in a wife when he sat by the sea with his mother, were precisely applicable to Diana, who had not yet been born – 'medium high . . . pale complexion . . black eyes' . . . dark would be more correct . . . 'She must not have an anaemic nature . . . She must be witty, sweet and musical.'

As a child Diana Gould went to a ballet school and until her marriage was well known as a ballerina and an actress. She has a great fund of knowledge, not only about music and ballet and acting, but of people and what's going on in the world. With a lively intelligence, witty, brilliant in her mimicry, she is a most entertaining companion.

Speaking to me over tea at her home, Diana said: 'I knew Puffin since I was sixteen years old. He used to come to Madame

Marie Rambert's ballet school and even in those days he had an ageless quality about him, which was a strange combination of being very, very old and very, very young. We always thought of him as a leprechaun and felt that he had materialised suddenly and was there. Whether it was winter or summer he always wore the same strange nondescript clothes and round his neck the everlasting muffler. No overcoat – I never remember seeing him in an overcoat. His head on one side as though he had to bend it to get through whatever aperture he had come through.

'He always picked up a friendship exactly where he left off. One would see him every day for three days and then one wouldn't see him again for goodness knows how long. But when you did meet again it was a most pleasant kind of contact because it was totally and utterly improvised: there was nothing prefabricated about Puff. He had ordered a table, of course, and he would arrive with the inevitable collection of newspapers under one arm and it may be that was what tilted his head to one side.'

Everybody was baffled as to why he carried that large, loose bundle of papers about. They consisted, I know, of all the daily papers ranging from *The Times* to the Communist *Daily Worker*. He bought a fresh batch every morning, but apart from tackling the crossword in *The Times*, he never looked at or even opened any of them. Yet he would arrive at 7.30 in the evening for an ACT meeting with the papers still under his arm and with the evening papers added.

'For a time,' Diana went on, 'he lived at the Mirabelle and after we had lunch we'd go up to his little flat where he had a small upright piano and he'd play little songs that he'd written – and the thing that struck me most as the daughter of a musician, whose mother was a pianist, was his tremendous frustration. Here was somebody born to be a musician and hadn't the equipment and this perhaps was what gave him that truly deprecating quality. My brother-in-law, Louis Kentner, felt that Puffin's knowledge of music was absolutely frightening; that he was the kind of person who said: "Oh no, Lou, but that was the *first* movement in Clementi's *third* sonata!" And Lou, who had an immense knowledge of music, would look at him and say: "My God, Puff. I can't remember the third sonata."

'The things I know most about him are his undisturbable manners. Nothing that ever happened to Puffin in the way of shock, in the way of feelings, in the way of his own condition could ever, ever affect his exquisite good manners. He was like one of those Russian dolls you knock over which immediately rights itself.'

Diana Menuhin's apt and accurate comment on his imperturbability will be endorsed by all who knew him, worked with him, or even met him casually. 'He talked to waiters and dustmen in the same way as he talked to a Duke,' Charles Hillyer told me. If he found there were barriers, such as being addressed as 'Sir' or 'Mr Asquith', he at once tried to break them down. 'I remember,' says Paul Dehn, 'how a young film technician, after being asked to address him not as "Mr Asquith" but as "Puffin", could only compromise by calling him from then on "Puffin, sir".' I myself found that most of the technicians couldn't quite get their tongues round 'Puffin': that was a family intimacy on which they refused to encroach. 'Tony' was the best expression, they felt, of their warmth and friendship.

Some thought that Puffin never married because he had homosexual tendencies. Others denied it emphatically. 'There was,' Terence Rattigan told me, 'an impenetrable side to Puff, however close one was to him. He certainly liked being with young men, but it never went further than talking or going to a concert, or playing cards. I knew Puffin as well as anyone could know him for close on thirty years, and to my personal knowledge there was never even the vaguest sign of any homosexuality.'

Lady Elliot of Harwood says: 'There are several reasons why Puff never married. He never fell in love with anyone – he was devoted to and loved many people, but that is a different thing. In his early childhood and indeed all his life he was dominated by his sister, Elizabeth, and by his mother. Not in any sense other than family devotion – but until they died, he never had a life apart from his mother, and I do not think he ever contemplated marriage. His love of his job, of music, and of his mother completely filled his life. No other kind of love ever came into his life.'

# 24

# The President's Rôle

PUFFIN WAS NOT at all politically-minded. By inheritance and by habit he was a Liberal, but he played no active part in it. Nor did his position as president of a film trade union, the Association of Cine-Technicians, which by now had taken in the television technicians and had added an extra T to the initials, involve him politically.

Almost always he took the chair himself at the meetings. Like most trade unions it had some militants and a small sprinkling of Communists. Puffin never took sides. He listened patiently however often the same argument was repeated; and saw to it that everyone had a chance to have his say. Sometimes, when an argument seemed extravagant or illogical, he intervened, in a gentle manner and apologetically.

I remember one occasion when there was talk of a strike. He listened carefully to all the arguments and, before putting it to the vote, gave his own analysis of the situation with which they were faced. The vote went against the strike. The man seated beside me said: 'Tony will go straight to Heaven. But he was wrong.'

His influence was strong, not only because they respected him but because they admired and almost worshipped him. They knew that his only purpose in joining the union was to identify himself completely with them. Though, as a director, he was in effect an employer, he refused to accept any differentiation between their position and his. Some may have thought that he dressed like them for that reason, but many of the technicians were much better dressed than he was and in any case even when he was at Oxford he dressed like that.

On the set and off he was one of them. He gave no orders, but said: 'Would it be more effective if we moved that light a little to the left?' Their response was an eager co-operation. After the council meetings and other meetings he always went to the pub with them, long after he had given up drinking alcohol. He had won through and kept rigidly to his 'coke' – one, perhaps two – but a cigarette was always between his lips.

Once, while he was making a film on location abroad, the possibility of a strike loomed over the horizon. In his absence I was sometimes voted into the chair and that night I was asked to take it. We examined and discussed all the pros and cons: it was obvious that there was justification for the discontent of the men engaged in one particular branch of work. Attempts to achieve an improvement in conditions had failed and it was necessary now to call a meeting of all ACT members to decide what should be done. Planning a strike is an appalling operation: one is conscious of the anxiety, the heartbreak and acute suffering not only of the strikers, however just their cause may be, but of their wives and children. They will receive messages of encouragement and sympathy from other unions, but on Friday they cannot feed their families on either encouragement or sympathy.

The mass meeting was fixed for eleven o'clock on Sunday morning. It was to be held at a cinema at Hammersmith. It was agreed that the president should not be informed of it: there was no need for him to stop work on location and come hurrying home. Moreover it was felt that if there was a strike in which he had played a part it might endanger Asquith's opportunities of being given another film to make.

It fell on me to take the chair at that vital meeting. While I was getting ready to leave for Hammersmith the phone rang. Puffin's voice said: 'I'm coming along to pick you up.' My surprise made me speechless for a moment.

'When did you get back?' I asked at last.

'About an hour ago. I didn't know anything about this until late last night.'

'It was thought unnecessary to bring you back . . .' I began.

'As president it is my responsibility,' he interrupted, 'and I am taking the chair. I'll be calling for you in fifteen minutes.'

He hung up. It was the first time I had heard him speak so firmly. In the car he said: 'I've examined the position thoroughly. The injustice has to be dealt with, and I'm going to stand by the men.'

There was surprise, of course, as he entered and went on to the platform and then a tremendous burst of applause. By almost complete unanimity the strike was endorsed. It lasted less than a week. The injustice was dealt with.

# 25

# An Adventure in Baghdad

His film *Carrington VC*, about a major accused of fraudulent conversion of Army funds, based on a play by Dorothy and Campbell Christie, was made in 1954, with David Niven and Margaret Leighton in the leading roles.

It was exciting and had the additional attraction of a court-martial setting; but it did not achieve the success expected, though the Press praised both the acting and the direction.

'David Niven is very good as Carrington VC,' said *The Times*, 'conducting his own defence and having just the spontaneous decency of reaction and the temperamental mixture of lightness and dash of which heroes are made.'

The *Spectator* thought David Niven, though he 'seems on the face of it to be miscast, gives one of the best performances of his career . . . Margaret Leighton as his neurotic wife makes treachery feasible.' Frederick Majdalany said the film's virtue was due to Anthony Asquith's resolution 'that the subject matter kindles its own interest and needs guidance rather than force.'

Tribute to him was also paid by Dilys Powell in the *Sunday Times*. These words provide her summing-up: 'Anthony Asquith is one of the first of his generation in this country, who loved films from the start and understood what could be done on the screen.'

'I feel very strongly about music,' said Asquith, 'but in this film and in *The Browning Version* I used hardly any music. *Carrington VC* had just "Reveille" at the beginning and "Last Post" at the end. *The Browning Version* had music only when the titles were being shown on the screen: no more than that in either of those films. I hate useless music. One must be frightfully careful how it is used – to heighten a drama *possibly* or as a comment in a comedy. There are some moments when the emotional stress becomes so great that music becomes a metaphor of speech, a substitute for language. In *The Young Lovers* I had a scene in which we see the boy and girl go into a French restaurant together. There is a man there playing an accordion and while the boy and girl talk you see the man playing and coming closer and closer to them. But instead of the music getting louder, you don't hear it any more because, although he keeps on playing, they are too interested in each other to hear it.'

An impressive array of awards was won by his next film, *Orders to Kill*. It is about a young American bomber pilot (played by Paul Massie) who is sent to Nazi-occupied Paris to kill a man believed to be betraying his colleagues in the French Resistance. Before being parachuted into France the young pilot is given a rigorous training for his assignment of murder.

The film is most exciting. Based on an original story by Donald C Downes, it was adapted for the screen by George St George. Paul Dehn wrote the film script and Anthony Havelock-Allan was yet again Asquith's producer.

After arriving in France the young pilot begins to realise that there is a difference between killing a lot of people ('When I dropped bombs I wasn't there at the other end') and killing just one man with a knife or with bare hands. He finds his selected victim is a gentle, henpecked husband, who dotes on his daughter, and he begins to feel that the man may not be guilty.

Lilian Gish is the pilot's mother, Irene Worth plays Leonie, an experienced agent in the French Resistance. The victim is played by Leslie French, and James Robertson Justice is Paul Massie's chief instructor. The location was in Paris with Paul walking through the roughest streets dressed as a French labourer.

'The whole first section of *Orders to Kill*,' said Asquith, 'apart from a scene in the aeroplane which has over it a little nursery song, has no music at all. The music starts when the hero, Paul Massie, is alone in Paris, and as you get more and more inside his personality, gradually, and I hope unobtrusively, we change the photographic style until finally the cameraman, using a hand-held camera, hares up the stairs of the Metro and we are right "inside" Paul Massie.'

The film was shown at the Cannes Film Festival and won three British Film Academy awards – Paul Dehn for the Best British Screen Play; Irene Worth for the 'Best Actress'; and Paul Massie for the 'Most Promising Newcomer'.

'*Orders to Kill* is a film you must see, both because it is breathtakingly exciting and because it deals with a very real problem which none of us in this day and age can afford to avoid,' said the *News Chronicle*.

'In *Orders to Kill*,' said *The Times*, 'it is the acting which scarcely reaches the required peak, but the director, Mr Anthony Asquith, brilliantly achieves a dramatic climax that becomes almost unbearable.'

'Lillian Gish occupies the screen for about five minutes. But it is a pleasure to see her,' said the *Evening Standard*.

'I was so delighted to be asked by Puffin to appear in *Orders to Kill*,' Lillian told me. 'His films are among the great classics – the Shaw films, *Orders to Kill*, and others.

'It was the only time I ever worked with and for him. I came to the Connaught Hotel because Katharine Hepburn said I should stay there as they'd serve breakfast at half past four or five o'clock in the morning before I went to the studio. Not many hotels can do that. The hall-porter used to make the coffee and toast and bring it up.

'When I arrived by plane for *Orders to Kill* and got to the hotel at five o'clock in the afternoon, there stood Puffin on the doorstep waiting to welcome me. He was in the middle of production yet he left the studio and came all the way back to London to greet me. Now that couldn't happen any other place in the world or with any other director. It was so touching and so like him.'

It was always Puffin's practice to hand a bouquet of flowers to the lady he had set out to see. When he arrived for dinner, he brought flowers: it was better, he felt, than leaving it to the florist's van to say his 'thank you' on the next day. Even when he was calling to take the Dowager Lady Harlech to a concert he had a corsage of flowers for her.

I remember an occasion when he went to meet a young actress who had been recommended to him for a part in his next film; and he took, of course, the flowers, which he always called 'a bloom'. In the lounge of the hotel where they were to meet, he looked about him. There were one or two businessmen, a plump bald-headed lawyer, a white-haired woman writing letters at a desk and at the far end, seated by herself and waiting for him, was a young woman, extremely well dressed. 'Ah!' he said with a shy wriggle, 'I've brought you a bloom.'

The woman looked at his boiler-suit, his hobnailed boots and rose from her chair in rage. 'How dare you!' she cried. 'How *dare* you!' and swept out of the lounge. The actress arrived as the angry woman went haughtily through the door.

* * *

Some months before the shooting of *Orders to Kill*, Puffin, Terence Rattigan and Tolly de Grunwald met to discuss the outline of a film treatment by Terry on Lawrence of Arabia. The sequences had been brilliantly worked out with a measured balance of exciting and emotional content.

Delighted to have yet another new Rattigan film in prospect, Puffin went to the Rank Organisation, who expressed their interest and waited for the script to be written. By the time *Orders to Kill* was completed, the script was ready. Everyone agreed it was one of the best things Terry had done; and Puffin and Tolly got ready to fly out to the Middle East in quest of suitable locations. Together with a cameraman they inspected and photographed certain possible settings, then flew on to Baghdad.

The town swarmed with visitors who had come to attend some royal occasion, for, in that early summer of 1958, Iraq had not yet become a republic. The hotels were so full that Puffin and Tolly had to share a bedroom. Their quest took them up mountain-tracks that climbed steeply higher and higher. Puffin, seated in front with the Arab driver, was as always unaware of any danger but it was clear to Tolly that the precipitous drop of thousands of feet on one side of the narrow track, which kept turning sharply and quite arbitrarily, must lead to the jeep whirling in loops over the edge and disposing of the Lawrence of Arabia prospectors finally and beyond recall.

Puffin kept talking incessantly, as was his way; Tolly was too scared to hear a word of it. He didn't even hear the Arab driver say 'Cigarette, sir!' to him, aware only that for a moment the driver had taken his eyes off that terrifying road. They got their shots and returned uninjured to the hotel.

On his return from the Middle East, earlier than I had expected, Puffin lunched with me and talked about the trip. I asked if he had found all the locations he needed. He wriggled and laughed, put his head to one side and then moved it to the other. 'We had to come back. We were interrupted,' he said.

'We had found a perfect spot on the fringe of Baghdad. I hopped around trying to select the right position for the camera. "Here!" I said. "We can shoot the King from here!"

'I heard a sort of gasp and turned to see what had happened to Tolly. Actually' – and he giggled – 'there was a large semicircle of Arabs who had been watching us and on hearing me say "We can shoot the King from here," they completely misunderstood us.'

Tolly came up to Puffin and said: 'Let's pack it up and get back to the hotel.' Puffin said: 'It won't take more than a few minutes to finish this.' But Tolly thought it was imprudent to stay where they were. 'Some of those men are talking angrily to their neighbours, telling them in Arabic what you have said you would do to their King.'

'I don't think it was really necessary for us to pack up and go,' Puffin told me. 'But perhaps he was right. The atmosphere in Baghdad the next day made me uneasy. Tolly said: "We'd better go to Egypt and find some locations there. We could come back here when things settle down." But, as you know, they didn't.'

On 14th July 1958, three or four days after Puffin and Tolly left Baghdad, the King was assassinated; and quite suddenly on his return Puffin was informed that the plan to make the Lawrence of Arabia film was abandoned.

'It was my greatest blow, and I think Puffin's,' Dirk Bogarde told me. 'We had already been slated to start this film. Puffin asked me to do it. Rattigan was not all that pleased. I was at the time more popular than Rock Hudson and Doris Day in England... but hardly the person, one would have thought, to play Lawrence!

'It was a magnificent script – starting in 1912 and moving to the climax. It was the greatest part I had ever been asked to do... and with Puffin's full approbation. He wrote to me at the very beginning and explained, carefully, that it had nothing to do with how I looked. "No one can look like Lawrence, but you can probably make us feel how he felt. Much more important." Those words sent a shaft of joy through me, and after a great many conversations together and with Rattigan, my severe doubts about my ability to play Lawrence had been put to rest, a little, by Puff's sureness.

'He sent me mountains of letters, books, paper-clippings. I read and read and read. People who had been friends of Lawrence's wrote and sent me marvellous details about him – fascinating, tiny little things. For over a year I steeped myself in the man, and Puffin used, constantly and tactfully, to ask questions. It was rather like being "crammed", with a very silvery-tongued professor asking you what you had studied! A fantastic wig was made, which cost a fortune, and which had an odd "essence" of Lawrence; and although I was the wrong complexion, and height, something began to build. We spent many evenings in the make-up rooms at Pinewood long after everyone had gone, fining things down.'

With some hesitation Dirk then asked Puffin a very personal question about Lawrence – 'out of the blue', to use his own phrase. 'Puff, tell me really and truly, now we have it all before us, was Lawrence homosexual?'

'Puffin's face,' Dirk told me, 'was a study in white horror. The cigarette dropped its ash; with an unsteady hand he removed it, then stubbing it out, he replied. "Not practising." I know that I should not have asked it.

uffin photographed while address-
ıg a film trade union meeting. On
ne right are Jennie Lee and George
lvin

photograph of the memorial
aque in the room at 'Glebelands'
ome of the Cinematograph
rade Benevolent Fund, endowed in
emory of Anthony Asquith.

his white Wedgewood cameo
ortrait of Anthony Asquith, on sage
reen Jasper, was flown to the
SSR in February 1969, accom-
nied by a delegation of the ACTT.
was presented to Russian film
chnicians. The plaque is a replica
f two awards made annually
y trustees of The Anthony Asquith
lemorial Fund to the composer and
rector of a film or TV feature
splaying the most apt and
aginative use of music.

A scene with John Mills (centre) from Asquiths' memorable *The Way to the Stars*. (*National Film Archive*)

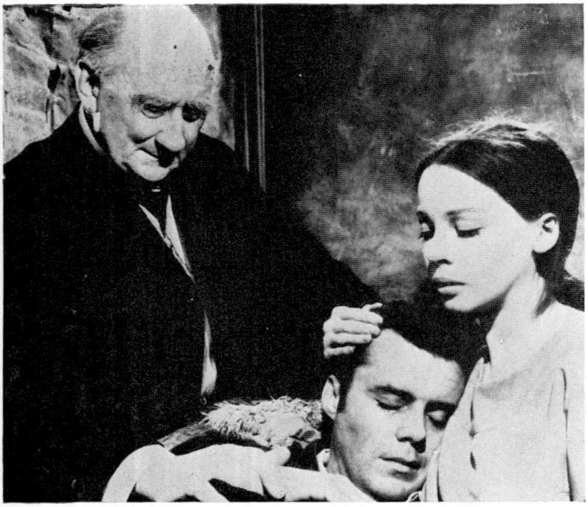

Felix Aylmer, Dirk Bogarde and Leslie Caron in *The Doctor's Dilem*
(*National Film Archive*)

Jack Warner (foreground) with (centre) Jim Laker and (right) Godfrey Evans in a scene from Asquith's *The Final Test*. (*Natio*
*Film Archive*)

'Eventually he left for the location and I went on with the costumes and other fittings. The day came for him to arrive back, only to be told that the film was "postponed". This he was told as he went through Immigration just after having found his sands, his railway, his living quarters – the entire background for his marvellous film, which sadly was not to be. I shall never judge his dissappointment or, to be more accurate, his heart-break.'

Dirk was deeply moved himself. 'We were a month away from shooting. The next morning "They" sent for us, one by one – Puffin first, de Grunwald second, myself last. I don't know, to this day, what Puffin was told. His interview lasted only half an hour, and he never mentioned it afterwards. Mine was longer, and I was offered a film called *The Captain's Table* instead. It was all over. The reason given, I think, was the budget – some £700,000. A fortune in those days.

'Rattigan, Puff and I were pretty desolate. Later the script became Rattigan's very successful play *Ross*, which had a long run at the Haymarket Theatre; so some of the glory was at least captured for Terry. But little for Puff and me. It was a bleak time. We had cancelled everything ahead for a full year to do *Lawrence*. But one day Puffin called with a very excited voice and suggested that we make a new film together' – which was in fact their next picture.

Terry Rattigan was just as disappointed and upset as the others and referred to it as 'the film we nearly made and which Puffin and I longed to make'.

He asked me if I had noticed a sort of similarity between Lawrence and Puffin. I felt there was in certain aspects of his personality some similarity.

Terry began to analyse it. 'There was the love and loyalty both Lawrence and Puffin inspired in people. There is also a similarity in their intellectuality' – both were classical scholars. After a reflective pause, Terry voiced his thoughts. 'The fact that in this toughest of all professions, which is the film director's, one would not have thought, certainly from the silent days onwards, this Oxford aesthete was able to command the passionate devotion of those very independent men who worked with him. They adored him. It seems remarkable to me. And *he* was devoted to *them*. He knew the names of each one's wife and children and never forgot their birthdays. As you know, none of this was sucking up: he was actually devoted to them and took a personal interest in everything they did.'

Michael Denison also noticed a similarity between Puffin and Lawrence. 'His recurrent trips to Joe's Café at Catterick seem to me very like T E Lawrence's escape into anonymity.'

Some years later David Lean made his famous film about Lawrence of Arabia with Peter O'Toole as Lawrence.

# 26

# His Second Shaw Film

FULFILLING HIS PROMISE to Dirk Bogarde, Puffin's next film was Shaw's *The Doctor's Dilemma.* Tolly partnered him on this, acting as producer and also adapting it for the screen.

Dirk was overjoyed. He wrote to me: 'With about three weeks preparation and with a marvellous cast ranging from Leslie Caron to Robert Morley, and with Cecil Beaton doing the costumes, we started to shoot. It was to be the turning-point in my life, and a film I adored. And so did Puffin.'

By putting more emphasis on the emotional scenes between Dirk Bogarde and his wife, Leslie Caron, than Shaw intended, Puffin provided an excellent counterpoise to the at times long-winded arguments of the doctors about 'stimulating the phagocytes'.

Interesting examples of Puffin's method while directing were vividly given to me by Dirk Bogarde. In the film he was Louis Dubedat, whose declining health is a matter of grave concern to his wife, and the dilemma of the doctors is to decide on the right treatment to save his life.

'When I was playing the big scene in the third act – the "Beauty of Light" speech – Puffin told me not to rehearse it. I was lying on a sofa thing and he said that we would shoot it in one. If it didn't work we'd do it again.

'The scene ran seven minutes. When it was over, I lay there waiting for the word "cut" from Puff . . . Nothing happened and I thought something awful had gone wrong. My eyes were closed, so I was not able to see . . .

'I sat up. There was dead silence. Puff had his back to me, one arm raised across his eyes. I said "Shall we go again?" He just shook his head and walked away into the shadows. None of us went near him. They started to break up the set and get ready for something else.

'Later, when he had composed himself, we carried on as if nothing had happened. He never spoke of it again to me . . . or indeed ever. At the end of the day he grabbed my elbow and simply said: "Lovely, quite lovely," and went scuttling off to his car.'

Dirk then told me of the shooting of two other scenes, one of which was the most moving scene in the film.

'When the time came to do the big speech to the doctors, which again he shot in one huge swooping take, I was in terror. I had sweated at it for days . . . line by line . . . word by word – you cannot "wing" Shaw! And when the day to shoot it came, I went in misery and fear to Puff and told him, very humbly that, having dissected the speech to the last comma, I found that it really didn't make sense.

'Puff said, "I know, my dear, it never has in fifty years, but actors have always made it *sound* sense." So I did it.

'Leslie Caron played Mrs Dubedat beautifully. The almost final scene had me lying dead on a sofa, with all the doctors standing round me, sadly looking at their failure. She had to come from a door, high up in the room, walk along a gallery, come down some stairs, and then say to the doctors "I'm so sorry to have kept you waiting so long." It was a difficult shot for the camera . . . very mobile and fluid.

'Puff, as he almost always did, tucked himself like a pixie under the camera, on the dolly. He sat there hugging his knees to his chest, squashed under the camera caul. I was dead. The take started. I heard the door open and close. Then Leslie's feet walking measuredly along the gallery . . . slowly and with dignity coming down each tread of the stairs . . . and then the gentle swish-swish of her silk skirt as she came towards the sofa. As she said, "I'm so sorry to have kept you waiting so long", there was a great cry from Puffin. "No! Oh, no! My dear, you haven't at all!" and he leapt to his feet and knocked himself out on the camera! What a glorious man!'

After a time, having rambled over memories of their personal friendship, Dirk gave me one more cameo of *The Doctor's Dilemma*: 'Puffin wanted to do a fade-in of the complete table at Richmond – the entire cast sitting round a large circular table. Before the Shaw dialogue started he wanted us to *ad lib* a little until the fade-in was steady. He begged us to talk to the person on our right and speak about something which had to do with the period because the sound track was running.

'I thought about Bonnard and light. My doctor on my right was Robert Morley. On the word "Action" I turned to Robert to say my invented line about Bonnard and light only to hear him say to me: "Dubedat! What did Oscar Wilde do?" The take was in ruins. Puffin was ill with laughter, and tears sprang from his eyes.'

Among the other doctors were Felix Aylmer (his fourth Asquith film) and Alastair Sim.

'Sometimes,' said Asquith, 'someone says he'd like to try

doing the scene his way and I say, "All right – and then we'll do it the way *I* want. I may be wrong." And at times I have been wrong. It can also happen the other way. In *The Doctor's Dilemma*, Leslie Caron was quite, quite sure about which take was best – I had printed two takes – done *her* way and mine. It was an important scene and I was sure she didn't like it done my way. In this case, when she saw the two scenes on the screen during the rushes, she agreed that I was right. But it does happen the other way sometimes.'

The film was a triumph for Anthony Asquith. *The Doctor's Dilemma* was just as enthusiastically received by the Press as *Pygmalion*. 'Shaw,' wrote Campbell Dixon in the *Daily Telegraph*, 'for me at any rate, could never portray romantic love convincingly. (Did he ever feel it?) Nevertheless, thanks to Mr Asquith's direction and well-judged performances by Dirk Bogarde and Leslie Caron, I found myself for the first time half-believing in the unprincipled artist's love for his wife and her patient devotion.'

The *Manchester Guardian* said: '*The Doctor's Dilemma* could scarcely have done more to circumvent whatever accusations there might be about whatever is dated in Shaw's theme. For it reduced to a minimum the pursuit of medical red herrings in the conversation among doctors and has concentrated more than Shaw did, on the life or death of Louis Dubedat.'

'Where the film succeeds best,' said Majdalany in the *Daily Mail*, 'is in the depth of feeling brought to the part of the artist and his wife by Dick Bogarde and Leslie Caron. Miss Caron's trembling sincerity splendidly offsets the artificial context against which it has to pull: Mr Bogarde, especially in the closing scenes, manages to counterpoint the Shavian wit with a beautifully-controlled display of unShavian emotion.'

*The Times* view was that the film owed what unity it possessed not to Shaw but to Cecil Beaton 'whose dresses and *décor* have converted this most barbed of theatrical polemics into the most polished and visually delightful of period pieces.'

# 27

# Sophia Loren and Peter Sellers

Yet another Shaw production was to follow, but it was preceded by *Libel*, in which Dirk Bogarde starred together with Olivia de Havilland (as his wife); Robert Morley again; and Paul Massie, whose fine acting in *Orders to Kill* had won him the award of 'Most Promising Newcomer'.

Sir Mark Lodden (Dirk Bogarde) is suspected by Paul Massie, who sees him in a television programme about his lovely home, as being an imposter. Paul and Dirk and a third man, who resembled Dirk in features but not in personality, had been in a prisoner-of-war camp together. An attempt to unmask the present Sir Mark leads to a libel action during which Olivia de Haviland reveals that Dirk is not really her husband.

The story was certainly enthralling and his acting earned Dirk the *Evening Standard's* verdict that 'he gives the performance of his career'. Dilys Powell was not so enthusiastic in the *Sunday Times*. '*Libel* offers a puzzle with excitement,' she wrote, 'and some neat twists . . . I don't myself think this kind of set-piece suits the director's ironic and elegant yet powerful gifts. But Mr Asquith doesn't make any mistakes.'

'When we finished filming *Libel*,' Olivia de Havilland told me, 'I tried to think of an appropriate gift for Puffin. I wanted it to be a gift of love, and, though only an amateur, I decided eventually to paint a view of my garden in Paris from my boudoir window. When I saw it hanging on the wall in his home I felt that he was really pleased. He was a kind, sensitive, witty, imaginative, affectionate person, – a hard worker and a devoted friend.'

His third Shaw film *The Millionairess*, starring Sophia Loren and Peter Sellers, won a place among his best films. Sophia played the title role; Peter Sellers was the Indian doctor. Also in the film were Vittorio de Sica and Wally Patch, who was with Asquith in his very first film, *Boadicea*, which was made thirty-five years before. Puffin was loyal to Wally and found parts for him in quite a number of his films – seven in all, including *Tell England*, in which he had the role of sergeant-instructor and expressed his annoyance with the recruits in rhyming slang like 'Stick it up his Khyber'. Puffin interrupted him, asked him what it meant, got him to write out a complete list of such phrases and sent them to the censor, who passed them on the condition that the rhyme itself was not supplied. Wally appeared in *Pygmalion* too, *Quiet Wedding*, and *Cottage to Let*.

The excitement over *The Millionairess* began when it was announced that Sophia Loren would be playing opposite Peter Sellers in her flirtatious scenes. The Press was agog. On her arrival in London, long before the shooting of the film began, the Press was invited to witness the introduction of Peter to Sophia.

The entire length of the reception room separated the two stars. Best known for his brilliant comedy in the Goon Show on radio, Peter Sellers was too shy to make any move towards her. 'I don't normally act with a romantic glamorous woman. You'd be scared too. She's a lot different from Harry Secombe, you must admit.' Later he picked up courage and was taken to her and introduced. It appeared to be too formal. Under pressure from the photographers, he gave Sophia a hesitant peck on the cheek.

Sophia Loren's entire collection of jewellery, valued at £750,000 and not insured, were stolen midway through the shooting. It was not just a Press sensation; it actually happened. There were tears, of course; but the show had to go on, and bravely and gaily, with saucy banter and laughter, she went on. There were stories about Peter Sellers falling madly in love with her, which possibly had no basis at all. She was anyway too much in love with her husband Carlo Ponti to be interested in anyone else. The acting of Peter and Sophia on the screen was arrestingly delightful: Peter's Indian accent was faultless: and after the release of *The Millionairess* Sophia and Peter recorded the song, 'Goodness, Gracious, Me!', which could so easily have been worked into the film – but Shaw had not written it. The friendship between them has endured and Peter Sellers often goes to stay with Sophia and Carlo at their magnificent house just outside Rome.

Pierre Rouve, who produced the film, told me: 'It was my first film as producer. Not only was Puffin extremely kind in helping and guiding me, but when it was completed he wrote to pay tribute to what he called *my* film – meaning *me*. It was of course *his* film; what he said could not be supported by any evidence, but only what was in his heart.

'One day something happened on the set which shows Puffin working with the workmen as a team. We had to take some close-ups of Sophia Loren in the water with Dennis Price. We discovered at the last minute that he was not well enough, so we called his stand-in, only to find that he couldn't swim. Sophia was getting more and more impatient because, as she had to go out that night, her hair had to be done; and while the usual chaotic confusion was going on, the beginner-producer (that's me) was rushing up and down the corridors of the studio trying to pacify people. When I returned to the set I found that something quite unexpected had happened. A new stand-in was swimming happily in the water and was being directed by the camera-operator. "Move to the left . . . Now to the right . . . Slightly forward. That's it!" The man in the water was wearing little white pants. It was Puffin.'

Referring to the theft of the jewels, Pierre Rouve said: 'It took place on Saturday night. On Sunday morning I was called by the police to the studio and I was there until Monday morning. Very tired – I had not slept all night – and still involved in discussions I was interrupted by the doorman who rushed in at seven o'clock that morning to say that Sophia Loren's Rolls-Royce had arrived. I was too upset and too distracted and waved him away. But in fact Sophia Loren had arrived in it for the day's filming. She went straight into the dressing-room to get dressed and be made up, and carried on as though nothing had happened, though we all knew how shattered she was when she learned on the Saturday night about the loss of her jewels.

'Later that morning somebody else's nerves cracked – those of Peter Sellers! He fainted and had to be taken to hospital. We had, of course, to go on with the shooting. The shooting could not be stopped. We spent the rest of the day taking close-ups of the tired, greatly upset Sophia Loren – and the close-ups were really beautiful.'

The film was an enormous success both with Press and public. C A Lejeune said in the *Observer*: '*The Millionairess* is something of an occasion. This lark, this farcical comedy . . . can in no way be considered GBS's work. On the whole it is a prank of an elderly gentleman.'

'Miss Sophia Loren,' said *The Times*, 'is in the role of one of those masterful, combative Shavian tomboys prepared to carry the war into masculine territory. She possesses a natural talent for rumbustious comedy but here she cannot compete with Miss Katharine Hepburn and Mrs Patrick Campbell.'

Alexander Walker in the *Evening Standard:* 'As I watched I nearly imitated Mr Khruschev and began thumping my seat. But not in anger. In delight. Delight at the best film of a Bernard Shaw play since *Pygmalion* – a play that has been refurbished inside and out by Anthony Asquith and now fizzes with effrontery and dances a jig with absurdity.'

'Peter Sellers is the magnet,' said Dilys Powell, 'the one you can't and mustn't miss. And we have to thank Anthony Asquith, most sympathetic of actors' directors, for letting Sellers be Sellers.'

Sophia Loren, to mark their happy association, gave Puffin, when the shooting was over, a small hobbyhorse on four wheels, to which she gave the name Shaw had given her in *The Millionairess* – Epifania. Puffin was so delighted with it that he always had it with him on the set and would ride round on it, joyous as a child.

The making of that film remains an enduring landmark in Sophia's memory, which she expressed to me later: 'I cannot talk about Puffin without feeling deeply moved and I cannot but call him Puffin. This familiarity is not a sign of disregard: very few directors have ever commanded deeper or truer respect. But very few have also stirred an equally deep feeling of sincere affection. He never ordered actors about. He guided them – gently and intelligently, but above all unselfishly. Artistic integrity and personal unsefishness made him what he was – *unique*. They also make him unforgettable.'

Carlo Ponti added his tribute: 'Anthony Asquith was a *signore*. This Italian idiom is not rendered by the English "gentleman".

It means more because it includes human qualities and intellectual abilities which transcend conventional class distinctions. It also implies an inborn reluctance to boast and a natural inclination to avoid the limelight. Asquith had all these qualities. In the somewhat harsh world of the cinema he brought something of the unobtrusive and unprepossessing dignity of a bygone age. I deeply regret that I never had the opportunity of having him direct any of my productions. It would have been a pleasure and a privilege.'

Peter Sellers, who always speaks of Anthony as 'Dear Puffin', found it difficult to express his feelings in words, but gave a realistic imitation of him on one of his records on '*The Critics*'; Newton Tweedale is quite easily recognisable as Puffin – rapid flow of words, whooping-cough laughs, and the nibbling *m–m–m* before speaking.

# 28

# Mind and Body

THE UTMOST DEVOTION to Puffin did not keep you from becoming aware that he lived in the mind rather than the body. The body did not seem to interest him at all. His boiler-suit covered his nakedness and one feels that he wore it for that purpose alone and relied on his muffler to keep him warm. He was indifferent to food: when he sat at the table as guest or even host, he toyed with what was served, nibbling perhaps two or three mouthfuls. The strawberry icecream always followed; but his incessant chatter reduced it to liquid and he had to drink the rest of it with a soup spoon. His hair was always untidy. Lillian Gish noticed the condition of his teeth: 'He needs somebody to look after him. I suppose his mother used to and now there is no one.'

It was not easy to look after him. He had Mary Brierley, and nobody could be a more dedicated housekeeper. She and her husband, John, did their best to make his home comfortable. 'You ought to have your bathroom alongside your bedroom. You ought not to be going down a flight of stairs to the toilet in the middle of the night!' Puffin would smile. He could not have cared less. He was not aware of the discomfort – never aware of any discomfort.

'Puffin was born to be a mind,' Pierre Rouve told me. 'The body was there as an appendage, which he dragged behind that mind all through his life. Consequently everything that was a concern of the body, a pleasure of the body, seemed alien to him. That explains in a way his total inability to deal with practical matters. Such violence as he depicted on the screen always seemed to me to be an attack by him on that enemy of his, the body, to prevent it taking possession of the mind and destroying the mind. I used to ask him jokingly why he betrayed his principles by shaving, having a bath, brushing his teeth. Music was away from anything that was corporal.'

The body was used for playing games, like golf and cricket and driving a car, however badly; but that was a way of working off his restlessness. His home life was erratically varied. When he was working on a script he would spend hours, even days, in his study at the back of the house, sending messages to ACT to say he couldn't come to the meeting that night. When there were gaps between films, and sometimes there were gaps of a year or even two years, he didn't relax at all but worked harder than ever in quest of something really worthwhile for his next film. He would fly to Paris, Berlin, Rome, Scandinavia. Numerous trips were made to New York and California for discussions with film magnates for backing and with film stars for casting. And almost always shooting on locations abroad kept him from home for weeks at a time. Nor must we forget that his passion for music took him to the opera or to a ballet or a concert whenever he was able to snatch the time.

Generally, during the weeks before going on the floor with his new film, Puffin used to rehearse some of the scenes in his house in Thurloe Square with the artists involved – often, even after the shooting had begun in the studio, he would devote the weekends to rehearsals at home of scenes to be shot during the coming week.

His book-lined study was much too cramped for this: there were piles of books on tables and chairs in untidy heaps, with barely room for him to hop about in, but if only one actor or actress was involved they were put through it there. When there were more artists he would take them to the large, orderly drawing-room upstairs and spend hours with them, often going on until the small hours of the morning, with Mary bringing up trays of tea and sandwiches.

'If he had an evening completely free, it was a joy to have him at home,' said Mary. 'The first thing he did when he entered the house was to come straight down to the kitchen, talk to us, join us in a cup of tea, and watch television in our sitting-room.

'After Ernie, his mother's coachman, retired, Mr Asquith bought a small car and used to drive it himself. We tried to stop him driving, but he would not listen. He loved driving. He was really a terrible driver. Material things didn't mean anything to him. At night when he came home, John would go out and look at the car. Sometimes he found the car doors had been left wide open. Most times all the lights had been left on and he never could remember to lock the car.'

John took over from her at this point. 'Quite apart from the fact that the battery would have been dead by the morning with all those lights on, there was the police to consider. They used to ring the bell and fetch me out of the kitchen, sometimes out of bed, and talk to me about those lights.

'I spoke to Mr Asquith yet again about it. He looked a little sheepish and said: "I'm sorry, John. I forgot." I said: "You know I ought to fine you for forgetting. If I fined you £1 every time the lights were left on or the doors left open . . ."

Vendy Hiller as flowerseller Eliza Doolittle
Asquith's film of Shaw's *Pygmalion*.
*Vational Film Archive*)

Edith Evans in Asquith's film *The Importance of Being Earnest*. (*National Film Archive*)

Iichael Redgrave with one of his pupils in
Asquith's screen version of Terence Rattigan's
*he Browning Version*. (*National Film Archive*)

Penelope Ward and Laurence Olivier in *The Demi-Paradise*, directed by Anthony Asquith. (*National Film Archive*)

(Right) Flora Robson with Anne Casson in a scene from the early Asquith film, *Dance, Pretty Lady*. (*British Instructional Films Limited*)

Paul Massie and Irene Worth in Anthony Asquith's film, *Orders t Kill*. (*National Film Archive*)

Omar Sharif and Ingrid Bergma meet in Asquith's *The Yellow Ro Royce*. (*National Film Archive*)

'He said: "Splendid idea, John," and laughed quite a lot. "You'll see, I shan't forget again." The next night when he came in, he called out: "All the lights out and I've *locked* the car too." He had come in with a pile of scripts and papers and went into his study to do some work. I went in with him and lit the gas-fire – that's all that room had, just one small gas-fire. When I came out I heard something come clattering through the letter box. It was his car keys. I opened the front door very quietly. The policeman was just moving off. He turned and told me the car was locked all right, but the keys had been left in the door.

'The next morning Mr Asquith told Mary: "I've lost my keys." Mary handed them to him. He was a little uneasy. "I hope John didn't pick them up." I told him I had and said I must fine him £1 as we'd agreed. I had put a poor-box in the hall for these fines. He said: "Of course. Just fine me every time I forget anything." He didn't dive into his pockets for the money, but called out to Mary: "Do be a dear and give John a pound for the poor box. It's my fine."

'Mary *always* paid these fines for him,' John went on. 'We knew of course that he never had any money on him. Twice a week a registered packet would arrive for him, containing his allowance. I didn't know how much was in them, but by the end of the day it was all gone. He didn't spend any of it on himself – he kept buying all sorts of things for his friends – endless quantities of flowers, scarves and gloves for women, cigarette lighters, long-playing records, books, very handsome and costly books most of them, for men as well as women. He didn't need any money for himself. When he took friends out for lunch and dinner, he always signed and added the tip for the waiter on to the bill. If the car broke down and he needed a taxi he'd borrow the money from Mary – he always paid it back, of course, though occasionally what with the fines, and his borrowing money to give it away, it mounted up quite a bit at times. He was constantly buying flowers for Mary.'

Mary smiled sadly: 'No one could have had a better, a dearer man to look after. He needed mothering really, so did Mr Peter Russell.'

After Peter Russell's death, a firm of accountants took over his finances.

There were evenings when he had friends round either to play cards or to listen to music or just merely to sit and talk and argue. Big parties were infrequent. There were some when an entire theatrical company from abroad were his guests and the audience included many distinguished members of the British and American and French theatre.

'Mr Asquith enjoyed himself on those evenings,' said Mary. 'He loved company. It was such a joy to see him among them hopping about like a little bird. The large rooms used to be full of people and we saw that there was plenty for them to eat and drink. There were two or three big Russian parties. He never missed any of the Russian dance displays and generally invited the entire cast to come and spend the evening here.'

Occasionally when he was away whether abroad or in Yorkshire, John would paint his bedroom and some of the other rooms. It was done furtively. On one occasion a phone call told them that he was returning much earlier than they expected, and John had to stay up all night to get it finished.

They did more than mother him. Puffin was in Scotland when Sir Winston Churchill had his ninetieth birthday. Mary, fearing that Puffin might forget to send a greeting, sent one for him. Her telegram said: 'Further congratulations, dear Winston – Anthony Asquith.'

When Puffin returned he found among his letters this telegram: 'Thank you, dear Puffin – Winston.'

He looked puzzled and turned to Mary. 'Did I send it?' he said.

# 29

# Sweden, Moscow, Spain

ON FINISHING *The Millionaires*, Puffin left for Sweden, taking the wooden horse on wheels Sophia Loren had given him. He had that horse on the set of every film he made until the end of his life. Attaching a lead to it, he used to take it all over the set, as though it were a pet dog. It came in useful though. While a shot was being taken he used in the past to crouch uncomfortably under the camera or sit on the floor, his knees raised with his arms round them. Now he sat on Epifania.

In Sweden he was to film *Two Living, One Dead*, with Virginia McKenna, Bill Travers, and Patrick McGoohan as the stars.

'It was based on a very interesting novel which won the Nobel prize,' Virginia McKenna told me, 'with no sex and no violence in it.' It tells of a small Swedish post-office being raided by two armed men. One of the post-office's three clerks is shot and dies. Another (played by Patrick McGoohan), who is married, has a child and is afraid of losing his life, hands over the cash-box to the raiders. The third clerk is regarded as a hero because he has a bandage round his head; whereas the man who handed over the money is treated by the people of the small town as a coward: his wife (Virginia McKenna) and his young son get the backwash of the public's hostility. It turns out that the hero is really a coward too. For, sickened by the so-called 'hero's' pride and boastfulness, the clerk who has been treated as an outcast, draws a gun on him and discovers that he is not prepared to risk his life either.

When the film was completed, Asquith took it and the leading members of the cast to Moscow. 'The film was shown,' said Virginia, 'in the Sports Stadium there. Puffin made a speech and the film seemed to be well received.

'We spent four marvellous days in Moscow. Our hotel was very old-fashioned, though some of the rooms had completely modern furniture. In Puffin's suite there was a grand piano which had been brought in specially for him. When he wasn't playing Schubert and Chopin, we would plunge into wild games of Racing Demon.

'He was wonderful to work with. The film was shot in a small town in Sweden and took ten bitterly cold weeks in the winter to make. As a director he was creative and sensitive and gave tremendous confidence to the actors. Everything he said was gentle and kind. His one concern was the feelings of the actors. When we left he gave Bill and myself two beautifully illustrated books as a thankoffering.'

On saying goodbye to the members of the Swedish cast and the Swedish technicians, he gave each one of them a small token of remembrance. They were so fascinated by his wooden horse, Epifania, that they all signed their names on various parts of it.

The film was shown only on television in Britain. Puffin was acutely disappointed, but plunged promptly into his next production, *Guns of Darkness*, which was made in Spain, where of course Epifania went too.

The scene, set in a South American republic, was shot in Malaga in five weeks. Based on a book called *Act of Mercy*, it was scripted by John Mortimer and produced by Thomas Clyde. It tells of a swift and violent coup which has put the Army revolutionary chief in control and focuses on the personal crisis of an English planter, Tom Jordan (played by David Niven), and his French wife, Claire. The marriage is disintegrating; the wife plans to leave her husband, but eventually reaches an understanding.

'I did not know Puffin really,' Tommy Clyde told me. 'In fact the first time we met was when he and I motored to Stratford-on-Avon to cast the part of Claire. What? Oh, I was driving the car. Puffin was busy with *The Times* crossword. "If we get this crossword out," he said, "we'll get Leslie." He was referring to Leslie Caron. The crossword was not solved, nevertheless we got Leslie. She was married at the time to Peter Hall, who was producing at the Shakespeare Theatre at Stratford-on-Avon.

'Puff is best at romance or comedy. He was faced with a predicament because *Guns of Darkness* was an adventure story and he tried to give it overtones. In that he was very successful. He was delightful to be with, endearingly boyish, always kind and considerate. It became an embarrassment, for whenever he came to see us he brought my wife flowers.'

With the group on location was Adza Vincent, a friend of Puffin's for many years and soon to manage his business affairs as his agent. The thing that impressed her and the others was the farewell party there. Years later they still went on talking about it.

'Pedro Vidal was our first assistant,' Tommy Clyde told me, 'and talked to the local crew in Spanish. Puffin, dressed as usual in his boiler-suit even in that very hot weather, with a belt round his waist, was not their idea of a film director, but they accepted him. He spoke to them in English.

'The party was given in the restaurant of our hotel. It was to offer our thanks to the Spanish crew. Puffin said he wanted to make a speech and thank them personally. We had our doubts whether many of them who knew barely a word or two of English, would understand the speech.'

'He stood on a chair,' said Pedro Vidal, 'and talked for twelve minutes in perfect Spanish – and cultured Spanish at that. We had not the vaguest hint of it. Everyone went wild with delight when they heard him speak Spanish.'

'The speech was impeccable,' Tommy Clyde said, 'and the way Puffin expressed his thanks was so moving that everybody was crying.' Presents were given, as usual, to everybody. To Pedro Vidal he gave cufflinks with A.A. and P.V. on opposite sides. 'They are the most beautiful links I have ever had,' Pedro told me. Leslie Caron's gift to Puffin was a lovely gold clock.

The Press did not care much for the film. 'Too many hares started here, I think,' said the *Daily Telegraph*. 'No blame for dissatisfaction on David Niven, whose Jordan needs some more writing rather than better acting, nor on the supporting players.'

'Anthony Asquith,' said Dilys Powell, 'uses all his professional skill to make it exciting. John Mortimer's script is shaped to put the emphasis on conscience. The exercise of violence: is it ever justifiable, is the human race capable of rejecting it, or are we trapped in violence? Not for the first time has Anthony Asquith presented this question on the screen.'

# 30

# Talking Shop

THE ACTT, THE trade union of the cinema and television technicians, took up a great deal of Asquith's time. The Council met at first every week but adjusted later to once a month, and as a rule he was in the chair. In addition he served on numerous committees. Even when he was filming, he would arrive breathless from the studio and listen patiently and sympathetically to the long and often heated arguments, pouring oil hopefully and often successfully on the troubled waters.

When there were crises in one of the sections – and there were many sections: cameramen, sound-men, laboratory-men, and so on – he would lead a delegation of three or four technicians from the section, together with George Elvin, the general secretary, and fight the battle for pay or conditions or both, always frank and always fair, not only to the union men but to the employers as well; that is why he was admired and loved by both sides.

At the annual general meeting, which went on for two days, he was in the chair for the entire time, acting as the Speaker does in the House of Commons; and doing indeed more than that, for the Speaker is not required to open the proceedings with a presidential address.

Everyone of Puffin's presidential addresses was a gem. With skill and adroitness he was able to blend wit and humour with the serious and at times critical problems that confronted the film industry. One could quote at random: the assembled Press found it quite easy to do so. But let us look at what he said when the association came of age:

'I doubt if any of you who attended the birth would have predicted that the tiny and feeble infant would survive so long, let alone grow into a fine upstanding youth. Before ACT was born there had been more than one abortive attempt by technicians to bring into the world a trade union organisation, beginning in 1918 with the Kine-Cameramen's Society. Unfortunately the parents put their funds into a bank which promptly went into liquidation, so that ill-fated toddler died of malnutrition.

'When ACT was born twenty-one years ago it seemed probable that it would suffer a like fate. Indeed, George Elvin reminds me that when he was appointed nanny to the sickly child he was unable to get into the office because the door was guarded by a liftman placed there by the landlord to whom heavy arrears of rent were owing. Luckily, a fairy godmother disguised as Thorold Dickinson was able to lend George a magic wand in the shape of a £5 note and by waving this under the liftman's nose he was able to get in to find that the records showed only eight fully-paid members – barely enough to provide the baby with a bottle of milk.'

He then struck a more serious note. 'Those who joined ACT in recent years can hardly appreciate the difficulties which we met in our early days. There were no employers' federations with which to negotiate. Studios and production companies had to be tackled one by one and, remember, we were a small and highly suspect body. Before 1930 there was not a single trade union agreement negotiated with a film studio or producer apart from one held by the Electrical Trade Union for their membership at Elstree . . . It was not until 1939 that the first collective all-industry agreement was signed, when the laboratory-workers got their trade union agreement.'

Frank Fuller, elected chairman of the Laboratory committee in that year, told me: 'When I began to work with Tony I began to admire his obvious sincerity and concern for the general welfare of our organisation. He showed a readiness to identify himself with the problems particularly of those who were less fortunate. During the war a freely negotiated agreement had been turned down by the laboratory employers and we had to go to arbitration. Tony, who instantly declared that he would lead our deputation, asked me endless questions so that he would have all the facts at his disposal. We won a complete victory. It was from that time that a close bond of friendship was established between us which lasted until the end of his life.

'We worked closely together for more than twenty years. Of course we did not always agree, but it didn't affect our relationship at all. He handled the meetings gently and was able to establish and maintain a close friendly line with the members, however turbulent some of them may have been before his intervention. His infinite patience and wonderful sense of humour carried him through everything. Never at any time has anyone seen Tony Asquith in a temper.'

And he still went round lecturing, sometimes to ACT members, or groups of young men and women who were interested in making films their career, or it might be at the Edinburgh Festival, to which he was a constant visitor from North Berwick.

One of his addresses there was on 'Director, Actor, and Audience', and he illustrated what he said with excerpts from his films.

In the early days of silent films, he said, the relationship between the actor and the audience was a very simple one, because the audience were delighted with pictures that moved at all. The invention by D W Griffith of the close-up established a new relationship between the audience and the actor. 'It gave the director the great power to impose on the audience what he wants them to see.'

The relationship between the director and the actor, he went on, is basically the same as that between the conductor and the orchestra. The director and the conductor must have the whole work in their minds all the time. But it is more difficult in a film because it is done not in sequence but in tiny bits, without any continuity, and spread out over a long period of time.

Speaking of his way of directing he said: 'I found that the most successful thing to do with good actors, and I have been fortunate enough to work with many, is to discuss each scene. I work out the pure mechanics of the camera and leave the actor absolutely free to do the scene as he feels it should be done.'

But, having worked with Puffin on the set, I know that, while the good actor or actress is given free rein to indicate how he or she plans to interpret the scene, it has to fit in with Puffin's own interpretation of it. With gentle guidance and almost apologetic persuasion – 'Let's just try it this way and see how it works' – he was able in the end to get the performance he wanted.

Paul Massie, who made his film début in Asquith's *Orders to Kill*, described his direction in these words: 'In almost every detail he shows consideration for the feelings of the artistes working with him. An acute sensitivity for human fears and emotions permeates his whole personality . . . When you hear the words, "Just one more" you know that something has gone wrong. But however many times it's wrong or however stupid you may be about some part of a scene, he is always calm and always wholly polite.'

David Lean said to me: 'I have worked with Anthony Asquith. I'd describe him as a very fine director, not a great director. He was too gentle with the artistes.' I shook my head. 'Gentle, yes,' I said, 'but also dogged. He never gave in.' A film critic shared my view. 'Puffin,' he told me, 'was an Iron Butterfly. He had a will of iron in spite of his wonderful courtesy and charm.'

# 31

# His Star-strewn Film – *The VIPs*

ELIZABETH TAYLOR, RICHARD BURTON, Orson Welles, Louis Jourdan, Elsa Martinelli, Maggie Smith, Rod Taylor, Margaret Rutherford, Linda Christian, and even David Frost, were in this glittering film *The VIPs*, written by Terence Rattigan and set entirely in London's main airport, Heathrow.

The idea for it came to Rattigan when he found himself fogbound at the airport and unable to leave for New York; and he whiled away the long hours of weary waiting by creating characters who, for varying reasons, were desperately anxious to to get away – Orson Welles because he had to leave the country before midnight in order to avoid paying very ruinous taxes; Elizabeth Taylor who was eloping with Louis Jourdan, but being unable to get away, had to spend the entire night with her husband Richard Burton in the airport hotel.

It was a cleverly worked-out story, rather on the lines of *Grand Hotel*. Though many would not place it among Asquith's best films, it attracted a vast public all over the world. The film was made for Metro-Goldwyn-Mayer and Anatole de Grunwald was once again the producer.

It was Elizabeth Taylor's and Richard Burton's first film together since *Cleopatra*, which had been shot in Rome. Puffin found her delightful to work with. 'She was always on the set in time and always word perfect,' he told me. He made no comment about Richard Burton other than to say that he played the part well.

Richard and Elizabeth bought him a magnificent new overall, feeling that it was time his old faded and frayed boiler-suit was discarded. Puffin was delighted. He showed it with pride to his friends, but never wore it. Throughout the film he dragged his wooden horse along the set and sat on it from time to time.

The Press did not greet the film with much enthusiasm. The *Spectator* said: '*The VIPs* seemed very much contrived, unbearably glossy, a sophisticated essay in emotional triviality, its only virtues being Margaret Rutherford, Maggie Smith and Richard Wattis.'

Cecil Wilson said in the *Daily Mail*: 'This immaculate film has nothing very serious to say. Its sole object is to entertain and in its romanticised, larger-than-life way it admirably exploits the box office value of an impressive cast.'

Leonard Mosley in the *Daily Express:* 'All hail to this film for providing the lushest, most lavish and most extrovertingly easy entertainment which has been seen on the screen for years. *The VIPs* will leave no scum on your hands from kitchen-sink dramatics. It will deposit no grit in your mind for worrying about the psychological problems of the characters . . . Its laughs come easy. Its weepy moments will have dried on your cheeks by the time the lights are up.'

'*The VIPs* is,' said *The Times*, 'as British films go very glossy and proficient; it is quite viewable (the names of Anthony Asquith as director and Anatole de Grunwald as producer guarantee that), but it is never really compulsive. Margaret Rutherford is excellent in her usual role, Orson Welles is wasted in an uninventively written minor role as a tempestuous film director and Maggie Smith does wonders with a thankless part as a devoted unnoticed secretary. Neither Richard Burton nor Elizabeth Taylor strikes any sparks in the central romantic tangle, but at least for anyone eager to see them together the film can be recommended as about an hour and a half less boring than *Cleopatra*.'

Margaret Rutherford told me that she had refused at first to play the part offered her as Duchess of Brighton. 'After reading it I didn't like it. There were just one or two gags and nothing very amusing in it. The part didn't interest me. It was not really a character part. Gags are not enough. So I turned it down.'

Tolly de Grunwald took it to Terry Rattigan and together they built it up. 'It was much, much better then, but still a small part,' she said. But it got her an "Oscar," the only person in the film to get an award.

Margaret Rutherford's husband, James Stringer Davis, played the part of a waiter in the airport scenes and kept bobbing up every time Richard Burton called for a drink. 'I'm afraid,' Stringer Davis told me, 'I must have overacted. Puffin looked at me very thoughtfully and came up to me from the camera. "Too much," he said. "Not quite so much next time."'

* * *

Some weeks after the *première* of *The VIPs*, on Friday, 23rd December 1963 to be exact, Puffin left for Catterick to spend Christmas with Joe and his family at their café.

He had already begun to prepare his next film, *The Yellow Rolls-Royce*. As always he worked for long hours and had spent part of the day talking to Tolly de Grunwald, who was to produce it, and to theatrical agents about the casting of the picture. But most of his time was devoted to shopping. With Christmas Day only hours away, he kept popping in and out of shops buying presents for his numerous friends. For Joe he bought some bottles of whisky, for his wife and daughter, both named Rita, he got some blouses, for the two sons cigarettes, had them packed carefully and placed them in the back of his new cream Sunbeam saloon car with its familiar red band round its waist.

Then a tour began to various parts of London to deliver personally the gifts he had for friends who were still in town. He did not return home until very late. Paul Massie had come to stay with him until Sunday when he was to fly home to Canada, with him was his friend Richard Easton. Puffin joined them and talked for hours, then put his bags into his car and set out for Catterick.

On the way he called at Adza Vincent's house near Regent's Park to give her her Christmas present.

'He had phoned me during the day to say he would be coming,' she told me. 'I waited for him until well after midnight and then went to bed. I was awakened from a deep sleep by the dogs barking. I looked at the time. It was four o'clock in the morning. I couldn't believe he would come at *that* hour. But it was him. He looked all in. After giving me his present and wishing me a Happy Christmas, he hurried towards the stairs. I said: "You *can't* set out on that long journey to Yorkshire on this dark, cold, foggy night. You are terribly, terribly tired. Why don't you sleep for a while in the spare room?" He wouldn't listen. He even refused to stay for a cup of hot coffee. "I'll be all right," he said, and rushed off,'

No one knows exactly how the accident happened. The Press reports differ. The car was a total wreck. In it, unconscious and hanging upside down in a roofless saloon car, was Puffin. Blood was all over his face: there was a great gash on his left cheek which stretched from above his cheek bone to underneath his chin. There was broken glass all over his hair. His right arm was limp and lifeless.

The accident occurred on the bypass outside Grantham. His car was hurled from his section of the dual carriageway on to the other section facing the direction from which he had come, and mounted the verge beyond it. Men in passing cars, not many at seven o'clock on that foggy December morning, shuddered as they saw the wrecked car with a man hanging so obviously dead in it. They pulled up at a telephone-box and called the police. He was taken to Grantham General Hospital and did not regain consciousness until an hour and a half later.

When able to speak he asked the Sister to telephone Mary Brierley, his housekeeper. The shattering news spread quickly through the house. Paul Massie phoned Adza Vincent and together with John Brierley they set out at once for Grantham.

'By the time we arrived,' said Adza, 'they had had an X-ray examination and found that there was no brain damage. Puff was unconscious and I could not bear to see the frightful cut right down his cheek. The surgeon operated on him that afternoon. It took three hours. I talked to the surgeon afterwards. He did a marvellous job. Puff's damaged arm and fingers took a long time to get right.

'Later that day, for a brief moment, Puffin regained consciousness. He looked up at me and asked: "Was there anyone else with me in the car?" I said: "No – only you." That was all he wanted to know. He couldn't have borne to think that anyone else had been hurt.'

Adza went to the police-station. They wanted her to come and collect the things he had in the car – his suitcases and the Christmas presents which had been scattered all over the car.

'I asked where the car was and they directed me to the garage.

When I arrived there I was told, "It's in the graveyard." The car they took me to was *not* his car, I insisted. "His car is a saloon car – this one has no roof." Then I saw a little figure of St Christopher lying on the floor by the front seat and recognised it as the one Mary had given him.

'Long afterwards Puffin told me what had happened. Being desperately tired, he had fallen asleep while driving behind one of those huge lofty lorries. When the lorry pulled up at the red light Puffin's car shot forward, went underneath the lorry and came out on the other side without its roof. It then swung across to the south-going carriageway and landed on the verge beyond it. He had the window by the driving seat down and that's how his arm and fingers were injured.'

Puffin was kept in hospital for eleven weeks. Adza stayed with him part of the time and visited him often. On 10th March he left hospital and went to stay with his youngest aunt, his mother's half-sister, Lady Crathorne, who lived in Yorkshire and was near enough for his Christmas presents to be given to Joe and his family at Catterick. Later Puffin went to Scotland to stay with his mother's other half-sister, Lady Elliot of Harwood, at Hawick.

# 32

# Rex Harrison, Ingrid Bergman and Shirley MacLaine

DESPITE HIS TERRIBLE accident and long stay in hospital, Puffin was able to begin the shooting of *The Yellow Rolls-Royce* at the appointed time – early in April.

Written by Terence Rattigan, it presented three stages in the life of the Rolls. We saw it first in a West End shop-window, where its impressive dignity and hypnotic appeal arrest the eye of Rex Harrison, an English peer and Secretary of State at the Foreign Office. He buys it as an anniversary present for his pretty French wife (Jeanne Moreau). At a vast and magnificent dinner-party given by Rex we discover (but the husband does not) that Jeanne is having an affair with Edmund Purdom, a member of his Foreign Office staff. At Ascot the next day Rex's horse wins the Gold Cup. In his excitement he looks for his wife and finds that she is not in the box. His frantic quest for her leads to the yellow Rolls-Royce, where Jeanne is found clasped in Edmund Purdom's ecstatic embrace. The marriage breaks up and Rex sells the Rolls-Royce. Also in the cast of that sequence are Moira

Lister, Roland Culver, Michael Hordern, and Lance Percival.

The next sequence shows us the Rolls-Royce for sale in a shop-window in Genoa. An American gangster (George C Scott) buys it to take his moll (Shirley MacLaine, fair-haired and chewing gum) on a tour of Italy. At one of their stops, they meet a persistent Italian roadside photographer (Alain Delon) who pursues Shirley from town to town. Afraid of the gangster, she resists the photographer, but when George Scott leaves for America to bump off a rival, Shirley eludes the guard he left behind to keep an eye on her. The gangster's early and unexpected return reveals what has been going on in his absence. He sells the car.

The next time we see the Rolls is during the war and it looks pretty run down by then. Ingrid Bergman, a very determined American millionairess, in Trieste with her companion (Joyce Grenfell), is on her way to Yugoslavia where she has been invited as a guest of the royal family. Transport is unobtainable; but, determined to get there, Ingrid buys the shabby Rolls-Royce, and engages a chauffeur. As she is about to set out, Omar Sharif comes up and asks her to take him with her in the boot of the car. He is undaunted by her successive refusals and finally she submits and they set off together, Omar in the boot, as he is a partisan and is wanted by the Yugoslav authorities.

The Rex Harrison sequence was shot at Cliveden, Lord Astor's home on the River Thames; at Ascot too of course; and at the Metro-Goldwyn-Mayer studio at Elstree. A physiotherapist used to come to the studio two or three times a week from Barnet to treat Puffin's elbow and fingers. The long scar across his cheek, though sadly disfiguring, was forgotten when one saw Puffin laughing and jesting and twisting in the old infectious way.

Rex Harrison told me: 'He was very brave and quite unaware of what a terrible time he had been through. It was a joy to work with him. I shall always remember *The Yellow Rolls-Royce* as one of the nicest films I've been in.'

Ingrid Bergman didn't like the part when it was offered to her. 'I turned it down,' she told me, 'but it was sent back to me. The producer, Anatole de Grunwald, asked me to read the part again. I said it seemed silly to me that I should be sitting at a table with my dog seated beside me, both the dog and I eating while bombs are falling and the walls of the hotel are crumbling down. People would thing it ridiculous. "And so it is," he told me. "The whole idea of that scene is to make the audience laugh." I read the part again very carefully and realised that he was right. I am glad I agreed to play it. I think it was the best sequence in the film.'

When she signed the contract, Ingrid stipulated that she should have John O'Gorman to do her make-up, as he always attended to her. On her first morning at the MGM studio in Elstree, while she was in the make-up chair at the unearthly hour of the morning when actors and actresses have to be got ready, there was a knock at the door and one of the technicians came in with a magnificent bouquet of flowers. 'I was quite taken aback,' she said. 'I felt he must have worked on an earlier film I made in London – possibly in some minor capacity for I would certainly remember the cameraman, the sound-man and others. I thanked him and after glancing at his frayed, bleached, torn boiler-suit, I wondered how he was able to spend so much money on such lovely flowers. I was very moved and said to John O'Gorman: "It was nice of him to do it. He remembers me, but I don't remember him at all." When the make-up was done, I rose and said: "Now to face the director. I wonder what he's like." O'Gorman said: "You don't have to wonder. He brought you those flowers."

'It was a tremendous change for me to be working with a kind, gentle director. Some of the directors in Italy and elsewhere yell and scream at the actors and technicians all the time. They are very rude and most offensive. Puffin was so different that for a moment I could hardly believe it was true. Nothing like that had I ever encountered on the studio floor. He addressed us as "Ladies and Gentlemen" and said "Do you *mind* coming up? We have *seats* for all of you and also some *coffee*."

'He used to drag a little wooden horse along the set' – I told her its history; 'I don't know why he dressed so badly, with a cigarette always in his mouth and a banana sticking out of his pocket. When I asked him why he never came to lunch, he would smile and wriggle and tap his banana and say, "This is my lunch!" but he never ate it. It was still sticking out of his pocket at the end of the day.'

For the location work they went to Austria and used the mountains adjoining the Yugoslav frontier. 'But we weren't allowed to take any shots of Yugoslavia," said Ingrid. The camera was pointed to another part of the Austrian mountains to represent Yugoslavia. On one occasion while waiting we couldn't find Puffin. We looked everywhere for him. After a time somebody happened to go to the Rolls-Royce and saw him curled up in the back seat fast asleep.'

Gladys Pearce, Tolly de Grunwald's secretary, who was in Austria at the time, tells me that a piano was moved into Puffin's suite at the hotel and he used to play on it for hours. 'The injured fingers of his left hand prevented his playing as well as he used to, but the physiotherapy helped a lot and they were becoming supple rather slowly.'

The Moscow Arts Theatre company was in London and in the evenings after shooting at Elstree was over, Ingrid Bergman and Omar Sharif used to go to the Aldwych Theatre to see them. 'That's the way to learn how to act,' Omar told her. 'We saw all three plays – *Dead Souls* by Gogol, *The Cherry Orchard* by Chekhov, and *Kremlin Chimes*,' Ingrid said. 'Puffin asked me to go to concerts with him, but my knowledge of music was not up to his standard. When we told him how much we enjoyed the Russian plays, he gave a big supper party at his house on a Sunday night and invited the entire Moscow Arts Theatre company to it. He also had more than a dozen interpreters so that we could all talk to the Russian players.

'Why was he called Puffin?' she asked me. I told her and she laughed. 'There's a bird in Sweden called Lunnefagel – a rare bird; I wonder if it's our equivalent of Puffin.'

Ingrid's companion in her sequence, Joyce Grenfell, said that when Puffin engaged her for the part he asked: 'What sort of accent do you think you should use? Ingrid is married to a rich American in this picture.' Joyce said she would use a Southern accent. 'I tried it on him and he seemed to like it. I used to go to his house in Thurloe Square for the readings. If the others were late, Puff played the piano and I sang. It was usually "Who is Sylvia?"

'I read the scenes with Ingrid and another time I read most of it through with Omar Sharif. The script was revised a little as a result of these readings and some small cuts were made. On my first day on the set Puffin arrived with red roses for me.

'It wasn't my first film with Puffin. In *While the Sun Shines* I was a silly deb and rode a bicycle up and down the set. I was also in *The Demi-Paradise* with Larry Olivier.'

Shirley MacLaine travelled to many parts of Italy in the Yellow Rolls-Royce – Genoa, Florence, Pisa, Monte Catini Alto, and Livorno. A second unit under Pierre Rouve was taking background scenes on location. Pierre told me that when it rained at Pisa Shirley spent the time in the hotel lounge waiting for the rain to stop. 'Puffin, as usual, was walking up and down, talking to her continuously. Shirley MacLaine just looked at him with large round schoolgirl eyes, not taking in one word of what he said.'

When I told her this, she said: 'I wasn't listening to anything he said. His actions told me much more than his words. His actions revealed what was going on *inside* him. Aware of the cruelty that lurked everywhere, his twisting and restless movements, the ceaseless pacing of the room, gave the impression that subconsciously he was trying to escape from it all and get right into the woodwork.

'To adjust the world immediately around him he wanted to be, and was in fact, one with all classes – and that's why he dressed in a boiler-suit. He was always deferential to people, and even to things, as you know, for if he tripped over a cable or a lamp, he immediately turned and apologised to it.

'He refused to face cruelty and tried to see how he could help others to overcome it. He was tender to everyone and *never* got as much as he gave. He gave more than anyone else I know. It was impossible to have bad vibrations when one was with Puffin.'

'You sent him,' I told her, 'flowers every week for a year. They were tea roses, I believe . . .'

'Who told you that?'

'I saw the tabs attached to them with the words "To Puffin – with love, Shirley.'

She was silent for a moment. 'I knew he loved flowers. I spent four or five hours with him in his house in Thurloe Square, looking through a book of flowers with beautiful illustrations, a *History of Flowers*, and I could see the joy it gave him to look at the pictures of the flowers and talk about them.

'I was conscious of the great tension in him – by the way he moved, by the way he walked, by the way he formed his words, the phrasing of his sentences. He was not a simple man, he was very complex. He was really a synthesis of complexity. One of the most intelligent men that ever came down the pipe. He always got what he wanted, but got it the sweet way. The music he loved gave a clue too. It was music which never hurt. I never heard him play Wagner or Beethoven, only Schubert and Mozart. And he loved flowers because they hurt no one.

'Puffin never understood himself. He controlled himself to avoid facing the truth about himself, whatever that might have been. His outstanding quality was extreme self-control.'

These were the comments about the man by those who had worked with him on *The Yellow Rolls-Royce*. Now let us turn to what the Press said about the film.

'The film is so smooth,' said the *Daily Express*, 'I couldn't hear my watch ticking . . . It is the finest thing Mr Rattigan has given us since *Separate Tables* and, as so often happens with Mr Rattigan, its theme is unhappy love: three love affairs, all linked by a glorious queen-like Rolls-Royce.'

*Variety*, the American show-biz journal, said: 'It was on budget within a few coppers and on schedule give and take an hour or two, and this is considered a remarkable achievement for a major production which was set up within the record time of two and a half weeks.'

'Each of these increasingly lunatic tales offers a tiny but undeniable pleasure,' wrote the *Sunday Telegraph*. 'The first has a faint but saving twinkle, glinting through the gloss and only collapses in its final moments when it pleads to be taken seriously. The second has the best performances. And the third is so splendidly foolish that it suggests some kind of MGM renaissance. Anthony Asquith directs the English episode with aplomb and is content to trundle the rest along with anonymous assurance.'

Kenneth Tynan in the *Observer*: 'Miss MacLaine is often touching, especially in moments of silence, but when she couples with M Delon, the director is ready with a thunderous cliché (waves crashing on the rocks) to sabotage her efforts.'

Pierre Rouve told me that while Puffin and Tolly were in the

Middle East looking for locations for Rattigan's *Lawrence of Arabia*, Puffin tried to get the original Rolls-Royce Lord Allenby had used in Palestine. This could not be found, but they found a contemporary Rolls-Royce which could be adapted to look like the original one. 'After the Lawrence project fell through,' said Pierre, 'the thought of the Rolls-Royce lingered in Terence Rattigan's mind, and this film eventually was the outcome.'

Margaret Rutherford, though she was not in *The Yellow Rolls-Royce*, was invited on to the set to attend a party given specially for her. She was working at the time in another studio but was brought on to the Rex Harrison Ascot scene in the first sequence of the film. 'Margaret,' her husband told me, 'was invited there for the presentation to her of the award for the best character actress in *The VIPs*. It was quite a celebration and she was photographed with Anthony Asquith, Anatole de Grunwald, and Terence Rattigan.

'And a strange thing happened when Margaret, who had just had her hair done, was lunching with me at the Ritz. Tolly de Grunwald, seated at another table, came up and invited us to the *première* of *The Yellow Rolls-Royce* that night and to the party that was to follow. To our surprise, when we were ready to leave home, we found the actual yellow Rolls-Royce used in the film waiting at the door to take us to the cinema.'

# 33

# The Film That Appealed Most To Him

NOT LONG AFTER *The Yellow Rolls-Royce* was finished, George St George, the American writer who had brought Puffin the story of *Orders to Kill*, arrived with a new project that appealed instantly to Puffin.

'The idea originated in Russia,' St George told me. 'The story – a fairy story – was written by Sergei Mikhalkoff, the brilliant writer of children's stories, and his son, Andrei Konchalovsky, who is now a well-known Soviet film director. I was greatly attracted by the story because it was unusual and imaginative, but I realised that it was unfilmable as it was.

'Victor Pahlen, after reading the story, felt that it could be adapted and made as a joint Anglo-Soviet or Soviet-American film production. He suggested that I should discuss the idea with Puffin, who was very highly respected in Russia. As the story was written in Russian which Puffin could not read, I translated it for him verbally. He was most interested in the general idea, but said the story in its existing form could not be made into a film.

Another story would have to be devised, based on ballet and Tchaikovsky's music, rather than the original fairy tale.

'During the following weeks Puffin and I evolved a new story – quite different from the original. It was given a theatrical background, Tchaikovsky's *Nutcracker* ballet was incorporated and some magical elements were brought in quite effectively.'

Puffin turned over in his mind who would be the best person to write the shooting script. He thought of Terence Rattigan, but realised there wouldn't be any point in asking him to tackle it, because on the outbreak of the Second World War when the Royal Sadlers Wells Ballet company was stranded at Rotterdam, Puffin had thought of making a film about the vicissitudes of a stranded ballet company. He discussed it with Rattigan at the time, but found not a trace of enthusiasm in his reaction. He next approached Frederick Ashton, who had worked with Puffin before as choreographer and technical adviser on the ballet sequences in *Dance, Pretty Lady*; Ashton liked the idea and felt something could certainly be done with it. Tolly de Grunwald was next approached, but dismissed it contemptuously. 'You are all mad,' he snapped. 'All of you!' For some time the thought of making the film hovered in Puffin's mind. Now, a quarter of a century later, something much better and with far greater possibilities had been brought to him.

Tony Warren, well known for his work on the very popular television serial *Coronation Street*, took an early hand in developing the story written by Puffin and St George. Later, when more work was required William Douglas-Home, whose plays *The Chiltern Hundreds* and *The Reluctant Debutante* had sweeping successes, was called in.

Equipped with a synopsis of the new story and the assurance from Puffin that he would direct the film, George St George and Victor Pahlen set out for Moscow. 'Sergei Mikhalkoff liked the revised version of the story and took it to the Maxim Gorky Studio where, after very careful negotiations, a preliminary co-production agreement was worked out and approved by Ekaterina A Furtseva, the Minister of Culture of the USSR who insisted, as an absolute condition, that Puffin would have to direct the film.

'Victor Pahlen had a company in London known as Ariadna Film Productions and it was arranged that it would act as an intermediary with the Soviet group. At that stage its finances were limited but there was enough money for the promotion of the project, which, it was expected, would in due course be underwritten by the distributors of the film.'

Puffin, who knew nothing about finance and business, left it to his agent, Miss Adza Vincent, to deal with the details of his contract. When finally completed and signed it undertook to pay Anthony Asquith the total sum of £40,000, of which £1,000 was to be paid on the signing of the contract; a further £4,000 during the preparation of the script; £25,000 during the production of the film; and the final £10,000 a year after the completion and final release of the film. It was an excellent contract, from which at this stage he received only £1,000.

While work on the script was in progress, Puffin began to look for a film star with outstanding qualities as a ballet dancer and an actress. Shirley MacLaine, who had been in *The Yellow Rolls-Royce*, happened to be in London. She had been trained as a ballet dancer since the age of two. Puffin had a long talk with her about playing the leading role of the ballerina, Parlipata. She liked the idea but could not decide until she knew the dates for filming.

Puffin next thought of Natalie Wood, the star of *West Side Story*, and flew to Hollywood to discuss it with her, but she too was unable to decide until she knew the shooting dates.

Puffin discussed it next with Leslie Caron, who had appeared in two of his films. She too had been ballet-trained and had starred in *Undine* on the New York stage, but he was out of luck with her too. In time one of these three, he felt, *might* be available. In the meantime he went in quest of actors and actresses for other parts. He flew to the South of France to ask Peter Ustinov to join the cast, and he told Joyce Grenfell, 'I may well have something for you in it.'

Invited by the Russians to Moscow for the Film Festival, he went with Kip Gowans, who was to be his assistant director on the film. Puffin's status as President of the Association of Cinematograph and Television Technicians made a great impression on his Russian hosts, who were even more impressed by his personality and his charm. They entertained him royally and when they, in their turn, came to London, they were entertained at Thurloe Square at an enormous party which included Vivien Leigh, Lady Diana Cooper, and many other stage, film and social celebrities.

Many more trips to Russia were made with George St George; also with Jimy Komisarjevsky, the son of the famous Russian theatrical producer.

On one of his visits he was entertained at lunch at the Moscow Arts Theatre. Baroness Moura Budberg, who had been a close friend of Puffin's sister Elizabeth, and her husband Antoine Bibesco, was at that lunch.

'The meal began at twelve o'clock and went on till four,' she told me. 'The food was lavish and so was the wine. Puffin was in the best of form. He left the drinking to the others, touched no alcohol himself and was really in splendid form.

'His Russian hosts made a great fuss of him; and he was given a charming souvenir – an elephant made of bone. It was most attractive and seeing that I admired it Puffin very sweetly presented it to me.

'He talked to me about his ballet film most excitedly. How sad that nothing came of it.'

George St George said that 'Ariadna Film Productions were unable to get distributors and the project was taken over by an American group headed by Unger and Landau, with which I was not associated.'

For two and a half years the business talks went on; and for those two and a half years Puffin had no film to make nor did he receive any money beyond the £1,000 paid to him on the signing of the contract.

There were talks with American film producers and there were differences between the Americans and the Russians, and quite suddenly the project was abandoned. Financially Puffin had nothing to show for the two and a half wasted years. His agent and ACTT insisted that he should be paid; and after months of correspondence £4,000 was finally paid to him – two days *after* his death.

# 34

# In Rome for *The Shoes of the Fisherman*

Picking up the bits and pieces, fragmented by the ecstasy that became a trauma, Puffin accepted an offer to direct the filming of Morris West's bestseller *The Shoes of the Fisherman.*

A remarkable novel, it tells the story of Kiril Lakota, who while still very young had been raised to the exalted office of Archbishop of Lvov, near the Polish border of Russia. The stern, cruel leader of Soviet Russia, Kamenev, arrests him and deports him to the distant eastern edge of Siberia. There he is held for twenty years in prison and in labour camps. Only once in all those years was he able to celebrate Mass. By a dramatic twist in circumstances he is elected Pope – the first man who is not an Italian to be made the Vicar of Christ in four and a half centuries. Laurence Olivier was cast to play Kamenev, the Soviet Premier, and Anthony Quinn his tormented victim. Also in the cast were John Gielgud, Vittorio de Sica, and Leo McKern.

Puffin went to Rome in the autumn of 1967 to work out the locations for the film, taking a small film unit with him.

On reading in the newspapers that Puffin was to make a film in Rome, Lillian Gish, in Rapallo at the time with her sister, Dorothy, could not resist going there to join him. 'I can't tell you how excited I was at the very thought of seeing him again,' she told me. 'Puffin, I found, had not yet arrived but I saw Morris West, whom I knew well and often saw in New York. His chief character in *The Shoes of the Fisherman* was based to a large extent on the personality of Pierre Teilhard de Chardin, a most wonderful man whom I had had the good fortune to meet and talk to: he was a Jesuit priest and his philosophical and scientific speculations were posthumously published. Morris and I talked about the book and the film.

'Puffin arrived a day or two later and came to dine with me. He was looking very ill. He ate hardly anything, but then he never ate much, as you know. But I was worried about the state of his health and I wondered if he was really fit to undertake the making of the film. It is such a strenuous job to direct a film. He discussed the script with me. His ideas were very clear-cut, but he looked so very, very tired.'

He was in fact ill, though not yet aware of it. A few days later, while talking to Adza Vincent on the telephone, he told her that he had not been feeling well, but was a little better now. By the end of the week, acute pains in the stomach made him decide to return to London for a check-up. Nevertheless, he spent all that day looking for locations and flew into London in the evening. The next morning, after being examined by the doctor, a room was booked for him at the Harley Street Nursing Home for a full and thorough check-up.

It was found to be cancer. He was operated on and was said to be making a satisfactory recovery. Those of his friends who asked if they could call and see him for a few minutes were told that he was able only to see one member of the family for just a few minutes a day and they worked it out among themselves which one should go. A little before Christmas I was told on the phone that he was very much better and it should be possible for me to see him. When I phoned again I learned that there had been a set back and that another operation was necessary.

There were in all three operations and although to those who eventually saw him he gave the hopeful assurance that he would soon be well and about again, his emaciated face, so heartbreaking to look at, made one doubt if he would recover. In fact Puffin doubted it too, and began to write his will.

Many friends called. Others, like Larry Olivier, talked to him on the phone. Artur Rubinstein told me that he had come to London for one of his concerts and, just as he was going on, a large bouquet of flowers and a note were handed to him. It was from Puffin saying: 'I am sorry to miss your concert tonight.' As he told me of this, Artur Rubinstein began to cry. 'It was that night that he died and yet – yet – he –' He was unable to say any more. Later he said: 'For me he is absolutely irreplaceable. London has become empty without him.'

Freddie Young called to see him at the nursing home but was told by the Sister in charge that he was not well enough to see any visitors that afternoon. 'The following week,' says Freddie Young, 'he telephoned me asking me to visit him that afternoon. When I arrived he was sitting propped up in bed surrounded by papers. He looked very frail but quite cheerful. "I'm feeling much better," he said, "and I expect to be home by the end of next week, so don't bother to call again. I'll call you. I so want to see little David and Joan" – he was referring to my two-year-old son and my wife. Pointing to the papers on his bed he said, "My secretary has just left and I have to remake my will which is completely out of date." He said how sad he was that he couldn't make *The Shoes of the Fisherman*. He had been working on the script in

Rome and had flown back to London. "I didn't want to be ill in Rome," he said. Michael Anderson, who had worked on many films with Asquith took over the direction of the film Puffin had to abandon.

Among others who called at the nursing home was Frank Fuller, who had been on the ACTT Council with him for many years. Frank was not allowed to see him but left a note, and Puffin, writing in bed, thanked him for coming, assured him that he was '100 per cent better and beginning to feel *really* well . . . I shall never forget, or be grateful enough, for all your kindness and invariably wise advice' and sent affectionate wishes to Frank and his wife; then 'I've just seen I've given you my (I hope!) temporary address,' meaning the nursing home. Frank was so moved by the letter that he called again and was allowed this time to see him.

Puffin died during the night of 21st February 1968. The funeral service was held at the lovely old church of All Saints at Sutton Courtenay, near The Wharf where he had spent most of his childhood. It was a bitterly cold morning, snowing when I left home, with a bitingly cold wind whistling through the trees and slicing one's body with iced scimitars. I could almost hear Puffin's voice say as we walked across the churchyard: 'I am *so* sorry that it's such a cold day for you all.'

Apart from the few front rows reserved for the family, the church was filled by film executives, ACTT members consisting of the General Secretary, George Elvin, the vice-presidents, Sid Cole, Charles Wheeler, and Frank Fuller, the Assistant Secretary Alan Sapper, and Paddy O'Gorman the Treasurer; as well as representatives of the distribution and exhibition side of the cinema industry and members of all the affiliated trade unions such as NATKE and the electricians' union. The family section, despite the sprinkling of young girls and men, had a distinctly Edwardian air. Like oases among them one saw Jo

Grimond, the former Liberal leader who was married to Puffin's niece, Laura, and Mark Bonham Carter (Laura's brother), Mark's wife and family. Violet, Puffin's only surviving sister now a life peeress as Lady Asquith of Yarnbury, was not yet there. Her son Mark, being told that she had arrived, went out to escort her to her seat. A tall, erect woman even at the age of eighty-one, she was today bowed and shrunken to half her size and was led in slowly by her son. She died exactly a year after Puffin.

The long winding path from the church door to the grave was lined on both sides with large wreaths and beautiful flowers that splashed colour on a day that was dark and bleak. Puffin was buried alongside his father and his mother.

# 35

# In Memoriam

TRIBUTES POURED IN from all parts of the world, many to the family, others to Adza Vincent, his agent and his friend.

Richard Burton phoned three times to Adza on the night Puffin died, leaving messages because she wasn't in, and, on his third call, was able to say personally how grieved he and his wife, Elizabeth Taylor, were at the sad news.

Christopher Fry, the poet-playwright, wrote: 'I am torn in two by sorrow that our world has to go on without someone as rare as Puffin.'

There were telegrams and letters from Larry Olivier and his wife. Edith Evans, Ingrid Bergman and her husband Lars Schmidt, and this from John Sutro, a prominent figure in the world of the theatre and of film production: 'It's a tragedy, for he represented the very finest qualities in films and had such a marvellous record – a unique person, respected and loved by all classes. I do hope some memorial connected with films may be created to his memory.'

The Anthony Asquith Memorial Fund was launched by his Union ACTT. The contributions, made by film companies, actors and actresses, various trade unions of the entertainment world, and hundreds of individuals including twelve long-distance lorry-drivers whom Puffin had served with coffee and sandwiches at Joe's Café (they contributed half-a-crown each), totalled more than £12,000. Part of this was used to endow a room in his name at the Cinema and Television Benevolent Fund convalescent home at Glebelands in Berkshire, and the rest was invested to provide an annual Award of £1,000 to be shared by the Composer and Director of the Film or Television feature showing the most imaginative use of music. The first of the awards adjudicated by the British Film Academy was made in the year following his death, and further awards have been made since: the second of them went to Theodorakis, the composer of *Zorba the Greek*, who was in prison at the time in Greece.

Margot Fonteyn's letter to Adza said: 'One evening I returned home late to find the Laura Knight painting and your letter waiting for me. I was so upset by your news about Puffin and wanted to phone you immediately the next day, but the next day Puffin was dead. You cannot imagine how touched I am that he should have thought of me in those last days and hours and that he should have struggled to send me a message about the picture. It is a picture of Lydia Lopokova, who married Lord Keynes and is now his widow. I am very deeply moved by your letter.'

To his goddaughter, Elizabeth de Grunwald (Tolly had died the year before), he left the manuscript of Terence Rattigan's play *French Without Tears*, which Terry had given him when the film was made. Elizabeth, greatly gifted musically, used to play duets with Puffin when she was a child: they had the same taste in music. She was hardly able to speak when she told me of Puffin's bequest.

There was a letter from the famous pianist Lili Kraus writing from Rochester, Minnisota: 'Brave, admirable and believing to the very end, our Puffin delivered the last proof of his superiority and lovable and loving sweetness.'

Executives of Metro-Goldwyn-Mayer, for whom he was to have made *The Shoes of the Fisherman*, wrote too. One of them, George England, wrote a few days before Puffin died: 'Shooting has been under way for some weeks now. I think often of you and even have the feeling I am in conversation with you as if to say, What do you think we should do about this? I miss your presence, your graciousness and your laughter . . . You have this illness to get over and my dearest hope is that all is going well.'

There were numerous tributes in the Press. Dilys Powell wrote in the *Sunday Times* an affectionate, intimate analysis of the man and his work. 'He cared deeply about the cinema. Sometimes he handled themes scarcely of his own choice and the results were scarcely worthy of his gifts.' Almost in every line there were happy memories. 'There are so many things to remember,' she wrote. 'Few people die leaving so much affection behind.'

And there was a brilliant appraisal of his personality by Lord David Cecil in *The Times*: 'Anthony Asquith had a child-like simplicity and innocence, a child-like power of enjoyment, a love of boyish pleasures – playing and watching games, telling and hearing favourite jokes – and a childish unselfconsciousness at once comic and delightful. But there was nothing child-like about the depth and richness of his culture, his critical penetration, the subtle refinement of his sensibility and the vigilant, unprejudiced fairness of his judgment.' He spoke also of his dedication to art. 'Like Keats, he loved the principle of beauty in all things.' And he summed up in these words: 'Up to the very day of his death, to see him was to have one's faith in human nature strengthened. There are people in this confused and distracted age who question the possibility of human goodness. No one could do so who knew Anthony Asquith.'

During my long association with him, no matter what problems he faced, no matter what wrong may have been done to him, plunging all he was trying to achieve into complete chaos, he was disappointed of course, frustrated naturally, but never said anything unkind about the person who had been the cause of what had happened. The unkindest thing I ever heard him say about anyone was, 'He is not my favourite person.'

At St Margaret's, Westminster, a memorial service was held four weeks after his death. In that vast congregation law and politics were conspicuously represented; the cinema and the theatre, of course, and all the Asquiths and Bonham Carters were there. Those who had been with him in films included Dame Edith Evans, Miss Marie Lohr, Dirk Bogarde, Rex Harrison, Sir Felix Aylmer, Marius Goring, Cecil Beaton, Phyllis Calvert, Michael Balcon and Victor Saville.

The lessons were read by Sir Michael Redgrave and Sir Laurence Olivier. The first from the Wisdom of Solomon, in Redgrave's gentle pleasing voice, told us that 'God proved them and found them worthy of himself.' The second, from I Corinthians, read very slowly by Olivier, was deeply moving. Each pause – and some of them were very long – made us aware how moved Larry was too . . . 'charity envieth not; charity vaunteth not itself, is not puffed up, doth not behave itself unseemly, seeketh not her own, is not easily provoked, thinketh no evil; rejoiceth not in iniquity, but rejoiceth in truth; beareth all things, believeth all things, hopeth all things, endureth all things.'

At the end of the service Yehudi Menuhin played Bach's *Chaconne* (Partita in D Minor): many in the congregation wept.

# 'PUFFIN' ASQUITH

## *A Filmography*

# 'Puffin' Asquith – A Filmography

## THE SILENT PERIOD

**BOADICEA, 1926**

*Production;* British Instructional *Producer:* H Bruce Woolfe *Director:* Sinclair Hill *Assistant Director:* Victor Peers *Photography:* Jack Parker *Property Master, Assistant Make-Up Artist, Assistant Cutter, Stunt Man:* Anthony Asquith *Distribution:* Pro Patria *With:* Phyllis Neilson-Terry (*Boadicea*), Lillian Hall-Davis, Clifford McLaglen, Wally Patch, Cyril McLaglen.

**SHOOTING STARS, 1927**

*Production:* British Instructional *Producer:* H Bruce Woolfe *Director:* A V Bramble *Assistant Director:* Anthony Asquith *Original Story:* Anthony Asquith *Screenplay:* Anthony Asquith and J O C Orton *Photography:* Stanley Rodwell and Henry Harris *Art Director:* Walter Murton *Lighting:* Karl Fischer *Design:* Ian Campbell-Gray *Distribution:* New Era *With:* Annette

Benson (*Mae Feather*), Brian Aherne (*Julian Gordon*), Donald Calthrop (*Andy Wilks*), Chili Bouchier, Wally Patch. *Length:* 7200 ft.

*Story summary:* Mae Feather, famous British screen actress, is publicised as a perfect wife, and is seen everywhere with her husband, Julian Gordon, a Western star employed by the same studio. Actually she is having an affair with Andy Wilks, a star comedian. Julian discovers this and decides on a divorce, which could ruin Mae's position with her public. Desperate, she decides to kill her husband at the studios by inserting a real bullet into a 'prop' gun, used by the villain in the film to 'kill' Julian. The shot is fired, but the blank bullet is used, and Julian is unharmed. Instead, the gun is taken to another set, used in a comedy scene in Andy's picture, and the real bullet kills him. Mae has a nervous breakdown. Julian divorces her; she begins to slip down the ladder of success. As the years pass, he becomes a famous film director, while she is forgotten. She gets work as a film extra, and unknowingly Julian uses her in a crowd scene for his new picture. Mae waits until everyone has gone at the end of the day, and asks him: 'Will you want me any more?' Without looking at her, he shakes his head and she passes through the studio door, out of his life forever.

## UNDERGROUND, 1928

*Production:* British Instructional *Producer:* H Bruce Woolfe *Director:* Anthony Asquith *Script:* Anthony Asquith *Photography:* Stanley Rodwell *Art Director:* Ian Campbell-Gray *Lighting:* Karl Fischer *Distribution:* Pro Patria *With:* Elissa Landi (*Nell*), Brian Aherne (*Bill*), Cyril McLaglen, Norah Baring. *Length:* 7282 ft.

*Story summary:* Bert, an electrician at Lot's Road power house, and Bill, an Underground porter, both fall in love with Nell, a shop girl. Bill wins her love and Bert plans revenge. He gets Kate, his mistress, to pretend that Bill has assaulted her, but Nell does not believe this, goes to see Kate and persuades her to confess the truth. As a result, Bert abandons her. Kate seeks out Bill, confesses her lie and in her anger and unhappiness demands that he take her to the power house, where she hopes to persuade Bert to come back to her. Bill takes her there, and leaves her alone with Bert. After a quarrel, Bert kills Kate and escapes into the Underground tunnel. A chase follows, Bert is eventually trapped by Bill in an Underground lift and Bill and Nell are happily united.

## THE RUNAWAY PRINCESS, 1928

*Production:* British Instructional and Laenderfilm *Producer:* H Bruce Woolfe *Director:* Anthony Asquith *Assistant Director:* Victor Peers *Script:* Anthony Asquith, from the novel '*Princess Priscilla's Fortnight*' *Art Director:* Ian Campbell-Gray *German Supervision:* Frederick Wendhousen *Photography:* Arpad Viragh *Distribution:* Jury-Metro-Goldwyn *With:* Mady Christians (*Priscilla*), Paul Cavanagh (*The Stranger*), Fred Rains (*Professor*), Claude H Beerbohm, Norah Baring.

*Story summary:* Princess Priscilla objects to being betrothed to the Crown Prince of Savona, whom she has never seen, and runs away to London with her professor. During her stay there, she is followed everywhere by a mysterious and handsome stranger. She is intrigued, but the stranger refuses to reveal his identity. At length, the princess's money runs out and she accepts a job as assistant to a fashionable Bond Street milliner. During her calls on clients, she becomes the innocent accomplice of one of them – a woman at the head of a forgery gang. Unwittingly, the princess passes forged bank notes for her, and is arrested. The intervention of the mysterious stranger secures her release. He then reveals that he is the Crown Prince she was supposed to marry. Now in love with him, Priscilla returns with the Prince to her own country and is married with due splendour.

## A COTTAGE ON DARTMOOR, 1929

*Production:* British Instructional *Producer:* H Bruce Woolfe *Director:* Anthony Asquith *Script:* Anthony Asquith from a story by Herbert Price *Photography:* Stanley Rodwell and Lindblom *Art Director:* Ian Campbell-Gray *Continuity:* Ralph Smart *Technical Supervisor:* Max Stern *Distribution:* Pro Patria, 1930 *With:* Norah Baring (*Sally*), Uno Henning (*Joe*), Hans Schlettow (*Farmer*). *Length:* 7538 ft.

*Story summary:* In a small Devonshire town, Joe, a young hairdresser, falls in love with Sally, the pretty manicurist in the shop where he is employed. The young man finally invites her to go out with him for an evening. She accepts; but it is soon apparent that she does not return his interest. Nevertheless, Joe persists. Into the shop – with some frequency – comes a young farmer who does not disguise his interest in Sally. He takes her to the cinema (one of the new 'talking films') and Joe, filled with jealousy, follows them. From the row behind he watches their happiness, and rushes out of the cinema in great distress. Next morning the young farmer comes into the shop for a shave. Joe notices that Sally is wearing an engagement ring. Desperate, he leans over the farmer, a razor in his hand. There is a struggle, and the razor wounds the farmer. Sally is convinced that he had attempted to murder her lover, and Joe is sent to Dartmoor. A few years later, Joe escapes and finds his way to a cottage which he knows is owned by the farmer he attacked. Sally, now the farmer's wife, takes pity on him and hides him. Warders, however, trace Joe to the cottage and he is shot down while trying to escape. He dies in the arms of Sally, whom he still loves.

# THE SOUND PERIOD

**TELL ENGLAND, 1930–31** (US title: *Battle of Gallipoli*)

*Production:* British Instructional *Producer:* H Bruce Woolfe *Director:* Anthony Asquith, with Geoffrey Barkas *Assistant Director:* Teddy Baird *Script:* Anthony Asquith, from Ernest Raymond's novel of the same name *Additional Dialogue:* A P Herbert *Photography:* Jack Parker, Stanley Rodwell, James Rogers *Art Director:* Arthur Woods *Editor:* Mary Field *Sound:* Victor Peers *Distribution:* Wardour Films, 1931 *With:* Carl Harbord (*Edgar Doe*), Tony Bruce (*Rupert Ray*), Fay Compton (*Mrs Doe*), Dennis Hoey (*Padre*), C M Hallard (*Colonel*), Frederick Lloyd (*Captain Harding*), Gerald Rawlinson (*Doon*), Lionel Hedges (*Sims*), Sam Wilkinson (*Booth*), Wally Patch (*Sgt. Instructor*), Hubert Harben (*Mr Ray*). *Length:* 7850 ft.

*Story summary:* Edgar Doe and Rupert Ray, boyhood friends, enlist in the British army at the outbreak of war in 1914. Both receive commissions and are sent eventually as part of the Mediterranean Expeditionary Force to Gallipoli. The horrors of war begin slowly to damp their romantic enthusiasm, and Doe, the more idealistic and sensitive of the two, is nerve racked by months of inactivity and then by the cruel slaughter of his men by a Turkish trench mortar. He quarrels with Ray (a young, inarticulate Englishman) who has been promoted to captain, and breaks down; he regains self-confidence on learning that he has been chosen to lead a raid on the Turkish trenches. Doe goes over the top, is seriously wounded, but manages single-handed to put the trench mortar post out of action. Soon after his death, the British withdraw from Gallipoli. The expedition has been a military blunder and only the scores of English graves left behind commemorate a tragic campaign.

## DANCE PRETTY LADY, 1931

*Production:* British Instructional *Producer:* H Bruce Woolfe *Director:* Anthony Asquith *Assistant Director:* Teddy Baird *Script:* Anthony Asquith from Compton Mackenzie's novel '*Carnival*' *Photography:* Jack Parker *Art Director:* Ian Campbell-Gray *Choreographer and Technical Adviser on Ballet Sequences:* Frederick Ashton *Distribution:* Wardour Films, 1932 *With:* Ann Casson (*Jenny Pearl*), Carl Harbord (*Maurice Avery*), Michael Hogan (*Castleton*), Flora Robson (*Mrs Raeburn*), Moore Marriott (*Mr Raeburn*), Leonard Brett (*Alf*), Norman Claridge (*Danby*), Sunday Wilshin (*Irene*), Rene Ray (*Elsie*), Eva Llewellyn (*Aunt Mabel*), Alban Conway, Hermione Gingold and the Marie Rambert Corps de Ballet. *Length:* 5786 ft.

*Story summary:* Jenny, a ballet dancer of the Edwardian era, falls in love with a wealthy young artist, Maurice, but refuses to become his mistress. He tells her that he does not believe in marriage and she becomes extremely unhappy. At length he offers to marry her, but Jenny now doubts whether she can be happy with him. Maurice decides to go abroad. Jenny, realising then that she loves him, waits vainly for his return. She comes to believe that Maurice has deserted her, and in a moment of loneliness, becomes the mistress of his friend Danby. Afterwards, she regrets it. Eventually Maurice returns, hears of her affair with Danby, realises he was the cause of it, forgives her and offers her his love.

## THE LUCKY NUMBER, 1933

*Production:* Gainsborough Pictures *Producer:* Michael Balcon *Director:* Anthony Asquith *Assistant Director:* Marjorie Gaffney

*Script:* Franz Schulz *Photography:* Gunther Krampf *Art Director:* Alex Vetchinsky *Editor:* Dan Birt *Music:* Mischa Spoliansky *Distribution:* Gaumont-British-Ideal, 1933 *With:* Clifford Mollison (*Percy Gibbs*), Gordon Harker (*Publican*), Joan Wyndham (*Winnie*), Joe Hayman, Frank Pettingell, Esme Percy, Hay Petrie, Arthur Wellesley, Betty Hartley. *Length:* 6535 ft.

*Story summary:* Percy Gibbs, professional footballer, idol of the fans, is jilted by his girl. He cuts adrift from his usual life and takes a holiday in France. On his return to London he visits a funfair where he meets, and is attracted to, Winnie, a girl working in a sideshow. Later, while drinking with her at a pub, Percy finds he has lost his wallet which was full of money. The publican accepts in payment a ticket that Percy had bought in a French lottery. The next day it is discovered to be the winning ticket. Percy and Winnie use every kind of subterfuge to get the ticket back from the publican, and finally succeed – only to learn that the promoter of the lottery has absconded with all the money. Percy returns to professional football and marries Winnie.

## UNFINISHED SYMPHONY, 1934

*Production:* Cine-Alliance, Willy Forst Productions (Vienna) and Gaumont-British (London) *Producer and Director:* Willy Forst *Co-Director for English Version:* Anthony Asquith *Script:* Benn Levy *Screenplay:* Walter Reisch *Photography:* Franz Planer *Music:* Schubert *Distribution:* Gaumont-British, 1934 *With:* Hans Yaray (*Schubert*), Marta Eggerth (*Caroline*), Helen Chandler (*Emmy*), Ronald Squire (*Count Esterhazy*), Brember Wills (*his secretary*), Beryl Laverick (*Mary*), Hermin Sterler (*Princess Kinsky*), Cecil Humphries (*Saliere*), Paul Wagner (*Folliot*), Eliot Makeham (*Joseph*), Esme Percy (*Huettenbranner*), Frieda Richard (*Schubert's landlady*), Vienna Philharmonic Orchestra, Vienna Opera Choir, Vienna Boys' Choir. *Length:* 8175 ft.

*Story summary:* Schubert, poor and miserable, and an unsuccessful composer, falls in love with Emmy, daughter of a pawnbroker. A rich friend arranges for Schubert to play at a command performance organised by Princess Kinsky. Schubert plays a solo piano version of his new, uncompleted Symphony in B

Minor. Halfway through, the aristocratic Caroline Esterhazy is heard to be giggling at a private joke. The young composer leaves in a rage. Caroline, however, is impressed and persuades her father to engage him as music teacher. Schubert falls in love with her and completes his symphony under her spell. Though she returns his love, Caroline is obliged by her family to marry a fellow aristocrat. In despair, Schubert tears out the final pages of his symphony, wanting it to remain, like his great passion, unfulfilled.

## MOSCOW NIGHTS, 1935

*Production:* Denham Productions *Executive Producer:* Alexander Korda *Producer:* Alexis Granowsky *Director:* Anthony Asquith *Assistant Director:* Teddy Baird *Script:* Anthony Asquith and Eric Siepmann, from a novel by Pierre Benoit *Photography:* Philip Tannura *Art Director:* Vincent Korda *Costumes:* John Armstrong *Supervising Editor:* William Hornbeck *Editor:* Francis Lyon *Distribution:* General Film Distributors, 1935 *With:* Harry Baur (*Brioukow*), Laurence Olivier (*Ignatov*), Penelope Ward (*Natasha*), Athene Seyler (*Madame Sabline*), Kate Cutler (*Madame Kovrin*), Morton Selten (*General Kovrin*), Robert Cochran (*Polonski*), Walter Hudd (*Doctor*), Edmund Willard (*Prosecutor*), Hay Petrie (*Spy*), C M Hallard (*President of Court*), Charles Carson (*Defence Officer*), Morland Graham (*Brioukow's servant*), Richard Webster (*Confederate spy*). *Length:* 6765 ft.

*Story summary:* It is wartime. Natasha, a well-born Russian girl, is persuaded by her impoverished parents to become engaged to Brioukow, a prosperous middle-aged contractor. While nursing in a hospital, she falls in love with Captain Ignatov, a wounded officer. Though Ignatov loves her, she remains faithful to Brioukow. The young officer and the older man quarrel over her and Ignatov accuses Brioukow of being a war profiteer. Angered, Ignatov is goaded into gambling beyond his means. To his aid comes Madame Sabline, an aged eccentric who offers to finance him. Knowing that Natasha loves him, and that ignominy and death are the only alternatives, the young man accepts; later, however, it transpires that Madame Sabline is a German spy and Ignatov is arrested as her accomplice. The only man who can help him is Brioukow, and knowing of Natasha's love for the young man, Brioukow clears him at the cost of his own happiness.

## PYGMALION, 1938

*Production:* Gabriel Pascal Productions *Producer:* Gabriel Pascal *Directors:* Anthony Asquith and Leslie Howard *Assistant Director:* Teddy Baird *Script:* W P Lipscomb, Cecil Lewis and Anthony Asquith from the play by Bernard Shaw *Photography:* Harry Stradling *Editor:* David Lean *Art Director:* Laurence Irving *Assistant Art Director:* John Bryan *Costumes:* Professor Czettell, Worth and Schiaparelli *Music:* Arthur Honegger *Distribution:* General Film Distributors, 1938 *With:* Wendy Hiller (*Eliza*), Leslie Howard (*Higgins*), Wilfrid Lawson (*Doolittle*), Marie Lohr (*Mrs Higgins*), Scott Sunderland (*Colonel Pickering*), Jean Cadell (*Mrs Pearce*), Everley Gregg (*Mrs Eynsford Hill*), David Tree (*Freddy*), Leueen Macgrath (*Clara*), Esme Percy (*Count Karpathy*), Violet Vanbrugh (*Ambassadress*), Iris Hoey (*Ysabel*), Viola Tree (*Perfide*), O B Clarence (*Vicar*), Irene Brown (*Duchess*), Wally Patch, H F Maltby, George Mozart, Ivor Barnard, Kate Cutler, Cathleen Nesbitt, Cecil Trouncer, Stephen Murray, Eileen Beldon, Frank Atkinson. *Length:* 8609 ft.

*Story Summary:* Henry Higgins, professor of phonetics, wagers with Colonel Pickering, an authority on dialects, that he can pass off Eliza Doolittle, a Covent Garden flower girl, as a lady. The girl is persuaded to try the experiment and rigorous training eventually brings its reward. After a successful tea party given by Mrs Higgins, Eliza moves on to an ambassador's reception, where she is accepted as a princess. The experiment successfully over, Higgins decides to get rid of the girl. By this time Eliza has fallen in love with her benefactor, and upbraids Higgins for his selfishness: Higgins comes to see her in a new light – as a human being of intelligence and beauty. Finally he realises he has fallen in love with his own creation, as in the legend of Pygmalion and Galatea.

## FRENCH WITHOUT TEARS, 1939

*Production:* Two Cities in association with Paramount Pictures *Producer:* Mario Zampi *Director:* Anthony Asquith *Assistant Director;* Teddy Baird *Script:* Anatole de Grunwald, Ian Dalrymple and Terence Rattigan from the play by Terence Rattigan

*Photography:* Bernard Knowles *Editor:* David Lean *Art Director* Paul Sheriff *Assistant Art Director:* Carmen Dillon *Music:* Nicholas Brodsky *Distribution:* Paramount, 1939 *With:* Ray Milland (*Alan*), Ellen Drew (*Diana*), Janine Darcey (*Jacqueline*), David Tree (*Chris*), Roland Culver (*Commander*), Guy Middleton (*Brian*), Jim Gerald (*Professor Maingot*), Kenneth Morgan (*Kenneth*), Margaret Yarde (*Marianne*), Toni Gable (*Chi-Chi*). *Length:* 7757 ft.

*Story summary:* Alan, a likeable cynic, Chris, a sensitive youth, and Brian, pleasant fool, are 'cramming' French – each for his own particular reason – at Professor Maingot's establishment in the South of France. Diana, sister of Kenneth, another student, comes to stay at the villa for the summer. She sets her cap at Chris, who quickly responds. He is loved, meanwhile, without knowing it, by the professor's daughter, Jacqueline. When Commander Rogers, a 'typical' serviceman, arrives to study French for a naval examination, the situation grows complicated; Diana flirts with him and succeeds in setting Chris and the Commander at each other's throats. The cynical Alan, who fancies himself as an impartial observer of the scene, finds to his own consternation that he too is attracted to Diana, though he tells himself he knows what kind of girl she is. He manages to extract the Commander from Diana's net, unites Chris and Jacqueline and becomes Diana's unwilling victim. She confesses that she has been in love with him all the time, and that her flirtations were merely a skirmish to make him aware of her. Alan cannot escape his fate; he succumbs.

## FREEDOM RADIO, *1940* (US title: *Voice in the Night*)

*Production:* Two Cities and Columbia Pictures *Producer:* Mario Zampi *Director:* Anthony Asquith *In Charge of Production:* John Corfield *Original Story:* Wolfgang Wilhelm and George Campbell *Scenario Contributions:* Louis Golding, Gordon Wellesley, Bridget Boland and Roland Pertwee *Screenplay:* Anatole de Grunwald, Basil Woon and Jeffrey Dell *Photography:* Bernard Knowles *Editor:* Reginald Beck *Art Director:* Paul Sheriff *Music:* Nicholas Brodsky *Distribution:* Columbia, 1941 *With:* Clive Brook (*Dr Karl Roder*), Diana Wynyard (*Irena*), Ronald

Squire (*Speidler*), Derek Farr (*Hans*), Joyce Howard (*Elly*), John Penrose (*Otto*), Raymond Huntley (*Rabenau*), Bernard Miles (*Muller*), Clifford Evans (*Dressler*), Howard Marion-Crawford (*Kummer*), Reginald Beckwith (*Fenner*), Morland Graham (*Father Landbach*), Abraham Sofaer (*Meyer*), Muriel George (*Hanna*). *Length:* 7110 ft.

*Story summary:* Dr Karl Roder, a Viennese throat specialist, believes in freedom of thought, action and expression and is thus hostile to Nazism. His wife Irena, however, is flattered by the attentions of the Führer and accepts a political post in Berlin. The two of them become estranged. Karl meets Hans, a young wireless engineer, whose fiancée has been raped by a Gestapo officer. Hans builds a transmitter so that Karl can broadcast the truth on a secret radio station to the German people. The Freedom Radio is born, and with it an underground group of anti-Nazis who regard Karl as their leader. Meanwhile, Irena continues to believe in the Führer and his pronouncements on peace, but when Karl denounces Hitler on the Freedom Radio for preparing for war with Poland, she is disillusioned. They are reconciled and Irena helps him to run the radio station while continuing her political work. Her brother, Otto, is an ardent Nazi. He begins to suspect his sister of being a spy and through his intervention the Gestapo discovers the Freedom Radio Station. Karl and Irena die together. But that night Hans rigs up a transmitter in another part of Berlin. While the Nazis announce that the radio has been silenced, a new anti-Hitler broadcast is being made. The station lives on.

## QUIET WEDDING, 1940

*Production:* Paramount Pictures and Paul Soskin *Producer:* Paul Soskin *Director:* Anthony Asquith *Script:* Anatole de Grunwald and Terence Rattigan, from the play by Esther McCracken *Photography:* Bernard Knowles *Editor:* Reginald Beck *Art Director:* Paul Sheriff *Music:* Nicholas Brodsky *Distribution:* Paramount, 1941 *With:* Margaret Lockwood (*Janet*), Derek Farr (*Dallas*), Marjorie Fielding (*Mildred Royd*), A E Matthews (*Arthur Royd*), Athene Seyler (*Aunt Mary*), Jean Cadell (*Aunt Florence*), Margaretta Scott (*Marcia*), David Tomlinson (*John*), Peggy Ashcroft (*Flower Lisle*), Sydney King (*Denis*), Frank Cellier (*Mr*

*Chaytor*), Roland Culver (*Ponsonby*), Michael Shepley (*Marcia's Husband*), Muriel Pavlow (*Miranda*), Bernard Miles (*Policeman*), Roddy Hughes, Muriel George, Wally Patch, Margaret Rutherford, Hay Petrie, O B Clarence, Margaret Halstan. *Length:* 7200 ft.

*Story summary:* Janet and Dallas become engaged and decide to have a quiet wedding, but their parents think otherwise. The fittings, the interfering relatives, local busybodies, the wedding rehearsal – all result in Janet becoming overstrung. She quarrels with her mother, then with Dallas. The arrival of Aunt Mary removes the threat of a broken engagement; she advises Dallas to 'kidnap' Janet the night before the wedding. Dallas does so, and the young couple are reconciled. Arrested for dangerous driving by a dim country policeman on their way home, they finish up in the local police station. The family bails them out in time, and the 'quiet wedding' at last takes place.

(Asquith's next film was his first documentary, *Channel Incident*, taking its story from the Dunkirk withdrawal. During the wartime period most leading British directors made short documentary or semi-actuality films on war themes; Asquith directed four between 1940 and 1945. *Channel Incident* and *Rush Hour* (made at the end of 1941, after *Cottage to Let*) were both less than a reel in length.)

## CHANNEL INCIDENT, 1940

*Production:* D & P Limited, in association with the Ministry of Information *Producer Director:* Anthony Asquith *Story:* Bartimeus *Script:* Dallas Bower *Photography:* Arthur Crabtree *Editor:* Alfred Roome *Distribution:* Ministry of Information, 1942 *With:* Peggy Ashcroft, Gordon Harker, Robert Newton, Kenneth Griffith. *Length:* 859 ft.

*Story summary: Channel Incident* was a story of the 'little boats' that went out to Dunkirk and of an Englishwoman searching vainly for her husband in her motor boat as well as rescuing soldiers from the sea.

## RUSH HOUR, 1941

*Production:* Twentieth Century-Fox, in association with the Ministry of Information *Producer:* Edward Black *Director:* Anthony Asquith *Script:* Arthur Boys and Rodney Ackland

*Photography:* Jack Cox *Distribution:* Ministry of Information, 1942 *With:* Joan Sterndale-Bennett, Muriel George, Beatrice Varley. *Length:* 554 ft.

*Story summary: Rush Hour* was a comedy short about Britain's workers coping with the British transport system and social amenities during a typical rush hour on a working day. It was witty and entertaining and pointed a very definite moral; the necessity for staggering workers' hours.

## COTTAGE TO LET, 1941

*Production:* Gainsborough Pictures *Producer:* Edward Black *Director:* Anthony Asquith *Script:* Anatole de Grunwald and J O C Orton, from the play by Geoffrey Kerr *Photography:* Jack Cox *Editor:* R E Dearing *Art Director:* Alex Vetchinsky *Music Director:* Louis Levy *Distribution:* GFD, 1941 *With:* John Mills (*Flt Lt Perry*), Leslie Banks (*Barington*), Michael Wilding (*Alan Trentley*), Carla Lehmann (*Helen Barington*), Alastair Sim (*Dimble*), Jeanne de Casalis (*Mrs Barington*), Catherine Lacey (*Mrs Stokes*), George Cole (*Ronald*), Frank Cellier (*Forest*), Muriel Aked (*Miss Fernery*), Wally Patch (*Evans*), Muriel George (*Mrs Trimm*), Hay Petrie (*Dr Truscott*). *Length:* 8124 ft.

*Story summary:* During the war, an inventor named Barington is engaged to work on a new and secret bombsight on his estate in Scotland. A cottage in his grounds is commandeered as a military hospital, and the first patient there is Perry, a wounded RAF pilot. Barington's assistant, Trentley, is suspected of being a German agent, and Evans, a detective, poses as a butler to watch him. Dimble, a spy suspect, claims to have rented the cottage, but he is in reality a British agent. Subsequently it is revealed that the plausible Perry is not an RAF pilot but a Nazi agent after the plans of the bombsight. In the battle of wits that follows, a Cockney evacuee (Ronald) intervenes, and Perry and his associates are unmasked. Trentley is cleared and Perry and his two accomplices are killed in a gunfight at a bazaar.

## UNCENSORED 1942

*Production:* Gainsborough Pictures *Producer:* Edward Black *Director:* Anthony Asquith *Script:* Rodney Ackland and Terence

Rattigan, from a story and adaptation by Wolfgang Wilhelm, based on a novel by Oscar Millard *Photography:* Arthur Crabtree *Art Director:* Alex Vetchinsky *Editor:* R E Dearing *Music Director:* Louis Levy *Distribution:* GFD, 1942 *With:* Eric Portman (*Delage*), Phyllis Calvert (*Julie Lanvin*), Griffith Jones (*Father de Gruyte*), Peter Glenville (*Charles Neele*), Raymond Lovell (*Von Koerner*), Frederick Culley (*Victor Lanvin*), Irene Handl (*Frau von Koerner*), Carl Jaffe (*Kolmeier*), Felix Aylmer (*Von Hohenstein*), Eliot Makeham (*Abbé de Moor*), Walter Hudd (*Van Heemskerk*), Stuart Lindsell (*Press Officer*), J H Roberts (*Father Corot*), John Slater (*Theophile*), Phyllis Monkman and Kathleen Boutall (*The Pony Act*). *Length:* 9615 ft.

*Story summary:* Following the occupation of Belgium in the Second World War, the Nazis set up their own propaganda machine. To counter the Nazi press, a group of Belgian patriots revive '*La Libre Belgique*', with Delage, a popular Brussels entertainer, and Julie Lanvin, daughter of a newspaper editor, as principal members of its secret staff. The Germans offer a reward for the capture of the paper's sponsors. Delage's disgruntled cabaret partner, Charles, develops a grudge against him and gives him away. Delage and Julie evade capture, but their colleagues are arrested. While the Germans announce the end of '*La Libre Belgique*' Delage and Julie bring out a new edition in secret and make the Germans a laughing stock, so that they are obliged to release their captives. The group is re-formed and, under Delage's and Julie's leadership, the work goes on.

## WE DIVE AT DAWN, 1943

*Production:* Gainsborough Pictures *Producer:* Edward Black *Director:* Anthony Asquith *Script:* J B Williams and Val Valentine *Photography:* Jack Cox *Art Director:* W Murton *Supervising Editor:* R E Dearing *Music Director:* Louis Levy *Distribution:* GFD, 1943 *With:* John Mills (*Lt Taylor*), Eric Portman (*Leading Seaman Hobson*), Niall MacGinnis (*Corrigan*), Louis Bradfield (*Brace*), Ronald Millar (*Johnson*), David Peel ('*Oxford*'), Lionel Grose ('*Spud*'), Jack Watling (*Gordon*), Reginald Purdell (*Dabs*),

Cavan Watson (*Duncan*), Leslie Weston (*Wilson*), Norman Williams (*'Canada'*), Philip Godfrey (*'Flunkey'*), Robert Wilton (*'Pincher'*), Josephine Wilson, Beatrice Varley, Marie Ault, Frederick Burtwell. *Length:* 8794 ft.

*Story summary:* During the war, the *Sea Tiger*, a British submarine with Lt Taylor as captain, docks at naval port. Seven days' leave is given, various members of the crew go home to their families. Shortly afterwards they are all recalled to the submarine. They are given secret orders to pursue and sink the Nazi battleship *Brandenburg*. After sinking a German wireless buoy and taking prisoners in the North Sea, the submarine sights the battleship and fires its torpedoes. Conditions prevent the crew knowing whether they have succeeded in their mission. They evade German destroyers by playing 'dead', but run out of fuel off the Danish coast. Leading Seaman Hobson, who can speak German, goes ashore in one of the German prisoners' uniforms and reconnoitres. He discovers a Danish tanker in the dock and signals the *Sea Tiger* to proceed into the shore. The Nazis discover the submarine while it is refuelling but with the aid of friendly Danish patriots the *Sea Tiger* manages to refuel and submerge, finally arriving back to safety at an English port.

**THE DEMI-PARADISE, 1943.** (US title: *Adventure for Two*)

*Production:* Two Cities Films and Anatole de Grunwald *Producer:* Anatole de Grunwald *Director:* Anthony Asquith *Script:* Anatole de Grunwald *Photography:* Bernard Knowles *Art Director:* Paul Sheriff *Supervising Editor:* Reginald Beck *Music:* Nicholas Brodsky *Distribution:* GFD, 1943 *With:* Laurence Olivier (*Ivan Kouznetsoff*), Penelope Ward (*Ann*), Marjorie Fielding (*Mrs Tisdall*), Margaret Rutherford (*Rowena Ventnor*), Felix Aylmer (*Mr Runalow*), George Thorpe (*Herbert Tisdall*), Guy Middleton (*Richard Christie*), Michael Shepley (*Mr Walford*), Joyce Grenfell (*Mrs Pawson*), Edie Martin (*Aunt Winnie*), Muriel Aked (*Mrs Tisdall-Stanton*), Jack Watling (*Tom Sellars*), Everley Gregg (*Mrs Flannel*), Miles Malleson, Marion Spencer, Wilfrid Hyde White, John Laurie, David Keir, Brian Nissen, Aubrey Mallalieu, Josephine Middleton. *Length:* 10304 ft.

*Story summary:* Ivan Kouznetsoff, an enthusiastic young Soviet marine engineer, invents a new type of propellor and is sent to have it manufactured in England, traditionally the home of the finest craftsmen. He arrives in England in early 1939 and is invited by Ann, granddaughter of an eccentric and intelligent ship owner, Mr Runalow, to her country home for the weekend. Ivan is at first bewildered and at times repelled by the smugness, strange sense of humour, obsession with tradition and other complexities of the English people with whom he comes into contact. He returns to Russia without seeing his propeller as a workable proposition. In 1941 he returns and again stays at the Runalows' house. This time he sees a different England, a country at war. The class tensions, the laziness and indifference are gone. Ivan is delighted and his English friends, too, find a new interest in someone they had decided was a dour and humourless communist. Eventually his propellor is manufactured and tried out successfully. Ivan returns to the Soviet Union, promising to come back to England (and to Ann) when the war is over.

## WELCOME TO BRITAIN, 1943

*Production:* Strand Films, in association with the Ministry of Information *Producer:* Arthur Elton *Director:* Anthony Asquith, in collaboration with Burgess Meredith *Photography:* Jo Jago *Distribution:* US Office of War Information, 1943 (to US troops in Britain) *With:* Felix Aylmer, Burgess Meredith, Bob Hope, Beatrice Lillie, Carla Lehmann, Beatrice Varley, Johnnie Schofield. *Length:* 5201 ft.

*Story summary:* Burgess Meredith, a captain in the US Army, is given a roving commission as a Yankee private in Britain. He makes a point of visiting English homes, pubs, schools and places of amusement. As a kind of guide or *compére*, he shows Americans just what – and what not – to do in Britain, and his observations and experiences are humorously recorded. Examples include a GI taxing the hospitality of an English working-class family, a turn by Beatrice Lillie, a pub scene and an episode in which Bob Hope 'explains' the British currency system.

## FANNY BY GASLIGHT, 1944 (US title: *Man of Evil*)

*Production:* Gainsborough Pictures *Producer:* Edward Black *Director:* Anthony Asquith *Script:* Doreen Montgomery, from the novel by Michael Sadleir *Additional dialogue:* Aimée Stuart *Photography:* Arthur Crabtree *Art Director:* John Bryan *Supervising Editor:* R E Dearing *Music:* Cedric Mallabey *Distribution:* GFD, 1944 *With:* James Mason (*Lord Manderstoke*), Phyllis Calvert (*Fanny*), Stewart Granger (*Harry Somerford*), Jean Kent (*Lucy*), Wilfrid Lawson (*Chunks*), Margaretta Scott (*Alicia*), Nora Swinburne (*Mrs Hopwood*), Cathleen Nesbitt (*Kate Somerford*), Helen Haye (*Mrs Somerford*), John Laurie (*William Hopwood*), Amy Veness (*Mrs Heaviside*), Stuart Lindsell (*Clive Seymour*), Ann Wilton (*Carver*), Guy Le Feuvre (*Dr Lowenthall*), Peter Jones, Beresford Egan, Joan Rees. *Length:* 9668 ft.

*Story summary:* Fanny, a pretty young girl, lives in London of the 1870's with her parents William and Mary Hopwood, over a West End pub. Hopwood also owns the 'place' next door, a rendezvous for young Society blades. In a brawl here with the dissolute Manderstoke, Hopwood is killed. On her deathbed, Mrs Hopwood tells Fanny that Hopwood was only her guardian, and that her real father is Clive Seymore, a Cabinet Minister. Fanny, now penniless, meets her father and he offers her a place as a maid-servant in his household. Fanny soon learns that Alicia, Clive's wife, is having an affair with Manderstoke. The affair leads to the suicide of Fanny's father. Harry Somerford, a young aristocrat, falls in love with Fanny and proposes marriage, but out of deference to his family and position she refuses. They live together, however, in opposition to his family, and go to Paris. There they meet Manderstoke, who is living with Fanny's childhood friend, Lucy, now an actress. A quarrel breaks out, and Manderstoke forces Harry to a duel. The latter is wounded but Manderstoke is killed and at last his evil shadow is lifted from Fanny's life. She and Harry return to London and eventually his family agree to their marriage.

## TWO FATHERS, 1944

*Production:* Crown Film Unit, in association with the Ministry of Information *Producer:* Arthur Elton *Director:* Anthony Asquith *Associate Director:* Peter Boulton *Script:* Anthony Asquith, from a story by V S Pritchett *Photography:* Jonah Jones *Art Director:* Edward Carrick *Sound:* Ken Cameron *Music:* Clifton Parker *Editor:* Terry Trench *Distribution:* Ministry of Information, 1944

*With:* Bernard Miles (*The Englishman*), Paul Bonifas (*The Frenchman*), Paulette Pruney (*The Girl*), Margaret Yarde, Arthur Young, Everley Gregg, David Keir. *Length:* 1205 ft.

*Story summary:* The film centres mainly on the conversation of an Englishman and a Frenchman sharing a room in a small British hotel during the war. The Englishman has a son in the RAF. He sees a photograph of the Frenchman's daughter and remarks, 'It's better to have a daughter in these days of war.' The Frenchman shrugs and tells how his daughter became a nurse and is now working for the *Maquis* in France. He has just had news that she is alive. 'And that is your son?' the Frenchman asks. 'He bailed out over France yesterday', is the answer. After a moment, the Frenchman observes, 'There are many who will help a British airman in France'. Their eyes turn towards the photograph of the girl.

**THE WAY TO THE STARS, 1945** (US title: *Johnny in the Clouds*)

*Production:* Two Cities Films and Anatole de Grunwald *Producer:* Anatole de Grunwald *Director:* Anthony Asquith *Associate Producer:* Gordon Parry *Script:* Terence Rattigan and Anatole de Grunwald, from a story by Rattigan, based on a scenario by Rattigan and R Sherman *Poem:* John Pudney *Photography:* Derek Williams *Supervising Art Director:* Paul Sheriff *Editor:* Fergus McDonnell *Music:* Nicholas Brodsky *Second Unit Cameramen:* Guy Green, Jack Hildyard *Art Director:* Carmen Dillon *Distribution:* United Artists, 1945 *With:* Michael Redgrave (*David Archdale*), John Mills (*Peter Penrose*), Rosamund John (*Miss Todd*), Douglas Montgomery (*Johnny Hollis*), Renée Asherson (*Iris*), Stanley Holloway (*Palmer*), Basil Radford (*Tiny Williams*), Felix Aylmer (*Rev Charles Moss*), Bonar Colleano (*Joe Friselly*), Trevor Howard (*Carter*), Joyce Carey (*Miss Winterton*), Bill Owen (*Nobby Clarke*), Jean Simmons (*Singer*), Nicholas Stuart (*Wally Becker*), David Tomlinson (*Prune Parsons*), Jonnnie Schofield (*Jones*), Charles Victor (*Fitter*), Hartley Power (*Col Page*),

Vida Hope (*Elsie*), Peter Cotes (*Aircraftsman*), Anthony Dawson (*Bertie Steen*), Hugh Dempster (*Tinker Bell*). *Length:* 9810 ft.

*Story summary:* The time is 1942. Peter, a young RAF pilot, is sent to a station in the Midlands, where he becomes friendly with David, his squadron leader. David is married to 'Toddy', manageress of *The Golden Lion*, the squadron's favourite local inn. There Peter meets, and is attracted to, Iris Winterton, a London girl evacuated with her aunt. David is killed on operations, leaving his wife with a baby son. She is comforted by an American pilot, Johnny, party of a contingent that joins the air base. Peter, shaken by David's death, comes to believe that pilots should not marry and breaks off his affair with Iris. Johnny's friend, Joe, pursues Iris, but she is still in love with Peter. Life at the station goes on. New operations continue. Men are killed, new faces arrive, young pilots are sent into the air, some of them never to return; eventually Johnny is killed and Peter, even more bitter, decides to tell Iris that love between them is impossible. Toddy, victim of the two losses, finally makes Peter see things in a different perspective. He and Iris are reunited. Around and above these personal incidents in the lives of members of the station's command is delineated the comradeship of English and Americans, which from mutual mistrust grows into understanding and affection.

## WHILE THE SUN SHINES, 1947

*Production:* International Screenplays *Producer:* Anatole de Grunwald *Director:* Anthony Asquith *Associate Producer:* Teddy Baird *Script:* Terence Rattigan and Anatole de Grunwald, from the stageplay by Terence Rattigan *Photography:* Jack Hildyard *Art Director:* Tom Morahan *Editor:* Fred Wilson *Music:* Nicholas Brodsky *Distribution:* Associated-British-Pathe, 1947 *With:* Ronald Howard (*Earl of Harpenden*), Bonar Colleano (*Joe Mulvaney*), Barbara White (*Lady Elisabeth Randall*), Brenda Bruce (*Mabel Crum*), Ronald Squire (*Duke of Ayr and Sterling*), Michael Allan (*Colbert*), Miles Malleson (*Horton*), Margaret Rutherford (*Dr Winifred Frye*), Cyril Maude (*Old Admiral*), Garry Marsh (*Jordan*), Joyce Grenfell (*Daphne*), Amy Frank (*Mrs Finckel*), Charles Victor, Vida Hope, Wilfred Hyde White, Judith Furse, Clive Morton, Cecil Trouncer, O B Clarence, Tamara Lees,

Geoffrey Dunn, Beryl Measor, Hugh Dempster, Aubrey Mallalieu. *Length:* 7355 ft.

*Story summary:* While on special leave from the Navy in 1944, Lord Harpenden, an ordinary seaman, encounters Joe Mulvaney, an American officer, drunk on the pavement. He takes him home and next morning leaves early to appear before a selection board. Calling at the Albany during his absence his fiancée, Lady Elisabeth Randall, is mistaken by Mulvaney for Mabel Crum, a former girl-friend of Harpenden's. He gives her several drinks and makes love to her. A young French officer, Colbert, interrupts them and announces himself in love with Elisabeth. Harpenden returns to find he has two rivals for his fiancée and she, in emotional confusion, believes she loves the American. With the aid of the good-hearted Mabel Crum, however, Harpenden is able to win back Elisabeth and pair off Mabel with Mulvaney.

## THE WINSLOW BOY, 1948

*Production:* Anatole de Grunwald Productions *Producer:* Anatole de Grunwald *Director:* Anthony Asquith *Associate Producer:* Teddy Baird *Script:* Terence Rattigan and Anatole de Grunwald, from the stageplay by Terence Rattigan *Photography:* Frederick Young *Art Director:* André Andreyev *Costumes:* William Chappell *Editor:* Gerald Turney Smith *Exterior Photography:* Osmond Borradaile *Period Adviser:* Michael Weight *Music:* William Alwyn *Distribution:* British Lion, 1948 *With:* Robert Donat (*Sir Robert Morton*), Margaret Leighton (*Catherine Winslow*), Neil North (*Ronnie*), Jack Watling (*Dickie*), Frank Lawton (*John Wetherstone*), Nicholas Hannen (*Col Wetherstone*), Basil Radford (*Desmond Curry*), Kathleen Harrison (*Violet, the maid*), Walter Fitzgerald (*First Lord*), Francis L Sullivan (*Attorney-General*), Wilfred Hyde White (*First Clerk*), Mona Washbourne (*Miss Barnes*), Evelyn Roberts (*Hamilton, MP*), Billy Shine (*Photographer*), Ernest Thesiger (*Ridgeley-Pearce*), Lewis Casson (*Admiral Springfield*), Stanley Holloway and Cyril Ritchard (*Comedians*), Mary Hinton (*Mrs Elliot*), Hugh Dempster (*Agricultural member*), Cedric Hardwicke (*Arthur Winslow*). *Length:* 10642 ft.

*Story summary:* In the autumn of 1912 Arthur Winslow retires from the bank. His elder son Dickie is an Oxford undergraduate, his daughter Catherine interested in the Suffragette movement, his younger son Ronnie has entered the Royal Naval College at Osborn. Ronnie is expelled from Osborn, accused of stealing a 5/– postal order from a brother cadet. Convinced of his son's innocence, Arthur Winslow fights unsuccessfully for his son's honour with the Admiralty and through his MP; then he engages the famous KC, Sir Robert Morton, to take up the challenge. Morton makes a brilliant speech in the Commons which results in a Petition of Right being granted and Winslow being able to sue the Admiralty and fight the case in the courts. The attendant publicity, meanwhile, embarrasses the Winslow family. Catherine's engagement is broken off, Dickie leaves Oxford and goes into business as his father's savings dwindle. The celebrated case finishes with Ronnie's vindication, however, and a romantic attachment between Sir Robert and Catherine.

## THE WOMAN IN QUESTION, 1950

*Production:* Javelin and Two Cities Films *Producer:* Teddy Baird *Executive:* Earl St John *Director:* Anthony Asquith *Script:* John Cresswell *Photography:* Desmond Dickinson *Art Director:* Carmen Dillon *Editor:* John D Guthridge *Music:* John Wooldridge *Distribution:* GFD, 1950 *With:* Jean Kent (*Astra*), Dirk Bogarde (*Bob Baker*), Susan Shaw (*Catherine*), John McCallum (*Murray*), Hermione Baddeley (*Mrs Finch*), Charles Victor (*Pollard*), Duncan Macrae (*Superintendent Lodge*), Lana Morris (*Lana*), Vida Hope (*Shirley*), Joe Linnane (*Inspector Butler*), Duncan Lamont (*Barney*), Bobbie Scroggins (*Alfie Finch*), Anthony Dawson (*Wilson*), John Boxer (*Lucas*), Julian D'Albie (*Police Surgeon*), Josephine Middleton (*Mrs Hengist*), Everley Gregg (*Woman Customer*), Albert Chevalier (*Gunter*), Richard Pearson (*Fraser*). *Length:* 7884 ft.

*Story summary:* Alfie, son of Mrs Finch, discovers the strangled body of Astra. Scotland Yard is called in. Mrs Finch relates how Astra's sister Catherine, a self-centred girl, had recently quarrelled with Astra. Among the dead woman's other visitors had been Bob Baker, a vaudeville artist trying unsuccessfully to persuade Astra to team with him in a thought-reading act. The day before she died, Bob and Catherine had called on Astra, and left after a quarrel. Catherine's version of Astra and her life is then recounted: Astra's neglect of her bed-ridden husband, and Catherine's love for Bob Baker, who returned it but was waiting for a divorce that Astra was trying to obstruct. Bob Baker's version is substantially the same, and the next person to be interviewed is Pollard, keeper of a nearby pet store. Pollard tells that he first met Astra when she brought her sick canary to him, and after that they became friends. The day before Astra died, he had proposed marriage to her and been accepted. The case takes a new twist with the arrival of Murray, an Irish sailor who had been in love with Astra, who tells how he came back to see her after a long voyage and found her with another man. But Pollard is finally found to be the murderer; Astra had not accepted him, as he claimed, and he killed her in a jealous rage.

## THE BROWNING VERSION, 1950

*Production:* Two Cities Films and Javelin Films *Producer:* Teddy Baird *Executive:* Earl St John *Director:* Anthony Asquith *Script:* Terence Rattigan, from his own play *Photography:* Desmond Dickinson *Art Director:* Carmen Dillon *Editor:* John D Guthridge *Distribution:* GFD, 1951 *With:* Michael Redgrave (*Andrew Crocker-Harris*), Jean Kent (*Millie*), Nigel Patrick (*Frank Hunter*), Wilfred Hyde White (*Headmaster*), Ronald Howard (*Gilbert*), Brian Smith (*Taplow*), Bill Travers (*Fletcher*), Paul Medland (*Wilson*), Ivan Samson (*General Baxter*), Joan Haythorne (*Mrs Wilson*), Judith Furse (*Mrs Williamson*), Vivienne Gibson (*Mrs Saunders*), Josephine Middleton (*Mrs Frobisher*), Peter Jones (*Carstairs*), Johnnie Schofield (*Taxi Driver*), Russell Walters (*School Porter*). *Length:* 8070 ft.

*Story summary:* Andrew Crocker-Harris has been teaching at a public school for eighteen years, and is forced to retire prematurely owing to ill-health. Lack of success with his pupils has blighted his youthful ambition and promise and, with his embittered wife Millie, he faces a future of poverty and disappointment. Millie's desire for her own particular brand of love, emotional and physical, is as great as Andrew's desire for the fulfilment of his own platonic ideal. The tragedy is that neither can satisfy the other's needs. Millie has been seeking consolation in an affair with Hunter, the science master, who is about to discard her. Andrew finds his protective armour of indifference and lovelessness pierced by the action of a small boy, Taplow, who gives him a second-hand copy of Browning's translation of *The Agamemnon of Aeschylus*, his master's favourite play. The violent outburst of emotion which greets this little gesture of goodwill, and Millie's spiteful attempt to destroy its value in Andrew's eyes – by pretending the gift was only a piece of flattery calculated to evade a punishment – brings the marriage to a crisis. In the last few minutes before he leaves, Andrew makes an unexpected gesture of defiance towards the Headmaster who has constantly humiliated him, and finds in the applause that greets his frank apology for his failings to the assembled school, courage to face a new life. He rejects Millie, who has by this time also been cast off by her lover.

## THE IMPORTANCE OF BEING EARNEST, 1951

*Production:* Javelin Films and Two Cities Films *Producer:* Teddy Baird *Director:* Anthony Asquith *Script:* Anthony Asquith, from the play by Oscar Wilde *Photography:* Desmond Dickinson *Colour:* Technicolor *Art Director:* Carmen Dillon *Costumes:* Beatrice Dawson *Editor:* John D Guthridge *Music:* Benjamin Frankel *Distribution:* GFD, 1952 *With:* Michael Redgrave (*Jack Worthing*), Michael Denison (*Algernon Moncrieff*), Dame Edith Evans (*Lady Bracknell*), Joan Greenwood (*Gwendolen*), Dorothy Tutin (*Cecily*), Margaret Rutherford (*Miss Prism*), Miles Malleson (*Canon Chasuble*), Richard Wattis (*Seton*), Walter Hudd (*Lane*), Aubrey Mather (*Merriman*). *Length:* 8589 ft.

*Story summary:* Jack Worthing and Algernon Moncrieff, two wealthy and eligible bachelors of the 90's, are in love. The former with Gwendoline, who is the latter's cousin, and the latter with Cecily, who is the former's ward. Due to Jack's ignoble habit of representing himself as his imaginary brother, Ernest, when in town, and Algernon's adoption of Ernest's name and wicked reputation to speed his courtship of Cecily, both girls believe themselves to be engaged to the non-existent Ernest. When Jack discovers this, he goes into deep mourning, announcing that his brother has been killed by a severe chill in Paris, but the girls see through this deception. Obliged to admit that neither is really called Ernest, the two men separately agree to be re-christened in that name to prove their devotion. They reckon, however, without the intervention of the formidable Lady Bracknell, Gwendolen's mother and Algernon's aunt, who opposes everything until Miss Prism, Cecily's governess and a devoted family retainer, brings to light an old skeleton in the family cupboard and makes it clear that one of the men is, in fact, 'earnest'.

## THE NET, 1952 (US title: *Project M7*)

*Production:* Javelin Films and Two Cities Films *Producer:* Anthony Darnborough *Director:* Anthony Asquith *Screenplay:* William Fairchild from the novel by John Pudney *Photography:* Desmond Dickinson *Aerial Photography:* Stanley Grant *Editor:* Frederick Wilson *Art Director:* John Howell *Music:* Benjamin Frankel *With:* Pnyllis Calvert (*Lydia*), James Donald (*Heathley*), Robert Beatty (*Sam Seagram*), Herbert Lom (*Alex Leon*), Muriel Pavlow (*Caroline Cartier*), Noel Willman (*Dennis Bord*), Walter Fitzgerald (*Sir Charles Cruddock*), Patrick Doonan (*Brian Jackson*), Maurice Denham (*Carrington*), Marjorie Fielding (*Mama*), Cavan Watson (*Ferguson*). *Length:* 7698 ft.

*Story Summary:* *The Net* tells of a group of international scientists in the security net of a research station.

## THE FINAL TEST, 1952

*Production:* ACT Films *Producer:* R J Minney *Director:* Anthony Asquith *Screenplay:* Terence Rattigan, from his play of the same name *Photography:* Bill McLeod *Editor:* Helga Cranston *Art Director:* R Holmes-Paul *Music:* Benjamin Frankel *With:* Jack Warner (*Sam*), Robert Morley (*Alexander Whitehead*), George Relph (*Syd Thompson*), Adrienne Allen (*Aunt Ethel*), Brenda Bruce (*Cora*), Ray Jackson (*Reggie*), Stanley Maxted (*Senator*), Joan Swinstead (*Miss Fanshawe*), Richard Bebb (*Frank Weller*), Len Hutton (*Frank Jarvis*), Denis Compton, Alec Bedser, Godfrey Evans, Jim Laker, Cyril Washbrook (*Cricket players*) *Length:* 8172 ft.

*Story summary:* An ageing cricketer is playing in his last Test Match and his son, who fancies himself as a poet, goes to see a famous writer instead of watching the game on this crucial day.

## THE YOUNG LOVERS, 1954

*Production:* Group Film Productions *Producer:* Anthony Havelock-Allan *Director:* Anthony Asquith *Screenplay:* George Tabori & Robin Estridge from a novel by George Tabori *Associate Producer:* R Denis Holt *Photography:* Jack Asher *Music:* Benjamin Frankel and Tchaikovsky *With:* Odile Versois (*Anna Sobek*), David Knight (*Ted Hutchens*), Joseph Tomelty (*Moffat*), Paul Carpenter (*Gregg Pearson*), Theodore Bikel (*Joseph*), Jill Adams (*Judy*), David Kossoff (*Anton Sobek*), Betty Marsden (*Mrs Forester*), Peter Illing (*Dr Weissbrod*), Peter Dyneley (*Regan*), Bernard Rebel (*Stefan*). *Length:* 8682 ft.

*Story summary:* The Young Lovers struggle against the separation forced upon them by the cold war.

## ON SUCH A NIGHT, 1955

*Production:* Screen Audiences *Director:* Anthony Asquith *Screenplay:* Paul Dehn *Photography:* Frank North *Editor:* Anthony Harvey *Music:* Benjamin Frankel *Sound:* Maurice Askew and Bill Bristowe *Colour:* Eastmancolor *Distribution:* JARFID *With:* David Knight, Josephine Griffin, Marie Lohr. *Length:* 3330 ft.

*Story summary:* A young American visits Glyndebourne and hears excerpts from the 'Marriage of Figaro', as well as seeing the beauty of England.

## CARRINGTON VC, 1956 (US title: *Court Martial*)

*Production:* Remus *Producer:* Teddy Baird *Director:* Anthony Asquith *Screenplay:* John Hunter adapted from the play by Dorothy and Campbell Christie *Photography:* Desmond Dickinson *Editor:* Ralph Kemplen *Art Director:* Wilfred Shingleton *Sound:* A G Ambler and Red Law *Distribution:* Independent in association with British Lion *With:* David Niven (*Major Carrington VC*), Margaret Leighton (*Valerie Carrington*), Noelle Middleton

(*Captain Alison Graham*), Laurence Naismith (*Major Panton*), Clive Morton (*Lt-Col Huxford*), Mark Dignam (*The Prosecutor*), Allan Cuthbertson (*Lt-Col Henniker*), Victor Maddern (*Sgt Owen*), John Glyn-Jones (*Evans, the reporter*), Raymond Francis (*Major Mitchell*), Newton Blick (*Mr Tester-Terry*), John Chandos (*Adjutant Rawlinson*). *Length:* 9532 ft.

*Story summary:* In *Carrington VC*, David Niven plays a VC major accused of fraudulent conversion of army funds.

## ORDERS TO KILL, 1958

*Production:* Lion International Films *Producer:* Anthony Havelock-Allan *Director:* Anthony Asquith *Associate Producer:* R L M Davidson *Assistant Director:* Peter Polton *Screenplay:* Paul Dehn, from a story by Donald C Downes *Photography:* Desmond Dickinson *Art Director:* John Howell *Supervising Editor:* Gordon Hales *Music:* Benjamin Frankel *Sound:* George Stephenson *Consultant technician for US sequences:* Donald Downes *With:* James Robertson Justice (*Head Instructor*), Paul Massie (*Gene Summers*), Eddie Albert (*Major MacMahon*), Irene Worth (*Leonie*), Leslie French (*Marcel Lafitte*), Lillian Gish (*Gene Summers' mother*), John Crawford (*Major Kimball*), Lionel Jeffries, Miki Iveria. *Length:* 10046 ft.

*Story summary:* A young American is sent to Nazi-occupied Paris to kill an assumed informer, but completes his mission to find that his victim was innocent.

## THE DOCTOR'S DILEMMA, 1958

*Production:* Comet Films *Producer:* Anatole de Grunwald *Director:* Anthony Asquith *Screenplay:* Anatole de Grunwald, from the play by George Bernard Shaw *Photography:* Robert Krasker *Art Director:* Paul Sheriff *Editor:* Gordon Hales *Music:* Joseph Kosma *Colour:* Metroscope Eastmancolor *Distribution:*

MGM *With:* Leslie Caron (*Jennifer Dubedat*), Dirk Bogarde (*the painter Dubedat*), John Robinson (*Sir Colenso Ridgeon*), Robert Morley (*Sir Ralph Bloomfield-Bonington*), Alastair Sim (*Cutler Walpole*), Felix Aylmer (*Sir Patrick Cullen*), Michael Gwynn (*Dr Blenkinsop*), Maureen Delaney (*Emmy*), Gwenda Ewen (*Minnie*), Alec McCowen (*Redpenny*), Terence Alexander (*Mr Lancaster*), Peter Sallis (*Secretary of the art gallery*), Clifford Buckton (*the Butcher*), Colin Gordon, Derek Prentice. *Length:* 8917 ft.

*Story summary:* The story of a young artist, his wife and a doctor who, when the artist is suffering from consumption, uses his limited serum on a more worthwhile case.

**LIBEL, 1959**

*Production:* Comet Films *Producer:* Anatole de Grunwald *Director:* Anthony Asquith *Associate Producer:* Pierre Rouve *Screenplay:* Anatole de Grunwald and Karl Tunberg from a play by Edward Wool *Photography:* Robert Krasker *Editor:* Frank Clarke *Art Director:* Paul Sheriff *Music:* Benjamin Frankel *Sound:* A W Watkins and Gerry Turner *Distribution:* MGM *With:* Olivia de Havilland (*Lady Loddon*), Dirk Bogarde (*Sir Mark Loddon, Frank Welney and Number 15*), Paul Massie (*Jeffrey Buckenham*), Robert Morley (*Sir Wilfred*), Wilfred Hyde White (*Hubert Foxley*), Anthony Dawson (*Gerald Loddon*), Richard Wattis (*the Judge*), Martin Miller (*Dr Schrott*), Millicent Martin (*Maisie*), Richard Dimbleby. *Length:* 8969 ft.

*Story summary:* A courtroom drama, covering a libel suit brought by a baronet accused of being an imposter.

**THE MILLIONAIRESS, 1960**

*Producer:* Dimitri de Grunwald *Director:* Anthony Asquith *Associate Producer:* Pierre Rouve *Screenplay:* Wolf Mankowitz and Riccardo Aragno from the play by George Bernard Shaw *Photography:* Jack Hildyard *Art Director:* Harry White *Editor:* Anthony Harvey *Music:* George Van Parys *Colour:* Cinemascope/ Eastmancolor *Distribution:* 20th Century Fox *With:* Sophia Loren (*Epifania*), Peter Sellers (*Dr Kabri*), Alastair Sim (*Lawyer Sagamore*), Dennis Price (*the Psychiatrist*), Gary Raymond, Vittorio de Sica, Noel Purcell, Alfie Bass, Miriam Karlin, Virginia Vernon, Basil Hoskins, Diana Coupland. *Length:* 8115 ft.

*Story summary:* Comedy drama about an imperious heiress who has considerable trouble in winning an altruistic Indian doctor.

## ZERO, 1960

*Production:* Sapphire Films Limited *Director:* Anthony Asquith *Screenplay:* Samuel Beckett from his play *Mime without Words* *Photography:* Bob Navarro *Editor:* Douglas Myers *Music:* John Beckett *With:* Zero Mostel *Length:* 1080 ft.

*Story summary:* Zero is a fat man forever trying to reach a jug of water – and forever failing. Based on Samuel Beckett's *Mime without Words.*

## TWO LIVING, ONE DEAD, 1961

*Production:* Swan Films *Producer:* Teddy Baird *Director:* Anthony Asquith *Associate Producer:* Lorens Marmstedt *Screenplay:* Lindsay Galloway *Photography:* Gunnar Fischer *Art Director:* Bibi Lindstrom *Editor:* Oscar Rosander *Music:* Erik Nordgren *Sound:* Stig Flodin and Staffan Dalin *Distribution:* Lion International Films *With:* Virginia McKenna (*Helen Berger*), Bill Travers (*Anderson*), Patrick McGoohan (*Berger*), Dorothy Alison (*Esther Kester*), Alf Kjellin (*Rogers*), Noel Willman (*Johnsson*), Pauline Jameson (*Miss Larsen*), Peter Vaughan (*Kester*), Derek Francis (*Broms*), Michael Crawford (*Nils*), Alan Rothwell (*Karlson*), Peter Bathurst. (*Engelhardt*), John Moulder-Brown (*Rolf*), Isa Quensel (*Mlle Larousse*), Mariane Nielsen (*Miss*

*Lind*), Mikael Bolin (*Peter*), Mona Geijer-Kalner (*Mrs Holm*), Alan Bair, Georg Skarstedt. *Length:* 8235 ft.

*Story summary:* Psychological study of the effect of a bank robbery on a bank official who did not resist the raiders.

## GUNS OF DARKNESS, 1962

*Production:* Cavalcade/Concorde Production-Associated British *Producer:* Thomas Clyde *Director:* Anthony Asquith *Screenplay:* John Mortimer, from the novel by Francis Clifford *Photography:* Robert Krasker *Art Director:* John Herdell *Editor:* Frederick Wilson *Music:* Benjamin Frankel *Distribution:* Warner Brothers *With:* David Niven (*Tom Jordan*), Leslie Caron (*Claire Jordan*), James Robertson Justice (*Hugo Bryant*), David Opatoshu (*President Rivera*), Derek Godfrey (*Colonel Hernandez*), Ian Hunter (*Dr Swann*), Eleanor Summerfield (*Mrs Bastian*), Sandor Eles (*Lt Gomez*). *Length:* 9244 ft.

*Story summary:* An emotionally and politically naive Englishman, with his wife, is involved in a South American revolution.

## THE VIPs, 1963

*Production:* Anatole de Grunwald Productions *Producer:* Anatole de Grunwald *Director:* Anthony Asquith *Screenplay:* Terence Rattigan *Photography:* Jack Hildyard *Art Director*, William Kellner *Editor:* Frank Clarke *Music:* Miklos Rozsa *Distribution:* MGM *With:* Elizabeth Taylor (*Frances Andros*), Louis Jourdan (*Marc Champselle*), Orson Welles (*Max Buda*), Richard Burton (*Paul Andros*), Rod Taylor (*Mangam*), Maggie Smith (*Miss Mead*), Elsa Martinelli (*Gloria Gritti*), Margaret Rutherford (*Duchess of Brighton*), Linda Christian (*Miriam Marhall*), Robert Coote (*Commandant Millbank*), Ronald Fraser (*Joslin*), Peter Illing (*M Dancer*). *Length:* 10679 ft.

*Story summary:* Several people trying to leave the country for various reasons are faced with their problems when stranded at London Airport by fog.

## THE YELLOW ROLLS-ROYCE, 1964

*Production:* MGM *Producer:* Anatole de Grunwald *Director:* Anthony Asquith *Associate Producer:* Timothy Burrill *Assistant Director:* Kip Gowans *Screenplay:* Terence Rattigan *Photography:* Jack Hildyard *Art Director:* Vincent Korda *Editor:* Frank Clarke *Music:* Riz Ortolani *Sound:* Cyril Swern *Distribution:* MGM *With:* Jeanne Moreau (*the Marchioness of Frinton*), Shirley MacLaine (*Mae Jenkins*), Ingrid Bergman (*Miss Gerda Millett*), Rex Harrison (*the Marquis of Frinton*), George C Scott (*Paolo Maltese*), Omar Shariff (*Dovich*), Alain Delon (*Stefano*), Art Carney (*Joey*), Edmund Purdom (*John Fane*), Moira Lister (*Lady Simeon*), Isa Miranda (*the Duchess of Angouleme*), Roland Culver (*Norwood*), Riccardo Garrone (*Bomba*), Joyce Grenfell (*Hortense Astor*), Wally Cox (*Ferguson*), Michael Hordern (*Harmsworth*), Lance Percival (*Harmsworth's assistant*), Harold Scott (*Taylor*), Gregoire Aslan (*Albanian Ambassador*), Jacques Brunius (*Duke of Angouleme*), Richard Pearson (*Chauffeur*), Richard Vernon, Reginald Beckwith, Tom Gill, Dermot Kelly, Guy Deghy, Carlo Groccolo, Martin Miller, Andreas Melandrinos. *Length:* 11025 ft.

*Story summary:* The travels of a Rolls-Royce in the 'thirties, with three owners: an English peer; a gangster; a rich American widow involved with a Yugoslav partisan.

# Index

INDEX